PRAISE FOR

Almost Hereditary: A White Southerner's Journey Out of Racism:

"Bill Drake offers an important perspective from someone who grew up in a world poisoned by racism but learned to see others in a more tolerant light. *Almost Hereditary* has a significant moral: we should all make a greater effort to second-guess our judgments of others, and to think about where those judgments originated."

—**Benjamin Todd Jealous**, former President and CEO of the NAACP

"Bill Drake's exceptionally well written narrative . . . is an excellent examination of one person's successful journey to break free from racist socialization messages passed down through his family. . . . While painful at times to read, this book and the story it conveys can serve as a catalyst for how social change is possible. . . . Bill offers insightful discussion questions and activities for classrooms and workshops to examine white privilege and the reduction of racial and other stereotypes. *Almost Hereditary* has been a valuable supplement for my class on the Cultural Politics of Peace. It would be an excellent complementary reading for both undergraduate and graduate courses in race and ethnic relations, conflict resolution, and social inequality."

—**Jeffrey G. Toussaint, PhD**, Dept. of Sociology and Criminal Justice, Old Dominion University

"Bill Drake's articulate and well written book testifies to the capacity to break free from our assumed identities. His story of conditioned, privileged, white-skinned identity begins with his ancestors and their firm dogma of superiority, takes us with him on his recognition of the horrible consequences of his family's and his region's bias, and finally invites us to recognize whatever residue of racism lives within us. His story invites us to be willing, as he has been willing, to investigate the personal and collective suffering caused by both conscious and subconscious acceptance of different values for different races. I salute his redemption, and I embrace the lasting value of his awakening."

—**Gangaji**, author of *Hidden Treasure: Uncovering the Truth in Your Life Story* (Jeremy P. Tarcher/Penguin, 2011), spiritual teacher

"A compelling and provocative account of one man's courageous journey from a deep-seated and inherited prejudice to a giving, open heart. It should serve as an inspiration to all of us, not just to think the right thing, but to put our thoughts into action and make this world a better place. A true pleasure to read. "

—**Steve Sanfield**, author of *The Adventures of High John the Conqueror* (Orchard Books 1986, August House 1995) and *A Natural Man: The True Story of John Henry* (Godine, 1986), Civil Rights activist, one of the first Freedom Riders (in 1961)

"Bill Drake offers us some very valuable resources for our nation's still-to-be-completed transformation of its racist past and present, particularly in his honest account of some 180 years of his family's history—from being slave owners in the 1830s to Bill's own effort to confront and transform his racist conditioning in the last 50 years. He shares generously his own journey, with honesty, compassion, and insight, and offers a number of perspectives and tools for those who would share his journey to uproot racism."

—**Donald Rothberg, PhD**, author of *The Engaged Spiritual Life* (Beacon Press, 2006), teacher of Insight Meditation and engaged spirituality at Spirit Rock in northern California

"Bill Drake's story is an inspiration to our students and staff and lends hope and promise to a situation that can often feel despairing. His journey as a human being is a story that needed to be told, and I am glad it has been captured in this book. *Almost Hereditary* would be a valuable complement to appropriate high school and college courses."

—**Dan Frisella**, Principal, Nevada Union High School, Grass Valley, CA

"*Almost Hereditary*, as a book club choice, has generated lively group participation. The sheer humility of the author's inner search, openness, candor, and the fruits of his dedicated research touch a poignant chord for many readers, whether they lived through the Jim Crow era or feel haunted by its covert clutches on today's society. Because it is part memoir, the experiences Bill Drake lays out can resonate without indicting, thus inspiring meaningful introspection or group dialogue. *Almost Heredity* opens the door for readers to celebrate the transcendence of the human rights battles of an earlier era, while searching their own souls and cities to sand off the rough edges that crusted over as a result of those battles."

—**Teresa Langness**, author of *Nine O'Clock Blue* (Writer's Showcase 2001), Nevada County Baha'i Book Club Co-Convenor

"Bill Drake writes with a disarming humility that guides the reader into a real yet non-judgmental conversation about the nature of prejudice. . . . With support from his book I have found a greater courage to examine the prejudice that lives in me."

—**Rob Steffke**, youth therapist and mentor, Movimiento
(www.movimagine.org)

"*Almost Hereditary* [includes] an excellent historical survey of the problem of slavery in the South."

—**Bill Ellis**, author of *Paradigm Shift* and "Teaching Tolerance and Acceptance," www.timescall.com, June 5, 2014

"Beginning with the powerful story of one man's healing from racism, *Almost Hereditary* offers many inspiring tools to help others do the same. Thank you to Bill Drake for the courage and commitment woven into this book."

—**Sharon Salzberg**, author of *Real Happiness: The Power of Meditation: A 28-Day Program* (Workman Publishing Company, 2010), Cofounder of the Insight Meditation Society

"Bill Drake courageously and honestly addresses the racist conditioning he received from his family, as well as from social institutions. His commitment to freeing himself from the impact of racism and the thoughtful and intelligent guidance he offers in this accessible and well constructed book provides a model for healing that is possible for everyone to follow."

—**Ann Todd Jealous and Caroline Haskell**, authors of *Combined Destinies: Whites Sharing Grief About Racism* (Potomac Books, 2013)

"Bill Drake has more reason than most white southerners to be racist. His ancestors owned slaves and his parents passed along their bigotry like an infection. Drake worked for much of his adult life to overcome his conditioned racism. . . . *Almost Hereditary* describes the journey and offers valuable lessons in how to undo the bondage of prejudice."

—**Norma Watkins**, author of *The Last Resort: Taking the Mississippi Cure* (University Press of Mississippi, 2011), professor emerita at Miami Dade College (Miami, FL), creative writing professor at College of the Redwoods (Ft. Bragg, CA)

"A valuable, heartfelt reflection by a descendant of a Confederate officer."

—**Curtis Wilkie**, author of *Dixie* (Scribner, 2002); Cook Chair and Associate Professor of Journalism, Overby Center for Southern Journalism and Politics, University of Mississippi

"*Almost Hereditary* is a strong personal account of a descendant of slave owners' difficult path from racial prejudice and white privilege to his rejection of racism, reclamation of his humanity, and current work for racial justice."

—**Paul Kivel**, author of *Uprooting Racism: How White People Can Work for Racial Justice* (New Society Publisher, 2011), www.paulkivel.com

Almost Hereditary:
A White Southerner's Journey Out of Racism

A Guide for Unlearning and Healing Prejudice

Almost Hereditary:
A White Southerner's Journey Out of Racism

A Guide for Unlearning and Healing Prejudice

by Bill Drake

Almost Hereditary Press
Nevada City, California

Almost Hereditary:
A White Southerner's Journey Out of Racism
A Guide for Unlearning and Healing Prejudice
by Bill Drake

Cover: Photograph taken in Mississippi in 1911 of my mother,
Wilmoth Harvey FitzGerald (on the left), her sister Elizabeth (on the right),
and their Mammy, Margaret Williams, a former slave.
Family slave receipts are behind the title.

Cover Design: Katy Hight
Copyright 2014
and 2015 by Bill Drake
(William Robinson Drake)

Printed in the United States of America

Library of Congress Cataloging-in-Publication Data
Drake, Bill, 1945 July 30 –
Almost hereditary: a white southerner's journey out of racism, a guide for
unlearning and healing prejudice / Bill Drake. – Rev. ed.
Includes bibliographical references.
ISBN 9781494924010 (Paperback)
ISBN 9780692277706 (eBook)

Library of Congress Control Number: 2014914963
(paperback)
Library of Congress subject headings:
1. Racism—United States. 2. Racism—Psychological aspects.
3. Discrimination—United States. 4. Discrimination—Psychological aspects.
5. Prejudices. 6. Toleration.
7. Self-actualization (Psychology).
8. Southern States—Race relations—History.
9. Slavery—United States—History.
10. Plantation Owner—United States—Biography. I. Title.

∞ This paper meets the requirements of ANSI/NISO Z39.48-1992 (Permanence of Paper).

DEDICATION

This book is dedicated to:

My mother, Wilmoth Harvey FitzGerald,
who taught me about love

Nancy McDougall Robinson, my great-great-grandmother

All of the black people who were harmed
by me and my birth lineage

All children and young people of today;
may they learn to love one another

CONTENTS

PART I
MY FAMILY HISTORY AND ROOTS OF MY RACISM

PART II
MY PERSONAL GROWTH AND
JOURNEY OUT OF RACISM

PART III

UNDERSTANDING AND HEALING PREJUDICE

PART IV
THE JOURNEY CONTINUES

PREFACE TO THE REVISED EDITION

This edition includes minor corrections, additions, deletions, and improvements, many of which were suggested by readers. Especially helpful was feedback from Jeff Toussaint, PhD, and his students, who used the book for his class "The Cultural Politics of Peace" at Old Dominion University.

The original edition contained references to my great-grandfather being a member of the Ku Klux Klan. That information was provided by an aunt, who is deceased. She told me she had seen evidence of his involvement in that organization. As I have been unable to find proof of her claim, I have deleted the KKK reference from this edition. However, I have found proof that, as a Mississippi state senator in the 1870s, he helped lay the foundation for the Jim Crow era, a period of almost one-hundred-years, during which Southern blacks were systematically oppressed. Information on his contribution has been added to this edition.

INTRODUCTION

This book has grown out of my background as a youth with deeply held racist views who once yelled derogatory names at black citizens. After growing up in a Southern family that believed in white superiority to blacks, I came to question and reject the myth of white supremacy. The book's roots also lie in the five decades that followed as I learned to deal with the painful remnants of racism, some of which remain with me even today. It has also evolved from years of working to heal racism, primarily through writing articles, producing radio programs, working with like-minded individuals to help others "unlearn prejudice," and working with students.

It may appear at first glance that this book is written for white people — especially white people who have some degree of racism. That is not the case. While it is the story of one white man's struggle with racism, its discussion of the history of black-white relations in America offers insights to both white and black readers. In that it addresses the broader issue of prejudice, it is for people of all races and ethnic identities. Prejudice, which is probably part of the makeup of almost all members of every human society, can also exist between Democrats and Republicans, Protestants and Catholics, Jews and Arabs, homosexuals and heterosexuals, men and women, rich and poor, adults and youth. In that light, this book is about, and for, almost everyone.

Almost Hereditary is written for young people as well as adults. It is important for young people to avoid or discard the burden of prejudice and hatred that our society has carried for too long, both for themselves and for the sake of our country and our world.

The book is unusual in its scope, in that it includes history related to racism and my ancestors' role in it, my personal story of first learning and later challenging racism, and a guide for unlearning and healing prejudice, all in one volume. It may be read cover to cover, or specific chapters may be selected and read in the order that best meets the interest or needs of each reader or classroom teacher. (A detailed description of the organization of *Almost Hereditary* is included later in this introduction.)

The Roots of *Almost Hereditary*

I was born in Norfolk, Virginia, on July 30, 1945, to Wilmoth FitzGerald Drake and James Stoney Drake, Jr. My parents grew up in families with racist views. I have little knowledge of my father's grandparents, but I know my mother's grandfathers were deeply committed to white supremacy. My mother's paternal grandfather was a slave owner and a Civil War hero. As a Mississippi state senator, he supported measures that laid the foundation for what was called the Jim Crow era, during which blacks were oppressed and kept in an inferior position for almost a century. My mother's maternal grandfather also fought for the South in the Civil War and, like his parents and grandparents, owned slave plantations. It is clear to me that the racism of my youth was passed down from generation to generation. Beginning with my birth, the concept of white supremacy was as much a part of my family environment as food, air, and gravity were part of my daily experience. I have come to consider my racism as "almost hereditary," like a life-impairing disease that is passed down from parent to child.

The difficulty I have had in overcoming such thorough conditioning is evident in this reflection on racism I wrote in a journal in July of 1967, just before my twenty-second birthday:

> Even after [I intellectually rejected racism in June of 1964]…it was not an easy thing to be around Negroes. Although I approved of integration and equality in theory 100 percent, my effort to act naturally in the presence of Negroes was in itself unnatural because it involved a conscious effort on my part — and an act isn't natural if it is a conscious effort and if it has been conditioned against for nineteen previous years…. Prejudice is not an easy thing to get over.

Almost Hereditary begins over 180 years ago with the early diary entries of Nancy McDougall Robinson, my maternal great-great-grandmother, whose husband owned 136 to 200 slaves in Mississippi.[1] When my mother and her sisters donated the original diaries to the Mississippi Department of Archives and History in the 1970s, the state agency gave photocopies of them to me and my relatives as part of the arrangement. The photocopies were organized into eleven volumes that contained 1,350 diary pages. In the summer of 1995, I decided to use the journals for a special radio program that I planned to produce for Martin Luther King Day the following January. The idea intrigued me both because I imagined the diaries contained something of educational value to radio listeners and because I felt that they would give me a deeper perspective on my family and myself. After I committed to the project, I studied the material for the first time. Because of Nancy's handwriting and the occasional poor quality of the photocopies, the written reflections were difficult to read. I devoted about 150 hours to studying them and organizing and typing selected entries. In some cases, I spent several minutes with a magnifying glass trying to read a word or two that held the key to the meaning of an important paragraph — not always with success. This endeavor gave me an intimate experience of my ancestor (whose married surname, Robinson, is my middle name), and in time I became very fond of her. I even came to imagine that she was guiding me in the radio project and later on in the writing of this book. Surprisingly, she did not fit my image of a slave owner. Although her family participated in the institution of slavery, later she wrote that she was relieved that the slaves had been freed. She was in many respects a wonderful and remarkable person. While she had her inconsistencies, it seems to be the nature of human beings to be inconsistent to some degree or another.[2]

When my mother died at the age of ninety-five, on Christmas Day in 2001, my brother Stoney, a nephew, a niece, and I inherited part of my great-great-grandparent's Albin Plantation in Tallahatchie County, Mississippi. In 2002, we sold the land to a cousin who owned and farmed neighboring property. At that point, the last of our ancestral plantation land, which was passed down my family lineage during the previous one hundred and fifty years and was the most physical link we had to the horrific institution of slavery, ceased to be in our possession.

I believe we each have unique gifts that can be utilized to make a contribution to the world around us. As I have immersed myself in promoting the understanding and healing of racism through the media with which I have worked, I have realized that one of my gifts is being a white person who can offer a unique voice for racial equality and healing because of my personal and family background. Through learning about myself and trying to bring healing to others, I have learned more about racism and prejudice in general as well as the healing of racism. This book is my way to pass on that knowledge. It is also my attempt to compensate for the injustice of my own, my family's, and my birth lineage's racist history.

The experience of writing this book has been both educational and painful. From conducting research on slavery and the South's Jim Crow era of white supremacy I gained a deeper awareness of how horrible slavery and the Jim Crow era were in America. This gave me a broader view of my relatives who were slave owners who believed in white supremacy. It also made me realize how much our society is still dealing with unresolved attitudes and issues left over from those periods of history. These have affected people of all races (and mixed races).

Many of the descriptions of slavery and slaves' stories that I read were heart-wrenching. To gain a better understanding of the Civil War, and to contribute to my research for this book, I watched Ken Burn's PBS film series on the subject twice. Both times, I was transfixed by the hundreds of poignant images and their accompanying dialogue and was filled with immense sadness. Seeing the horrors of such a brutal war, and sensing the enormous losses suffered by each side, was difficult. As a Southerner, at times I was close to weeping for the incredible pain suffered by my native South, and by my ancestors, during what many of us from the South called the Northern invasion.

Writing this reflection on my family history and my life has helped me put into perspective my own journey away from racism and prejudice. It has allowed me to step back and look at the big picture of my evolution. Looking at the racism of my family lineage was not easy for me, nor was it easy to revisit some of the painful experiences of my childhood that I have shared in these pages. Although this book may seem critical of members of my family, it is important to keep in mind that some people are unable to overcome the effects of their experiences and that generally they do the best they can.

In 2003, after writing 98 percent of this book, I attended a workshop (discussed in Chapter 8) which gave me a deeper understanding of the nature of our stories about ourselves and others; it allowed me to soften my own judgments, especially toward members of my family. The change in me caused me to put my book aside for almost ten years.

At the end of 2011, after joining a black friend in starting an organization to counter examples of racism in our community, I began to revisit what I had written and change some of its flavor. There are ways our stories are not quite the "ultimate truth," and in spite of my recent revisions and my efforts to write as honestly as I can, I would discourage the reader from looking at the stories I share as "the truth." I can only offer you, the reader, "my truth" as I know it at this moment, and I hope you will benefit from whatever inspires or moves you.

Although part of this book reflects the pain of our nation, of my birth lineage, and of my own life, this book is also an expression of hope. If one ordinary Southerner can make a shift from harassing black people in his youth to producing radio programs related to healing racism in his adulthood, then other people can face and overcome their own prejudices too. My greatest wish for this book is that it gives the reader insights and encouragement to look for prejudices carried within his or her own heart and also a sense of hope that healing racism and unlearning prejudice are possible for us all.

Organization of *Almost Hereditary*

The book is divided into four parts:

Part 1, "My Family History and Roots of My Racism," provides the historical background for understanding our race relations today as well as the multi-generational, "almost hereditary," racist influences that resulted in my own racist beliefs and behaviors. The first two chapters cover the history related to slavery, the Civil War, reconstruction in the South after the Civil War, and the Jim Crow era of segregation, oppression, and injustice imposed on the black population in the South following the abolition of slavery. The first chapter is unique in that it includes the personal experience of slavery with excerpts from the diaries of my great-great-grandmother, a slave owner, and quotes from interviews of former slaves. These two chapters, which may be painful to read, are meant to deepen the understanding of the forces that have contributed to the tension and conflict that still exists between the black and white races today. The remaining three chapters of Part I cover my experience of growing up in my birth family and how it affected me, including the ways in which racist views were passed down to me through the generations of my ancestors.

In Part II, "My Personal Growth and Journey Out of Racism," I share many of the experiences and influences which have contributed to my journey out of racism and my current work of helping others unlearn prejudice. Some of the experiences described relate directly to prejudice and racism. Others taught me about human behavior and helped me to become more self-aware, open-minded, and compassionate.

In Part III, "Understanding and Healing Prejudice," some of the causes and effects of racism and concrete steps that readers can take to overcome prejudice, both in themselves and society, are presented. In some respects, this is the most important section of the book. It provides a possible way out of the morass of racism as presented in Part I. It gives the reader options for positive action and personal growth. It offers hope.

Part IV, "The Journey Continues," covers one of the results of my journey out of racism, the co-founding of an organization to help others unlearn prejudice.

An epilogue describes some reflections on my last visit to Mississippi.

In the appendices are over one hundred questions, arranged by chapter titles and subtitles, for class discussions, book clubs, or individual reflection; articles I have written related to Martin Luther King; my philosophy of social action; and ideas regarding prejudice that I like to share with young people.

My website, http://www.healracism.com (formerly www.almosthereditaryunlearningprejudice.com), offers the general reader, historians, teachers, and students an introduction to my family history; three hundred excerpts from interviews with former slaves, arranged by subject matter; and many entries from my great-great-grandmother's diaries which are not found in Chapter 1.

Additional Comments About the Writing of *Almost Hereditary*

The first two chapters of this book include excerpts gleaned from my study of over 575 interviews of former slaves. More than 2,300 slave narratives were collected in the 1930s by field workers for the Works Projects Administration, a government agency. Unfortunately, most interviewers were white, which was likely a variable in the fact that some former slaves were not forthcoming about their experiences. Although the white interviewers tried to accurately replicate the language of their subjects, at times the result was a white person's representation of black speech, which may have been influenced by unconscious racism in some cases. This should be kept in mind when reading the quotations. One thing that is evident when reading the narratives, and the quotes I have extracted, is that most white people in the slaves' environment referred to the black people with the derogatory term "nigger;" hence the slaves were taught to use the term for themselves and each other.

One of many decisions I had to make in writing this book was whether to use "African-American" or "black" as a term to describe slaves, their descendants, and other people of African descent. Because I wanted to avoid using a term that might be improper or offensive, I asked my black friends what they preferred to be called and also looked on the Internet to see what word the National Association for the Advancement of Colored People (NAACP), *Ebony* magazine, and other entities used. Because "black" was commonly used by most of the sources I polled, I decided to use that. I mean no disrespect to those who prefer the term African-American.

This book has several references to America's indigenous peoples. I talked with "native" friends and studied websites to try to determine the suitability of the designations "Indigenous Peoples," "Indians," "American Indians," and "Native Americans." There appears to be an ongoing controversy regarding this subject, and in some cases, older members of native cultural groups have different preferences than younger members. There are understandable objections to each of the names just mentioned, and I could not come up with one perfect choice.

There is also the problem of using terms like "racist" and "white supremacist," which could easily be associated with people described in this book. They can create stereotypes of individuals by casting them in a set category. In turn, this can keep us from seeing all of what makes up the individuals. (I discuss the problem with stereotypes in more detail in Chapter 10.)

Several of the book's stories tend to connect racism with the state of Mississippi. I discourage readers from developing a prejudice against this state or its residents. Mississippi is a great state and many wonderful people live there, including some of my relatives. Like all states, it has had, and continues to have, its positive and negative qualities. And, of course, it has gone through many changes since the times of which I write.

Furthermore, a danger in focusing on racism or prejudice in a southern state, or in the South in general, is the tendency to overlook the fact that prejudice has existed, and still exists, all over our country. In *Southern Stalemate*, Christopher Bonastia points out that whites in the North opposed integration just as strongly as whites in the South.[3]

My great-great-grandmother's diary entries, which are included in the first chapter, contain many spelling errors. Standardized spelling was not a priority in America at the time she lived. She misspelled so many words, and even used different spellings for the same words so many times, that I even wonder if the spelling she usually used for her son's name, "Duglas," is correct, since that name is commonly spelled "Douglas" in our contemporary culture. (Although she spelled her son's name "Duglas" numerous times in her diaries, on at least one occasion she spelled it "Douglas"!) His tombstone, which appears to be fairly modern and was created long after he died, has the spelling "Douglass Robinson." Her family plantations were also referred to with different spellings as well as with different names, which made identifying and locating them very challenging.[4] In most cases, I have kept her original spelling, punctuation, and underlining. Bracketed material relates to words or explanations that I have added to make her entries clearer or to make notations pertaining to her words that were illegible.

Throughout this book, I have done my best to adhere to the guidelines in *The Chicago Manual of Style*.

In addressing the causes and effects of prejudice and discrimination (Chapter 10) and healing prejudice (Chapters 11 and 12), I have relied on my own observations and what I have learned on my own journey out of racism as well as authors and teachers whose insights and information I have found helpful. My wife, a licensed psychotherapist, contributed her expertise to sections related to psychological phenomena.

PART I

MY FAMILY HISTORY AND ROOTS OF MY RACISM

The chapters in this section provide the historical background for understanding our race relations today as well as the multi-generational, "almost hereditary," racist influences that resulted in my own racist beliefs and behaviors. The first two chapters cover the history related to slavery, the Civil War, Reconstruction in the South after the Civil War, and the Jim Crow era. These two chapters, which may be painful to read, are meant to deepen the understanding of the forces that have contributed to the tension and conflict that still exists between the black and white races. The remaining three chapters of Part I cover my experience of growing up in my birth family and how it affected me, including the ways in which racist views were passed down to me through the generations of my ancestors.

CHAPTER 1

THE ROOTS OF
MY FAMILY'S RACISM [i, ii, iii]

Most of what I have learned about the roots of my family's racism comes from the surviving volumes of diaries (1350 pages) recorded by my mother's maternal great-grandmother, Nancy McDougall Robinson, and research that I undertook in order to better understand those diaries and their author's family. The entries begin in July 1832, when Nancy was twenty-three years old, and end in December 1873, the month of her death at age sixty-five. This chapter includes a brief overview of the diaries, primarily focusing on my ancestor's relationship to, and attitudes about, slaves, freed blacks ("freedmen"), and Northerners. In order to give a more complete picture of my ancestors, and the context for parts of the diaries, it also discusses the harsh reality of slavery, the Civil War, and Reconstruction. Excerpts from narratives by former slaves have been included to provide the slaves' perspectives.

---

i Over thirty-five sources were researched for background information on slavery, the Civil War, and the conditions in the South at the end of the war, including ten volumes of slave narratives. All of these sources are listed in the bibliography. Aside from what has been gleaned from the Nancy Robinson diaries, much of this chapter's information on these subjects consists of common knowledge, facts, or details that can be found in numerous references.

ii Since the focus here is on my ancestors' relationship to slavery, other aspects of the slaves' experience have not been addressed, such as the ways some resisted other than running away, and ways some maintained their own sense of community and avoided being totally dominated by whites. To learn more about those subjects, I direct the reader to some of the sources in the bibliography, including *Slavery Remembered* by Paul Escott and George Rawick's *From Sundown to Sunup*. *Slavery Remembered* offers a good overview of the themes in the narratives and analyzes what percentage of slaves had different conditions and experiences. It is an important book in that it dispels some of the popular misconceptions about slavery.

iii Please be advised that this chapter's graphic descriptions of slavery and photographs of slave receipts might be upsetting to some people.

Nancy's parents, Nicholas and Elizabeth McDougall, were born in New York. Nancy was born in Canada in 1808 and attended school, apparently college, in Ohio. At some point her family settled in Port Gibson, Mississippi, where her father was a judge.

While living in their home on Farmer Street, she began the first of the series of diaries that came into my possession with these words:

Miss Nancy McDougall
Vol. 4
This Book much like its owner
Too incapacious to be of any note
Port Gibson   July 1832
Claibourn County, Miss.

One of the first entries in that volume indicates Nancy's awareness of life's many difficulties:

July or August [?] 1832 - We are considered in ourselves very helpless and wretched beings. We are subject every moment to greate calamities & misfortuntes.

She also expressed sensitivity and occasional idealism:

September 30, 1832 - The ways of providence are mysterious. Would it but favor the brave, the generous & good. Could I be Rich, no one should want while I had it in my power to bestow. I would give to the homeless child of want. My coffers should be open to the destitute. How can the children of disipation behold the misery of their fellow creatures without paying to aleviate their suffering, to cheer the dying moments of those who are friendless, to sooth the afflicted, to dry the tear from the cheek of misery & dispence happiness. Such would be the wish of the kind hearted.

Slavery

In general, the whole South benefited from slavery because it brought prosperity.[1] Most of the crops the South exported were grown on slave plantations. Although two-thirds to three-quarters of Southerners were not involved with slavery, they supported the institution, in part, because it perpetuated the myths that whites were superior to blacks and blacks were sub-human. These myths comprised one of the main themes in the history of the South and justified the harsh treatment blacks received, as well as the belief, before and during the Civil War, that whites had the right to own blacks as property.[2]

In December 1832, Nancy married twenty-five-year-old Alfred Robinson, and they rode on horseback to one of the slave plantations he had inherited from his deceased parents. Some historians define a plantation as a farm where at least twenty slaves lived.[3] Plantations with fifty or more slaves contained about twenty-five percent of the South's slaves.[4] At least ten different Robinson plantations are mentioned in her diaries, one in Louisiana and the rest (with possibly one or two exceptions) in Mississippi. Sometimes different names or references are used for the same plantation, which makes it hard to determine their exact number. Her husband often owned two or more plantations simultaneously. One of my cousins who currently farms the family land estimates that Alfred Robinson owned at least six or seven thousand acres of plantation land on the Mississippi Delta in the north half of the state at one time. Alfred was the owner of the family's land and slaves, and when he died in 1858 at the age of fifty-one, his estate was valued at $600,000[iv], a considerable amount of money at that time. Although he may have owned as many as two hundred slaves, at the time of his death Nancy and her two sons, Jerry and Douglas, inherited 136. Nancy's account book, which lists slave names, notes a number of slave children born after Alfred's death.

---

iv Using the consumer price index to calculate what $1 in 1858 would equate to in 2014, the amount would be $27.30. Six hundred thousand dollars would equate to $16,380,000.

Nancy McDougal Robinson (1808-1873), wife of Alfred B. Robinson, my great-great-grandmother and author of the diaries.

Alfred B. Robinson (1807-1858), husband of Nancy McDougal Robinson, my great-great-grandfather and owner of the slave plantations.

*Brothers Jeremiah "Jerry" Robinson (1836-1905), my great-grandfather (left),
and Douglas Robinson (1838-1883), sons of Alfred and Nancy Robinson.
(Alfred and Nancy's first child, Alfred, died in 1837 at 3½ years of age.)
Like their mother, both brothers inherited slave plantations.*

*1852 deed granting 198 acres of Mississippi land to Alfred B. Robinson for
$1,190.16. This land probably became a part of his slave plantations.*

1854 deed granting 480 acres of Mississippi land to Alfred B. Robinson. The land probably became a part of his slave plantations.

Mississippi

Alfred and Nancy Robinson's Plantations
(Approximate Locations)

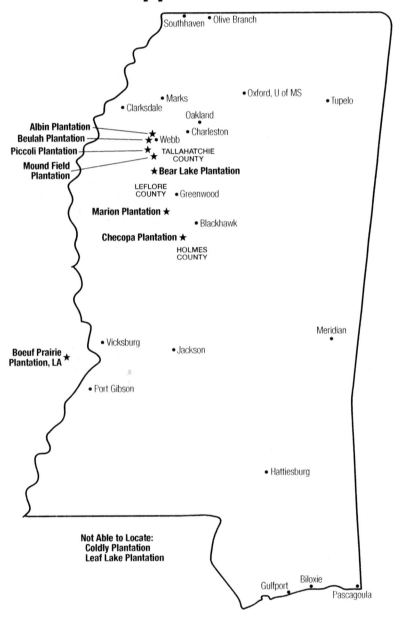

Southhaven • Olive Branch

• Oxford, U of MS • Tupelo

• Marks
• Clarksdale
Oakland •
• Charleston

Albin Plantation ★
Beulah Plantation ★ • Webb
Piccoli Plantation ★
Mound Field ★ TALLAHATCHIE COUNTY
Plantation

★ **Bear Lake Plantation**

LEFLORE COUNTY • Greenwood

Marion Plantation ★

• Blackhawk

Checopa Plantation ★

HOLMES COUNTY

Meridian
•

• Vicksburg
• Jackson

Boeuf Prairie ★
Plantation, LA

• Port Gibson

• Hattiesburg

Not Able to Locate:
Coldly Plantation
Leaf Lake Plantation

Biloxie
Gulfport •
Pascagoula

On a typical family plantation involving a husband, the husband owned the slaves and the land and had authority over the family while the wife took care of the house.[5] The wife of a plantation owner usually had a lonely life.[6] I do not know how true this was for my great-great-grandmother. She did write about entertaining company, visiting friends, sewing, and reading.

Five generations of slaves on a plantation in Beaufort, South Carolina, 1862. (Library of Congress).

The house of the slave owner, usually referred to as "the big house," could be a mansion or a large well-built house that was fairly modest. Housing conditions for slaves varied, and the structures could be made of boards, logs, brick, or stone. There were slave quarters with dirt floors and ones with wood floors. Simple cabins were common, yet some large plantations had basic wood or brick apartment-like buildings. My study of the slave narratives indicates that most slaves seemed to have adequate housing. While there are certainly examples of very poor living conditions, the popular view that all slaves lived in drafty quarters with dirt floors that encouraged illness does not appear to be true.

My mother described "dogtrot" houses, a type of slave housing used on the Mississippi Delta, where she grew up. These were also called "possum-trot" or "breezeway" houses. Dogtrot structures could be found in the southeast United States in the 1700s and 1800s. They consisted of two cabins under a single roof with an open area or breezeway in the middle. The covered breezeway contributed to ventilation and offered shade for those who wanted to sit under the roof to work or relax. The dogtrot or possum-trot names probably referred to the fact that those animals could run through, or trot through, the breezeway. Dogtrot houses for slaves were more primitive than those for whites.

Plantation house in Jefferson County, Mississippi. (Library of Congress).

Plantation house in Melrose, Natchitoches Parish, Louisiana. (Library of Congress).

Slave quarters in Montgomery County, Maryland. (Library of Congress).

Former slave cabin in Barbour County, Alabama, with later occupants. Photograph taken between 1936 and 1937. (Library of Congress).

Slave quarters in Grundy County, Tennessee.
(Library of Congress).

Slave quarters in Adams County, Mississippi. (Library of Congress).

Dogtrot style slave quarters in Butler County, Alabama.
(Library of Congress).

The diets of slaves varied. Some slaves were fed extremely well, whereas others were almost starved to death and were forced to steal food from the owners at risk of severe punishment. Some slaves did not receive a good nutritious diet due to the lack of knowledge about the subject on the part of their masters.[7] Some owners let their slaves leave the plantation to hunt or fish, and some slaves were allowed to grow their own food to supplement their diets. It seems that, in most cases, the slaves were fed adequetly.[8]

Clothes for slaves were generally made on the plantation. On a number of farms, slaves were given new clothes a couple of times a year. Some slaves were dressed well, while some were very poorly attired. Some had severe foot problems from not having shoes and suffered cold winter days without warm clothing. However, most slaves seem to have been provided clothes for their most basic needs.[9]

Here is a comment on inadequate food and clothing by Charlie Moses, who was a slave in Marion County, Mississippi, a county where one of my ancestors' plantations (the "Marion Place") was located:

> We never had much clothes 'ceptin' what was give us by the marster or the mistis. Winter time we never had 'nough to wear nor 'nough to eat.... The marster didn't think we needed anything, but jus' a little.[10]

Jennie Kendricks, who lived the life of a slave in Sheram, Georgia, had a very different experience. Here are the words of her interviewer:

> She stated that they all wore good clothing and that all of it was made on the plantation with one exception....
>
> There was always enough food for everybody on the Moore plantation. Mrs. Moore once told Jennie's mother to always see that her children had sufficient to eat....
>
> The houses that they lived in were one-roomed structures made of heavy plank.... The beds were well constructed.... [Jennie said that when they finished constructing each mattress] "it looked like a mattress that was bought in a store."[11]

Plantation slaves worked in the house or in the fields. Field workers were managed by a white overseer and/or a trusted black "driver," either of whom could be cruel to the workers. Charlie Pye, a former slave in Georgia, described the situation on his plantation:

> To see that everyone continued working an overseer rode over the plantation keeping check on the workers. If any person was caught resting he was given a sound whipping....
>
> The whipping was done by a "Nigger Driver," who followed the overseer around with a bull whip especially for this purpose.[12]

Slaves were given light work to do around the age of five or six. By the time they were about twelve, they were doing adult work as field hands. Typically they got up at four in the morning and worked from sunrise to sunset, five and one-half days a week. Some masters worked their slaves six or seven days a week. On some plantations, work extended into the evening. Often women and men worked equally hard in the field. One of the most common complaints of former slaves was the extreme work conditions.[13] Sarah Oteen, formerly a slave in North Carolina, gave this assessment:

> I nebbah knowed whut it wah t' rest. I just work all de time f'om mawnin' till late at night. I had t' do ebbathin' dey wah t' do on de outside. Work in de field, chop wood, hoe cawn, till sometimes I feels lak mah back sholy break....
>
> Law, chile, nobuddy knows how mean da'kies wah treated. Wy, dey wah bettah t' de animals den t' us'ns.[14]

Not all slaves worked on plantations; some worked in city homes, for businesses, and so on. Some slave women, often with lighter skin, were forced to work as prostitutes. They were referred to as "fancy girls."[15]

Speculators bought slaves from plantation owners or at auctions and then sold them for a profit. In many cases, husbands, wives, and children were sold separately, never to see each other again. Here is the recollection of former slave, W. L. Bost, from his slave days in North Carolina:

> The speculators stayed in the hotel and put the niggers in the quarters jus like droves of hogs. All through the night I could hear them mournin' and prayin.' I didn't know the Lord would let people live who were so cruel. The gates were always locked and they was a guard on the outside to shoot anyone who tried to run away. Lord miss, them slaves look just like droves of turkeys runnin' along in front of them horses.
>
> I remember when they put 'em on the block to sell 'em. The ones 'tween 18 and 30 always bring the most money. The auctioneer he stand off at a distance and cry 'em off as they stand on the block. I can hear his voice as long as I live.
>
> If the one they going to sell was a young Negro man this is what he say: "Now gentlemen and fellow-citizens here is a big black buck Negro. He's stout as a mule. Good for any kin' o' work an' he never gives any trouble. How much am I offered for him?"
>
> If they put a young nigger woman the auctioneer cry out: "Here's a young nigger wench, how much am I offered for her?" The pore thing stand on the block a shiverin' an' a shakin' nearly froze to death. When they sold, many of the pore mothers beg the speculators to sell 'em with their husbands, but the speculator only take what he want. So maybe the pore thing never see her husban' agin.[16]

Henri Necaise, an ex-slave from Mississippi, shared this story:

> I never knowed my mother. I was a slave an' my mother was sol' from me an' her other chilluns. Dey tol' me when dey sol' 'er my sister was a-holdin' me in her arms. She was standin' behin' de Big House peekin' 'roun' de corner an' seen de las' o' her mother. I seen her go, too. Dey tell me I used to go to de gate a-huntin' for my mammy.[17]

The woman who interviewed former Alabama slave Janie Scott described her story with these words:

> During the Civil War when supplies were scarce, especially salt, Marster John rode off taking her mother's sister Ca'line [Janie's aunt] with him, and when he returned alone his wife, Mrs. Meyers, wanted to know where was Ca'line, and Master John replied: "I sold her for a sack of salt." Sarah [Janie's mother] never saw her sister anymore.[18]

It was not unusual for my ancestors to pay $1,000 for an adult slave. Nancy referred to them as "negroes," "darkies" or "the People." (The term "the People" was also used to refer to her black and white tenants collectively after the Civil War.) At times she referred to blacks with the abbreviation "Col" (for "colored"). Once in awhile she used the word "family" in a context that included both her family by marriage and their slaves.

The journals contain several references to the purchase of slaves.

September 24, 1858 - [Richmond, VA] Today is cool. We have a fire in the grade for Mr. R. [her husband] complains of feeling chilly — in the evening he went out with Jerry to buy some more Slaves to bring home while I write June Baldwin and Duglas.

September 26, 1858 - We left Richmond on the [train] Cars at 5 o'clock. Jerry, Mr. R., myself & 29 slaves for our home.

January 17, 1860 - The next morning Jerry came and we went to see a family of negroes he had bought…. They belonged to Gov. Brandons son who sold them to us as his minority had expired. Duglas concluded to take them to Talahachie and we returned home to prepare for their journey.

February 8, 1860 - Jerry went to Black Hawk on business, and there met a man with some negroes, which he and I bought for the River place — and he gave up going to the City; and took the People home to Talahachie.

I remember one day in my childhood sitting on the sofa in my grandmother's Mississippi home on one of the family plantations as my mother proudly showed me receipts for some of the slaves my ancestors had purchased. At that time in my life, I did not question my family's values, and I found the receipts interesting and even a little awe-inspiring. They were physical artifacts — that I could actually hold in my hands — from an era of long ago that my mother was so proud of being connected to and that was part of her and our family's identity. When I was doing research for this book, I procured photocopies of these very receipts from the Mississippi Department of Archives and History and read them for the first time in over forty years. They made the idea of treating human beings like animals that were to be bought and sold more real to me than anything else I had seen pertaining to my family's history. Unlike when I was a naive child, I found them very disturbing.

FAMILY RECEIPTS FOR THE PURCHASE OF SLAVES
(Courtesy of the Mississippi Department of Archives and History)

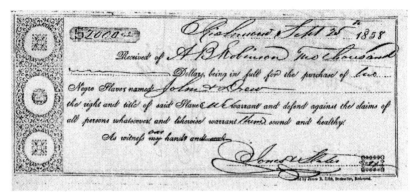

"Richmond, Sept. 25, 1858. Received of A B Robinson two thousand Dollars, being paid in full for the purchase of two Negro Slaves named John & Drew the right and title of said Slaves we warrant and defend against the claims of all persons whatsoever, and likewise warrant them sound and healthy. As witness our hands. Jones & Slater." (Drew died of pneumonia on October 24, 1858, a month after he was purchased.)

"Richmond, Va, Sep. 24, 1858. Received of A B Robinson twenty eight hundred Dollars being in full for the purchase of four Negro Slaves named Tom Eliza Phoebe and Ann the right and title of said Slaves I warrant and defend against the claims of all persons whatsoever, and likewise warrant them sound and healthy. As witness my hand and seal. Thos A Turk [seal]"

"*$10,800 Richmond Sept 24th 1858. Received Mr A. B. Robinson ten thousand and eight hundred dollars being in full for the purchase of twelve negro slaves named George Bob Paul George and John Jenny Nrify(?) Esarlespon(?) Jack Eliza Muriad(?) And Martha the right and title of said slaves I warrant and defend against the claims of all persons whatsoever and likewise warrant them sound and healthy as witness my hand and seal. E. W. Blackburn. Seal.*"

Receipt for slaves that apparently were brought to the Sidon plantation in Mississippi for Jerry Robinson. "Sidon, Miss. Feb. 11, 1860. $5,950. Received of Jerry Robinson his draft for five thousand nine hundred and fifty dollars due the first of [March?] next being in full for the purchase of four negro slaves named Carolina, Lilly, Calvin and Sophy. The right and title of said negro slaves I warrant and defend against the claims of all persons whatsoever and I likewise warrant said slaves sound in body and mind. So witness my hand and seal. John T.(?) Thomas. Seal. D. Robinson Witness."

Slave pen, Alexandria, Virginia, interior view showing the doors of cells where the slaves were held before being sold. Photographed between 1861 and 1865. (Library of Congress).

Slave sales and auction house ("Auction & Negro Sales"), Atlanta, Georgia. Photographed in 1864 during Union General Sherman's occupation of Atlanta. (Library of Congress).

Some of my great-great-grandmother's entries refer to slaves celebrating the Fourth of July and the Christmas holidays, to the playful activities of slave children, and to occasional slave weddings in either the slave quarters or her home:

December 15, 1853 - My mind is easy by hearing that my sons are contented and I sit alone to night and think of them. A lone with three <u>of the Sable children of Africa siting on the carpet</u> by the fire at my feet - and their merriment drives all care a way.

July the 4th, 1853 - A memorable day to all Americans. A day of <u>Liberty here</u>. The negros are enjoying it and banqueting on the good things on the place.

December 18, 1853 - We have been making cakes & preparing Christmas Cheer. All the negros are makeing ready their houses and clothes for gaiety.

December 26, 1859 - Dancing, feasting and pleasure is going on at the [slave] <u>Quarters</u>. The <u>Darkies</u> are very happy and joyous.

December 27, 1859 - The rain is falling and the people are indoors quilting and doing Christmas work, visiting each other and making merry.

April 29, 1859 - There is to be a wedding at the [slave] Quarters this evening (London weds Ester). Anna and I witness the ceremony — and the overseer.

February 11, 1865 - The Boys [her sons] are at Alban [Plantation] & we are preparing for the wedding of two servents, Agustus & Sopha. The supper table is set, Duglas, Walter & Daniel are come in a canoe — all are ready. At 8 o'clock Agustus & Sopha were married in the hall.

Slave marriages were never considered legal and could be disregarded or terminated by the owner. Because masters had total authority over their slaves, and owning a slave implied owning the slaves' sex life, slaves were susceptible to sexual exploitation, and sexual abuse was a frequent occurrence.[19] The owner could force female slaves to have sex with anyone he pleased, including himself or — for breeding purposes — another slave. Former Mississippi slave Mollie Williams related this story:

> One day Marse George an' his uncle, Mr. John Davenport…dey rid over to Grand Gulf whar dey was a sellin' slabes offen de block an' Mr. John tol' Marse George to pick hisself out a pair of darkies to mate so's he could get hisself a start of darkies fer to chop his cotton an' like. So Marse George pick out my pappy fust. My pappy come from North Ca'lina. Den he seen my mammy an' she was big an' strengthly an' he wanted her pow'ful bad. But…he didn' have 'nough money to buy 'em both, so his Uncle John say he'd buy mammy an' den he would loan her over to Marse George fer pappy. An' de fust chile would be Mr. John's, an' de secon' Marse George's, and likewise.[20]

John Bectom, an ex-slave in North Carolina, recalled:

> Some of the slave holders would have some certain slave women reserved for their own use. Sometimes children almost white would be born to them. I have seen many of these children. Sometimes the child would be said to belong to the overseer, and sometimes it would be said to belong to the marster.[21]

Ironically, during slavery and the later Jim Crow era, many people who were part Caucasian due to the rape of slave women by whites were persecuted by their own white fathers, siblings, nephews, cousins, etc.[22]

As one of many ways of asserting authority over the slaves, it was common practice for slave owners to name their slaves' babies.[23] When I studied the names of slaves Nancy's family owned, I discovered that, with rare exceptions, slaves were only given first names. The babies were never given a last name that would allow them to be publicly and officially connected to their birth families.[24, 25]

Life for Nancy was difficult and painful, as it was for many people of her time, regardless of race or social class. Sickness and death were common sources of suffering. Several of her entries mention diseases that had devastating effects on various cities, in some cases killing hundreds of people. Her husband's brother and sister-in-law lost five of their eight children before the children's fifth birthdays. In one year, Nancy lost seven of her relatives, including her mother. People died from pneumonia, smallpox, cholera, typhoid fever, measles, yellow fever, and other ailments.

Because of their harsh life, and, in some cases, their lack of proper nutrition, slaves were subject to more sickness and a much shorter lifespan than whites.[26] During eight months' time (September 1858 through April 1859), Nancy saw forty of her family's slaves die from sickness. While this represented a considerable financial loss, it was also a difficult emotional experience for her. She felt a strong sense of responsibility toward her slaves and spent many hours trying to nurse them to health. All of those named in the following entries, except for Nancy's son Jerry, are slaves.

October 18 through November 4, 1858 - I left home with Jerry for the Talahatchie Place, the wagon with 11 of our new People [slaves bought in Richmond, Virginia] started before us, Jerry drove me in the buggy the first days journey, and I rode on horse back the rest of the way.

The next morning one of the new boys Drew was sick with pneumonia....

Sunday [24th] The sick boy [Drew] died.

Tuesday Morning 26th Oct. – We came home ([to] Sidon) and found many of our sick family [the slaves] sick unto death. I went from one to another nearly all night, with all we could do (Charles Sykes died while I was gone) and Lilly his wife next morning. That evening Lucys infant died and they was buried.

Friday 29th - This morning at nine Lucy died. Peter her husband come to our door before light to tell us he was worse but medicine treatment could not save him. He died at 11 o'clock. Charles Baily, a favorite, with all our care died at 4 o'clock that evening. Maked a loss of three good servants that day. Lucy & Peter was taken to the grave together and Charles was buried the next morning.

Sat. 30th - Our remaining sick seemed better but Pneumonia is a fearful disease. I tended on them all day and though[t?] of sleeping at night. At 12 o'clock wearier with fatigue and anxiety I lay down But was soon aroused to be told Louis Sykes was dead.

Sun. 31 Oct. - The Sun shone brightly but fear and dread was in our hearts. Every one that took sick thought they would die. Pneumonia was indeed fearful. At nine o'clock Maria a young girl died and late in the evening Sister and I went to see her and Louis buried. With humble and crushed hearts we all knelt on the earth and never was a more humble prayer made for mercy. Claiborn [a slave and preacher] asked for the distruction to ceace and for our weary and grieved hearts to be healed. We all felt the weight of sorrow, and I tried to cheer them with the hope that the sickness was under.

Thursday - I have walked about the Place all day cheering, nursing, and having every thing changed in the [slave] Cabbins that would give a different and cheerful aspect and saying the sickness is over and not put a sick one in the sick house.

Another source of pain for both my great-great-grandmother and her slaves was the relocation of slaves from one plantation to another in order to meet the family's labor needs.

> **December 16, 1841** - A day of sadness truly has passed, yes, of grief in reality — the sepperation of Brothers, the parting of friends, of parents and children, the grief and lamentation of the negroes at leaving, for Jerry [her husband's brother] started for the Louisiana Place (with some of the people).

As a result of relocating slaves, they were often separated from their spouses, parents, children and/or siblings because of the needs of plantation owners. In the following entry, Nancy talks about having to move with some of her slaves from the Marion Plantation to the Tallahatchie Plantation (probably also known as the Beulah Plantation) after her husband's estate had been settled.

> **January 23, 1861** - I was much distressed during the week, and on Saturday at the discontent of the People that belonged to me, at going to the Talahachie Place, which I was to have [for] my division of the estate. They have rung my heart at the division, and were now to go to the only home I had for them or myself. I feel like a bird of passage, till I can have a house of my own.... I am to leave this Place, so long my home, to Duglas, and go to a new country…and live where I can, till my home can be made a home for me. It is a trial for me to go out alone and make for myself new friends for the little time I have to remain on earth.

During the dozens of hours that I spent studying the 1,350 pages of my great-great-grandmother's diaries, I discovered that there were no descriptions of her slaves' working or living conditions. There is not a single entry regarding the punishment, or lack of punishment, of the family's slaves. She does not say the slaves were treated poorly, nor does she say they were treated well, and I wondered if she felt uncomfortable writing about this subject because of the cruelty of slavery. (Her references to slaves celebrating July 4 and Christmas are not revealing, since most plantations gave their slaves these holidays regardless of how strict the masters and overseers were.)

One thing that stands out in the slave narratives is the variation in conditions slaves had to contend with. A very small percentage of slaves had a situation such as that of Anna Parkes when she was a slave in Georgia:

'Ole Marster'…'spained dat us wuz not to be 'shamed of our race. He said us warn't no 'niggers;' he said us wuz 'Negroes,' and he 'spected his Negroes to be de best negroes in de whole land….

…[He] never whipped none of his negroes, not dat I ever heard of. He tole 'em what he wanted done, and gave 'em plenty of time to do it.[27]

This was the experience of G. W. Pattillo, when he was also a Georgia slave:

(Interviewer:) With a few slaves and a small farm, Master Ingram was very lenient and kind to his slaves and usually worked with them in the fields. (G. W. Patillo:) "We had no special time to begin or end the work for the day. If he got tired he would say, 'Alright, boys, let's stop and rest,' and sometimes we didn't start working until late in the day."

(Interviewer:)…Mr. and Mrs. Ingram never punished the children, nor allowed anyone but their parents to do so. If the boy became unruly, Mrs. Ingram would call his mother and say, "Harriett, I think G.W. needs to be taken down a button hole lower."[28]

There are even examples of slave owners leaving their land to the slaves in their wills.[29] One such person explained to the slaves that they had made him prosperous and he wanted them to become prosperous.[30]

On the other end of the spectrum, you have incredible cruelty, even sadism, on the part of masters, their representatives, and even, in some cases, the master's wife. Former Mississippi slave Henry Cheatam told this story:

> Old Miss had a nigger oberseer an 'dat was de meanest debil dat eber libbed on de Lawd's green yearth.... Lots of times I'se seen him beat my mammy, an' one day I seen him beat my Auntie who was big wid a chile, and dat man dug a roun' hole in de groun' and' put her stummick in it, an' beat an' beat her for a half hour straight till the baby came out raght dere in de hole.[31]

An analysis of the slave narratives indicate that slave owners who whipped their slaves were the rule rather than the exception, and most of the owners fell somewhere in between the two extremes just described.[32] The whippings were one of the things that bothered former slaves the most about slavery.[33]

Slaves could be whipped for any number of reasons, including showing what was perceived to be the least bit of disrespect to the master or overseer through body language, facial expression, tone of voice, etc.[34] Some slaves were whipped because they were newly purchased, and the master wanted to let them know who was boss. On a number of plantations, slaves were whipped simply because they had not been whipped in awhile, even though they had done nothing wrong. The slave narratives have numerous examples of the master, driver, or overseer rubbing salt, pepper, or even turpentine into the fresh wounds of a severely whipped slave in order to increase the pain. Some slaves were whipped with a paddle that had holes in it. The holes caused blisters to form, which were then broken open with a cat-o-nine-tails, a whip with nine individual leather strips attached to the handle. Then salt or pepper would be applied. Some slaves were whipped to death. There are examples, one in the autobiography of Frederick Douglass, a former slave who advised President Lincoln, of slaves who were shot to death because they refused to be whipped.[35]

Wilson Chinn, branded slave from Louisiana. Shows instruments of torture used to punish slaves, including paddle with holes (described in this chapter), 1863. (Library of Congress).

Scars on a slave's back, wood engraving that was an exact replica of a photograph, 1863. (Library of Congress).

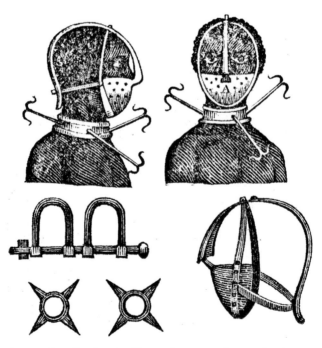

Iron mask, collar, leg shackles, and spurs used to restrict slaves, 1807. (Library of Congress).

While whippings, and in some cases torture, occurred on plantations, some slave owners used alternative forms of punishment. Some deprived their slaves of food and/or threatened to sell them and separate them from their families. In short, slaves and their families had no rights whatsoever, and any resistance to white domination resulted in brutal punishment.

Given the genuine sensitivity and kindness that is evident in some of her writing, it is very likely that Nancy was kind to the house servants with whom she interacted on a daily basis. But there is no way to tell from the diaries how her husband and sons related to the family's slaves. Even if they refrained from abusing their slaves — aside from the fact that ownership of other human beings is in itself abusive — the overseers on their plantations most likely would have been abusive. Ultimately, like all plantation owners, my ancestors would have been responsible for the abuse.

In order to keep blacks from advancing intellectually, a development that might make slaves less cooperative and challenge the myth that blacks were inferior, slaves in most Southern states were forbidden to learn to read and write. Slaves who were caught trying to read were generally sold and/or severely punished. One was told by his master he would be hung if he were caught with a book.[v] A slave account described in *Remembering Slavery* by Berlin, Favreau and Miller discusses a young slave who was caught trying to learn the alphabet. The overseer whipped the boy repeatedly and then put out his eyes.[36] Here is a testimony from former Georgia slave Henry Nix:

> When my Uncle stole a book and wuz a trying to learn how to read and write, Marse Jasper had the white doctor take off my Uncle's fo' finger right down to de 'fust jint'. Marstar said he fixed dat darky as a sign fo de res uv 'em![37]

In discussing numbers or "figures," and "ought" or "0," Andrew Boone, once a slave in North Carolina, told this to his interviewer:

---

v Rev. W. Northcross, *Alabama, Slave Narratives*, 230

I can't read an' write but dey learned us to count. Dey learned us to count dis way. "Ought is an' ought, an' a figger is a figger, all for de white man an' nothin' fer de nigger."[38]

It was dangerous for any slave to leave a plantation without a pass, even with permission and/or for a legitimate reason. To leave the plantation to visit a wife on another plantation, go hunting or fishing, run an errand for a master, or for some other legitimate reason, slaves were supposed to have passes or permits from their masters. Small groups of white patrollers (called "patty-rollers" by some slaves) were paid to roam the country and catch runaways and other slaves who were out without permission, break up illegal gatherings of slaves off the plantation, and even police slaves on their own plantations. (Some of the more humane slave owners would not allow patrollers to come on their land or harass their slaves when they were off of the property.) The patrollers usually beat slaves mercilessly when they left their plantations without permission and then took them back to their owners. Some slave owners as well as some patrollers kept dogs, referred to as "nigger dogs," specifically for tracking down an escaped slave. It was not unusual for the vicious dogs to be allowed to attack the person, causing considerable physical harm. George Young, formerly a slave near Livingston, Alabama, described his brother's attempt to run away:

My brother Harrison [ran away] an' dey sot de 'nigger dogs' on him…. Dey didn't run him down till 'bout night but finely dey cotched him, an' de hunters feched him to de [mistress'] do' an' say: "Mary Ann, here' Harrison." Den dey turned de dogs loose on him ag'in, an sich a screamin' you never hyared. He was all bloody an' Mammy was a-hollerin', "Save him, Lord, save my chile, an' don' let dem dogs eat him up." Mr. Lawler said, "De Lord ain't got nothin' do wid dis here," an' hit sho' look like He didn't, 'caze dem dogs nigh 'bout chewed Harrison up. Dem was hard times, sho'.[39]

Nancy's diaries note that her family's plantation overseers were not always the best of characters.

July 4, 1859 - Our overseer left yesterday from inability to attend to business caused by...drunkenness.

September 11, 1859 - I hear the overseer at Marion [Plantation] was a trifling fellow.

As noted in *Remembering Slavery*, starting in the late 1800s, whites in both the North and South began to develop the myth that slaves enjoyed their lot and their masters were kind.[40] In his book *The Hidden Wound*, Wendell Berry points out that, even if a slave owner was kind to his or her slaves, for that kindness to exist the slave had to be cooperative. If a slave would not cooperate, the owner controlled the slave with violence or, being unable to do that, sold the slave to someone else who could. In and of itself, this inescapable fact belies the myth of the benevolence of slavery.[41] Furthermore, some, if not most, of the more benevolent slave owners acted out of their own self-interest.[42] A former slave from North Carolina, Alex Huggins, explained it this way:

Nobody was bein' mean to me. No, I was'nt bein' whipped.... What pusson with any sense is goin' to take his horse or his cow an' beat it up? It's prope'ty. We was prope'ty. Val'able prope'ty.[43]

Another reason some owners were kind to their slaves was because it made the slaves more productive. In fact, for this reason most Southern writings recommended treating slaves fairly.[44] Obviously many slave owners ignored this advice.

People like my mother who justified slavery because of the belief that all slaves were treated well miss the essential point.

Whether slaves were treated well or horribly, it is wrong to buy, sell, and own other human beings. Here is how Green Cumby, formerly a slave in Texas, put it:

> I allus had de good marster. He sho' was good to us, but you knows dat ain't de same as bein' free.[45]

Former Virginia and Georgia slave Delia Garlic said:

> It's bad to belong to folks dat own you soul an' body.[46]

Two of my great-great-grandmother's diary entries make it clear that not all slaves on her plantation and in her community were happy with their situation.

> **December 27, 1856** - We have been disturbed in mind this week with the news of inserection and rebelion against the white comunty for Liberty by the Darkies. But I hope it is past, and no injury done in our Country. [At times Nancy used the word *country* in reference to a region or perhaps a county — not the whole United States]

> **March 28, 1860** - Duglas has not yet returned home, and the overseer is yet very sick, not able to be up — and I hear bad news from Talahachie [Plantation]. That 3 of the men had run off and Duglas caught them and took them back.

The Civil War

Southerners in the slave states of the South were horrified when Abraham Lincoln was elected president in November 1860 because he was opposed to the spread of slavery into new territories. (He was not opposing slavery in the states where it already existed.) On January 9, 1861, Mississippi became the second state (after South

Carolina) to secede from the Union. A total of eleven Southern states seceded, including Alabama, Arkansas, Florida, Georgia, Louisiana, North Carolina, Tennessee, Texas, and Virginia. On February 18, Mississippi Senator Jefferson Davis was sworn in as President of the Confederacy. Alexander H. Stephens was the Vice-President.

On March 21, Stephens gave what was called the "Cornerstone Speech," in which he stated:

> "The new [Confederate] constitution has put to rest, forever, all the agitating questions relating to . . . slavery[,] as it exists amongst us the proper status of the negro in our form of civilization. This was the immediate cause of the late rupture and present revolution....
>
> "Our new government is founded[,]...it's cornerstone rests, upon the great truth that the negro is not equal to the white man; that slavery subordination to the superior race is his natural and normal condition. Thus, our new government is the first in the history of the world based upon this great physical, philosophical, and moral truth."[47]

As well as defending slavery and its basic premises, the formation of the Confederacy related to a belief in the concept of state's rights, which supported the view that the South had the right to secede from the Union without interference from the North. On April 12, rebels fired on Fort Sumter, South Carolina, and the Civil War began.

It was difficult for Nancy to watch the South's young men, including her sons, go to war. (I only found Jerry's name among records of soldiers, but a post-war diary entry indicates that Douglas got a pardon for fighting in it.)

April 21-23, 1861 - There is much uneasiness now with regard to our political disentions. President Lincoln has issued his proclamation, that all the secession states come into the Union again, or he will [force] them back. He has now 70,000 armed men at the city of Washington ready for his orders. His war vessells are now round our southern coast. The secessionists will not go back without the purposed amendments to their laws, and must now contend against the armies of Lincoln. Our state calls for men to assist in this trial for ourselves. Jerry has left me this evening. He goes to Jackson, commissioned to see the governor for the company formed in this neighborhood, with regard to arms and orders.

April 28, 1861 - I have many things to distress me. I heard that a company was forming at Sidon to go to Charleston, S.C. Also a horse company, and I expect Duglas will join, as Jerry has. I feel the horror of the suffering if they do go. Capt. Dillon has called on his way up the Bayou to collect friends to fit out our county companys, to start immediately. Fort Pickens has been sustained with a great loss to our state's men. There has been a skermish at Baltimore, he said, in which Lincoln's men retreated. And the South, he said, would fight while she still has a man. Lincoln said he will fight the South as long as he has men and money, if they do not come back into the Union.

May 6, 1861 - The company of vigilence met here and we had forty to dine with us. Our flag for the Southern Confederacy floated in the breeze, and was hailed with cheers. Gov. Pettes sent back the company from Boliver County, saying he wished those of the valley to remain to protect themselves from Abolitionists [the opponents of slavery] and home troubles.

July 8, 1861 - Jerry began getting ready to leave his home for a year, and trust the uncertainty of war to ever return. Jerry was fine, though the grief of his people was calculated to make him regret leaving them, and he told them he must go.

July 15, 1861 - Our soldiers left in the morning for the camp, and my company of ladies went in the carriage and buggy at ten.... Mr. Helm addressed the company (the Sunflower guards [representing Sunflower County]), and presented them with a banner.... The dancing began. I went to see the dance and found that both my sons were dancing happily. How long, I asked myself, can they be so happy. These sad times, when our country is in a struggle for Peace on Earth. The time is uncertain. After the festivity was over I went with Mr. Wells to the Camp, where we were invited to see them drill and performed mock battle. I saw the company in their heavy uniforms and arms go through their exercises in double quick time, and the exertion and weariness they showed grieved me — dear children of the South raised tenderly. How can they be able to bear the druggery of camp life.

On September 22, 1862, Lincoln signed the Emancipation Proclamation, a declaration of freedom for slaves in the territory controlled by the Confederacy (which did not apply to any other states). It took effect on January 1, 1863. The proclamation also made it possible for those freed slaves to be hired to fight for the Union. Prior to this, slaves that had escaped to the North or to the Union army, had to be returned to their owners; although as of August 1861, slaves confiscated from plantation owners by Union troops could be freed.

Nancy's son Jerry (my great-grandfather) fought in the war for over a year, after which he was allowed to hire a replacement to fight for him so he could return to the plantation (or plantations) he had inherited when his

My great-grandfather, Lt. Col. W. H. FitzGerald (rear, center), commander of a Civil War regiment, signed the paper releasing my great-grandfather Jerry Robinson from military service.

father died. (Jerry's release from service related to the Confederate Congress' October 1862 law drafting able-bodied men of a certain age into military service. The law allowed a draftee who could afford it to pay someone to take his place and exempted those who owned at least twenty slaves. Because this law favored the wealthy, it was resented by nonexempted soldiers. Perhaps as much as anything, it reinforced the view among poor Southerners that the war was waged by poor men for the benefit of rich men.)[48]

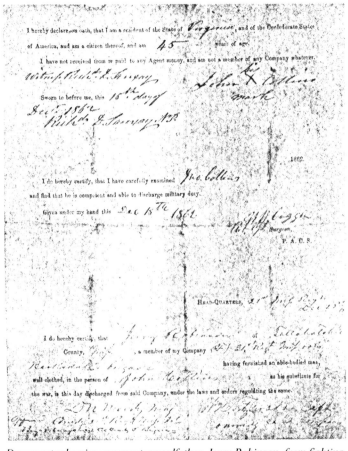

Document releasing my great-grandfather, Jerry Robinson, from fighting in the Civil War due to his owning over twenty slaves and hiring forty-five-year-old John Collins of Virginia to replace him. Jerry Robinson's daughter became my mother's mother. This release paper, dated Dec. 15, 1862, was signed by Capt. (later Lt. Col.) William Henry FitzGerald, whose son became my mother's father. (Copy of document courtesy of the Mississippi Department of Archives and History.)

Envelope, created from a newspaper or advertisement, that was used for a letter sent by my great-grandfather, Lt. Col. William Henry FitzGerald, to his wife, "Mrs. W. H. FitzGerald, Charleston, Mississippi," 1863. The five-cent Confederate stamp has an image of Jefferson Davis, president of the Confederacy.

Envelope used for a letter sent by Frances Wilmoth Harvey FitzGerald to her husband, Lt. Col. William Henry FitzGerald, when he was a prisoner of war at Johnson's Island, Ohio. The letter is postmarked May 27, 1865. ("Lt. Col. Wm H FitzGerald, Prisoner at Johnson's Island, Block 3, Room 4") (A relative wrote what appears to be "Series 1861" on the envelope, which may refer to the issue date of the stamp.)

When the South seceded from the Union, they printed their own currency. These two bills have remained in my family since the Civil War.

Like any war, the Civil War was hell. Of the 3,500,000 soldiers and sailors who fought in the war, recently conducted research indicates that between 650,000 and 850,000 died.[49] Several of the battles resulted in enormous casualties. After the three-day Battle of Gettysburg, over 51,000 men were dead, captured, missing, or wounded.[50] The battle of Cold Harbor, Virginia, in June of 1864, is another example. According to some sources, almost 7,000 Union soldiers, who charged well-fortified Rebels during the battle, were killed or wounded in about an hour.[51]

Soldiers were often organized by regions (in Mississippi, by counties). Because they fought and died together, great suffering was experienced in their home communities.[52] In 1866, the year after the war ended, 20 percent of Mississippi's state budget went to artificial limbs for war veterans.[53]

The following letter, written to my great-great-grandmother by her sister during the siege of Vicksburg, captures the painful experience of the war in terms of the Northern invasion and the Southerners' loss of assets.

Port Gibson [Mississippi],
June 26, 1863

Dear Sister Nancy,

I sit down to write you a few lines not knowing whether this will reach you. I know you must be anxious in regard to us but have had no opportunity to write you with any expectation that you would receive a letter.

We have not heard from you for a long time and would like to know what has become of you.

The Yankees as you are aware came here and fought Genl. Bimers at the Shaifer & Buck plantations on the 2nd of May 35,000 against 7,000. Our forces retreated and burned the Bridges across the Bayou and escaped. The Town was occupied by the Yankees who behaved as well as other thieves, merely taking all they wanted & destroying what they did not want. They have literally ruined the best half of the county and taken Thousands of negroes away.

I have not one [slave] worth a cent on the Dotson place and but <u>12</u> hands on the Haro Simes place. All or nearly all of our stock, waggons, &c &c including my old <u>Tooth</u> <u>Brush</u> have been stolen — 175 negroes have been taken off from the places which I own and control. My town negroes all remained except Argyle (the last I expected to leave me). <u>ALL</u> of David McDougall's negroes left him and Mrs. Ann McDougall has only Mary and child. Kenard Shreve & Mr. Hoopes lost <u>ALL</u>. Mrs. Session — <u>ALL</u>. Mrs. McAlpine <u>ALL</u>. Mrs. Valentine & Mrs. Crane nearly <u>ALL</u>. All along the road to Rocky Springs has been "cleaned out" — The Davenport Estate & Shields places are ruined — in fact a general stampede — Jeff Briscue lost say 200. Mrs. Daniels 400 &c &c It is sickening to add it up.

If we gain Vicksburgh and defeat them, as I believe we will, we will get many of them back. All except the men are put on plantations on the other side of the River above Vicksburgh. And we may get back those who don't die from exposure.

Sarah's negroes are all here — I wish to God she had them, as I wrote her long ago. They take negroes whether they wish to go or not — to my certain knowledge.

They have a gun Boat stationed at the Gulf and make raids into the surrounding country when they please — there are more in Jefferson County robbing and plundering. When this will end God only knows. I am ruined to all appearances & have lost not less than $150,000. I will go to Mrs. Valentine's tomorrow (Mr. V. is dead) with Parene. We are as usual since the Yankees came. They stole all of the provisions wherever they went. Write to me. The mail is expected this evening but may not come.

Yrs Truly S M Baldwin

My great-great-aunt's hopes for a Confederate victory at Vicksburg were shattered. The city surrendered to Union troops on July 4, 1863.

My great-great-grandmother's experience was no different from her sister's, as the following entry indicates. It was written three years after the war ended.

Slaves who escaped from slavery or were taken from their owner(s) by Union troops. 1862. (Library of Congress).

February 24, 1868 - I am having the silverware we have left cleaned. It has been abused by being thrown into the Bayou when a Yankee raid was coming — been in the house, hid in the woods, and buried in the earth — to keep it from Yankee robbers…. Col. Coats soldiers took all they could find & broke the china they could not take away & destroyed a bureau full of clothing belonging to me (at Marion) & tore up & carried off books to throw away — long, long will our injuries and wrongs be remembered — from those bigoted self-righteous Yankees — corrupted by a little money to pay them for killing people…& burning houses & destroying.

To be fair to the Yankee soldiers, it should be kept in mind that one of the worst atrocities of the war occurred at the hands of Confederates. Life at Andersonville Prison in Georgia, where Union prisoners of war were held, was so brutal that the number of deaths reached thirteen thousand in fourteen months.[54]

My great-great-grandmother was distraught because the South was not allowed to secede. She despised President Lincoln, who was trying to force the South back into the Union.

February 26, 1865 — By Sorrow of the Heart the Spirit is Broken. I think Mr. Lincoln can make no atonement to heaven or earth for the sorrow and suffering his sins has caused on this continent. He came to office with one intent, one hobby, to take or steal from the South their property [including slaves] & he will murder every Southern man, woman, and child and half the North before he will give up that dishonest intent. For half the money expended in this war would buy every slave in the South. President Lincoln sits in luxury at the White House & cares not for the thousands of helpless women & children he has had robbed & left in poverty & want, yes Starving. He has no thought for the sin of arming the slaves to fight against them that served and protected them. He has no soul to fear for the millions of lives he has caused to cease their usefullness in this life. All this he could have stayed by acting the good and just man when he came into office. The Savior says he that begins with the sword will end with the sword.

April 12, 1865 - David Wright brought us papers.... President Davis shows his want of confidence in our resources. Lincoln is a wicked murderer.

As the war drew to a close, my great-great-grandmother felt considerable apprehension.

April 1, 1865 — Jerry...brought some Federal papers which makes us fear falling into the clutches of such creatures as their own papers show they are.

April 17, 1865 - We hear that Richmond is lost to us & Mobile is taken, yet we hope never to return to the people of the Union. Where is the independence of the country if they force people to stay with them?

April 23, 1865 - Jerry received a letter from W. B. Miller. He is a soldier stationed near Richmond. Our soldiers are determined to fight till they are crushed out rather than go back to such people.... Duglas returned from Mr. Wright with news that Lincoln and Seward [Secretary of State]

Nancy Robinson diary, entry for Feb. 26, 1865: "By Sorrow of the Heart the Spirit is Broken. I think Mr. Lincoln can make no atonement to heaven or earth for the sorrow and suffering...."

were both assassinated — that the news came from the Yankees — it may be false, we hear many reports.

(Although Nancy received the news on April 23, Lincoln had actually been shot on April 14 and died the next day. Seward survived the attempt on his life.)

May 8, 1865 - Jerry was sad. He said some soldiers that staid all night said Gen. Lee...surrendered [our] armies

& we were now in Yankee lines. I tried to cheer him, said I did not believe it.

May 9, 1865 - Duglas came with a shout. Sayed the War was over & we were again in the Union. All our forces on this side of the Miss. River were surrendered.... [He said that] the Yankee boats were running the river as they once did before the war, that he was treated kindly & asked to trade, etc. The news astonished me, yet must be true.

(Gen. Lee actually agreed to surrender on April 9, a few days *before* Lincoln's assassination. It took awhile for everyone to get the news that the war was over — a month for my great-great-grandmother.)

May 12, 1865 - I feel a relief I cannot describe with the war being ended — and a horror as deep — at going into the Union — with the people the South has risked their lives to get from. The terms of the surrender we do not know, but cannot expect any justice or mercy from them that have none. Soldiers are here. Our table is spread to the furthest extent for our guests. Poor noble soldiers of the South.

May 21, 1865 - The uncertainty of the ultimate result of this overpowering the Southern people & forcing them to do what they do not wish to, is not freedom. But we must submit, for we are few and weak. The North are many & strong. This is submission. The South has nobly born her sorrows and her wrongs.

May 25, 1865 - The soldiers are disheartened, all are sad — they have nothing to expect from the Feds but to be crushed is the general opinion. When the wicked rule the land mourns. All are mourning for their hearts are crushed.

May 29, 1865 - Brother John McDougal came with a servant from Alban. He had left his wife and son well in New York City…. He told us much of the Northern people and their bitterness toward us. The Yankees have proclaimed our negros free & will try to confiscate our lands. They have robbed & ruined The People for revenge, which is ours. They have robbed me of 65 thousand dollars worth of negro property & left my lands useless to me I fear.

About two hundred thousand blacks fought for the Union, their bravery surprising white Union commanders. Even as Union troops, blacks experienced racism. As Richmond was being captured, the 7,800 black soldiers closest to the city where forced to allow white troops to go ahead of them so whites could gain credit for the capture.[55] The Rebels deeply resented blacks who fought them, and many blacks who surrendered or were captured were killed.

When I received from the Mississippi Department of Archives and History a copy of the document releasing Jerry from Civil War service, I was surprised to see that the name of the commanding officer who signed it was Capt. William Henry FitzGerald. Captain FitzGerald was later promoted to lieutenant colonel and was captured by Union troops on April 6, 1865, at the battle of Saylor's Creek in Virginia, three days before General Lee surrendered and the war ended. Lieutenant Colonel FitzGerald was initially imprisoned in Washington, D.C., but after President Lincoln's assassination, he was moved to Johnson's Island Prisoner of War Depot, in Sandusky Bay, Lake Erie, Ohio, until his release on June 18. His son, Fletcher Poitevent FitzGerald, married Jerry Robinson's daughter, Nancy McDougall Robinson (named after her grandmother), and they became my mother's parents.

Reconstruction and the Years
After the Civil War

About four million slaves were freed because of the Civil War, and the Thirteenth Amendment to the Constitution, abolishing slavery, was ratified the year the war ended.

After the Civil War, the South had to endure another period of hardship called Reconstruction. During these years (1865 to 1877), the North controlled the South by military rule. Much to the dismay of most whites in the state, Mississippi was patrolled by 9,122 black soldiers in Federal service.[56] Nancy Robinson's diary suggests that white Southerners suffered what to them were many injustices during this time, from being charged unfair taxes to having outsiders control who became governor of the state. Times were somewhat chaotic, and bands of freed slaves (called freedmen) as well as bands of whites committed violent acts.

Even though the slaves were free, nothing changed in regard to the dominant white Southern view that blacks were an inferior race and the deep commitment on the part of whites to keep blacks held down by any means necessary. Most whites feared that if blacks gained political equality, they would get social equality, which in turn would lead to the dreaded possibility of intermarriage and the dilution of the white race. Also, whites tended to inappropriately blame blacks for the South's painful situation (a phenomenon called "scapegoating").[57]

After having suffered the horrors of war, which included enormous financial losses, landowners now had to make their farms work without slaves. A number of former slaves were paid wages or offered part of the income from coming crop sales in exchange for helping to grow cotton and other crops. From this practice of offering payment based on crop sales comes the term "share-cropping." It was not unusual for unscrupulous former slave owners to find ways to make their tenants financially obligated to them, keeping them in bondage by ensuring that their debts remained greater than their income. Former slave Addy

Gill gives this description of his experience as a sharecropper in North Carolina after the end of slavery:

I caint read an write…. I haint had no chance…. I had to depend on white folks I farmed wid to look atter my business. Some of em cheated me out of what I made…. Dey got mighty nigh all I made. Mr. Richard Taylor who owned a farm near Raleigh whur I stayed two years wus one of em. He charged me de same thing three times an I had it to pay. I stayed two years an made nothing.[58]

Ann Ulrich Evans, who had been a slave in Alabama, related this story:

De white folks would pay niggers to lie to de rest of us niggers to git der farming done for nothin. He'd tell us come on and go with me, a man wants a gang of niggers to do some work and he pay you like money growing on trees…. Dey carried us by de droves to different parts of Alabama, Arkansas, and Missouri. After we got to dese places, dey put us all to work allright on dem great big farms…. [But] we always get through with fine big crops and owed de white man more dan we did when we started de crop, and got to stay to pay de debt. It was awful. All over was like that.[59]

Former North Carolina slave Andrew Boone also spoke of the exploitation of the black worker during and after slavery:

In slavery time they kept you down an' you had to wurk…. It's all hard, slavery and freedom, both bad when you can't eat. The ole bees makes de honey comb, the young bees makes de honey, niggers makes de cotton an' corn an' de white folks gets de money. Dis wus de case in slavery time an' its de case now. De nigger do mos' de hard wurk on de farms now, and de white folks still git de money dat de nigger's labor makes.[60]

My great-great-grandmother and many other white Southerners perceived the entire black race as inherently lazy, unintelligent, disloyal, and dishonest (although she did acknowledge some individual exceptions). The white Southern view that blacks were lazy is interesting in light of this comment by Sarah Gudger, a former slave in North Carolina:

> De rich white folks nebbah did no wok; dey had da'kies t' do it foah dem. In de summah we had t' wok outdoo's, in de wintah in de house. I had t' ceard an' spin [card and spin wool] till ten o'clock. Nebbah git much rest, had t' git up at foah de nex' mawnin' an' sta't again. Didn' get much t' eat, nuthah. Lawdy, honey, yo' caint know what a time I had. All cold n' hungry.[61]

Certainly many of the slaves were hard workers, in spite of being forced to work under the constant possibility of severe punishment, and it is evident that many black sharecroppers and farmers in later years worked hard. However, having suffered the considerable afflictions of slavery for 244 years — including the encouragement to feel inferior — some Southern black Americans may not have had the heart or will to continue to be hard workers for Southern plantation owners that had kept them in bondage with the overseer's whip.

Nancy Robinson believed that blacks could not really survive without help from whites and saw herself and her fellow pre-Emancipation plantation owners as the kind caretakers of inferior Negro slaves. In this light, she believed she and the other white landowners now deserved — but did not get — the support and loyalty of the freedmen whom they had once owned and enslaved. This perceived lack of loyalty was very painful for her. It was not unusual for slave owners to think that slaves were obligated for the care they allegedly received on the plantations. Of course, this view overlooked the fact that the slaves were forced to live and work on the plantation by an incredibly violent system. The desire of many slaves to leave her family's plantations after they were freed indicates that they had lived there all their lives against their will.

It is clear from the slave narratives that a number of the slaves that had kind masters (or mistresses) found it very hard to leave, or stayed on after the war and worked for years, in part out of a genuine sense of loyalty. The slaves were more prone to leave their former masters if they had been treated poorly. There is no way to know if this was a factor in the slaves leaving my ancestors' plantations. Some blacks stayed on plantations simply because they did not believe they had the resources to go off on their own and were desperate. A significant challenge for many ex-slaves who wanted to leave the plantation was the high rate of illiteracy, due to the denial of an education while slaves. (It has been estimated that less than five percent of Mississippi's 436,000 slaves were able to read.)[62]

A surprising number of slave owners withheld from their slaves the fact that they were free and kept them enslaved for months or even years after the war ended. In one case a master admitted to a slave he was supposed to be free, but told him if he tried to leave he would kill him.[63]

North Carolina ex-slave Sarah Debro describes her mistress' efforts to keep her after the war:

When de war was over....

One day my mammy come to de big house after me....

"Let her stay wid me," Mis' Polly said to Mammy.

But Mammy shook her head. "You took her away from me an' didn' pay no mind to my cryin', so now I'se takin' her back home. We's free now, Mis' Polly, we ain't gwine be slaves no more to nobody." I can see how Mis' Polly looked now. She didn' say nothin' but she looked hard at Mammy an' her face was white.[64]

Returning to my great-great-grandmother's diaries:

June 7, 1865 - Mr. McDougall [her brother]…& I went to Alban. When we got there the overseer was in the field. I saw Aunt Becky. She said they were all well & getting ready to go for they were FREE. I could not refrain from coughing when she told me that some was going to the city of Richmond [Virginia], to Charlston [South Carolina] & different places at a great distance. That day I called them all to the house. I then told them to stay & they should have their share of the cotton crop etc. All was satisfactory & they went to the field. We staid all night. The next day we all rode to Mr. Martin's store for we heard that he had President Johnson's Proclamation…. Brother read it aloud to us. I then fully felt our wretchedness. It was suffering acute with poverty in view, the wants & poverty of the thousands thus robbed…sickened my heart.

I feel bad, very bad. The prospects are gloomy. The Yankees have left us no consolation. All would gladly leave the country to get from their hateful government. But where can they go? They have impoverished us.

There is no alternative but to stay & submit to their dishonest tyrany with a hatred that is unChristian like the day is dark…. Our fields may have to lay untilled for we know the laziness of the negroes.

August 20, 1865 - Jerry called up the People [i.e., the freedmen] & told them about the contract & asked if any wanted to leave their home (for some of his was going). To my surprise almost all said they were going. I expostulated with them. Told them they were leaving friends & home to hunt their bread, that they could not get employment with more wages than I was giving if they got work & advised them to stay. Some said they had no fault with the place of the white folks but they wanted to travel, some to Virginia, others to Carolina, Georgia, Tennessee, etc. to see their friends & relatives. I was troubled for them. Many I had raised from infancy, watched over their orphan childhood & reared them to manhood. Now regardless of my feelings for them they seemed pleased with the change of going. Poor creatures. You still need the white people's care and protection. At sunset Jerry, Mrs. Bridges & I, weak and weary, mounted our horses & road to Beulah without speaking, so troubled & confounded at what I had seen.

September 17, 1865 - Jerry went to Alban to see the People that had come back, five grown ones & three children. Mary Jane, the house woman that always waited on me & slept in my room when I was at home, had started for Memphis to live....

December 2, 1865 - I made my farewell to the old Servants we had owned that was still there acting well, for many have gone [to] idleness & vagrancy, & none of them are disposed to hire for wages. The freed negroes are living on our substance without a care for our interest or their honesty.

December 5, 1865 - I road to Alban to see the manager & the People & was surprised to hear the Provo (Federal) had been sent for to make them do their duty & behave respectfull. Freedom has taken the last good trait from them here (respect for others & themselves). They are doing better now, though not well. The Federal Provo with 16 negro soldiers called at Beulah Wednesday & went back today to Charleston [Mississippi] I suppose. He can only manage them without chastisement, which he threatens.

December 17, 1865
My heart, within my fevered breast
Is beating, beating wearily
And memory with a sad unrest
Wails through its chambers drearily
(Nancy Robinson)

December 25, 1866 - At 11 o'clock a boat with 25 of Jerry's Freedmen pushed from his shore on their way to new homes.

December 30, 1866 - This morning an other boat load of negroes left here. Old Adam, a once faithful slave now free, by bribary is taking all the negros from this Place by the influence he has with them. There is no honesty, honor, or truth in the negro race is my experience.

July 16, 1868 - At night Winnie & I became alarmed needlessly. We carried the firearms in our room & I watched the night through. When the morning was come we could not think it foolish to be fearful of 30 persons of a different color, when we thought of the many cruelties & murders committed by them in our country.

July 26, 1868 -
There is a crop of heavy weight
for every human life to bear
There is a chaplet formed of thorns
for each & every brow to wear
(Nancy Robinson)

September 14, 1869 - Col. McLemore rode to the gate. He said there was trouble for...two hundred negroes had congregated at the Archer Plantation in Sunflower County. On Saturday 80 mounted [Negro] men with flags & horns, armed with guns, sabers, pistols & some with large knives rode from Boid's Store to Mr. Minters. There they shot many times without aim. They said a negro man called Combush that was with them had intended to speak to the negroes & had heard that the whites had forbid it. They made such noise at places & shot a pistol over two ladies heads, made many threats & many families left their homes & slept in the woods.

October 8, 1869 - We heard from Mrs. Boid that their sheriff was not killed (as we had heard). The negroes had been all waiting at places to hear negroes speak & preach. The negro man Combush had just gone when we got there. He was doing much to make the negroes think they were entitled to all the crops they had made or help work. Many was riding around the country instead of picking cotton.

November 29, 1869 - [Someone] had threatened to burn out Greenwood & kill the people with 500 negroes. Some companies had been organized for protection for they feared trouble at the election.

As I have indicated, after the Civil War, whites as well as blacks caused unrest. One white organization that fell into this category was the Ku Klux Klan (KKK). The KKK was a highly secret vigilante group that terrorized blacks as well as whites who tried to help blacks. Louisiana ex-slave Agatha Babino shared this story about the Ku Klux Klan:

De Ku Klux kill niggers. Dey come to take my uncle.... Dey don't take him but tell him to vote Democrat next day or they will....
    Dey kill my old Uncle Davis. He wouldn't vote Democrat. Dey shoot him.... Dey dare his wife to cry.[65]

Here is former Arkansas slave Betty Brown's story about her grandfather and the Klan:

He wuz a good man, my gran'fathur wuz.... An' he made a good mayer too; people all said so, an dey wuz gonna' 'lect him fo' foe mo' year, an' de 'Ku Klux'ers said dey wuz en' gonna have no 'nigguh' mayor. So dey tuk him out and killed him. Dey wuz awful times.[66]

Former North Carolina slave Martha Allen had this to say about the Klan:

I 'members dat de Ku Klux uster go ter de Free Issues houses [houses of former slaves?], strip all de family an' whup de ole folkses. Den dey dances wid de pretty yaller gals [mulatto, with white and black ancestry?] an' goes ter bed wid dem [rapes them]. Dat's what de Ku Klux wuz, a bunch of mean mens....[67]

The following is my great-great-grandmother's description of lawlessness committed by whites:

October 16, 1869 - Mrs. Martha Reading & Lilly Collier with Carrie called for a few minutes to see me & urged me to go home with them. Two [white] men on horseback came in sight, but delayed till the ladies left. They then rode in at the lower gate, left their horses. I soon saw them and they passed a house with Peter Sykes, a freedman, going before them. They had guns drawn on him & [were] heavily armed with pistols & knives. They broke the doors & searched all, breaking locks & doors. I went out when I saw them going to break a door & forbade it. One answered they had a right to do it. I asked for their authority. He said he would give me a receipt. (They were drunk.) They took the guns & pistols to the road where a mounted [man?] helped carry them. One was Alta Harris (a boy raised in this neighborhood), the other a refugee from Justice, the [boy] that is staying with them at the Crage farm on Black Bayou, his name is Murdock, the other's name is Rhodes. They rode away with many more [weapons] taken from houses up the bayou. Mr. Webb soon came, very angry that his freedmen had been robbed. At some places they had knocked down them that opposed them.

The following entries, several of which contradict her stereotype of blacks, pertain to former slaves Nancy respected:

June 16, 1868 - Mary our cook told me Dad Johnson died yesterday. He was a freedman of ours. His mother Percile served me from my marriage till she was free [about thirty years], faithfully. I had raised Dad & many more of her children. He was a good man & [his death is] a loss to the world. He died at Mr. Hawkins' where he was living this year.

June 19, 1873 - Margaret Brown went this morning with George Shere [?] to see her father & mother who live at Oakland [Mississippi] & to see a long absent brother who was sold when young from the family then in North Carolina & was brought to Mississippi, Yazoo County, where he has remained ever since. He is a good & trustworthy man like his father Daniel Crider [?].
Mag was so unhealthy I was very willing for her to go with the hope of her getting well, though I miss her very much to comb my hair & help me dress & sew etc. etc.

July 30, 1873 - I saw a wagon driving to Maggy's house & sent to know if she was in it. Yes, she was in it dead… her sisters & many friends had brought her home to bury her by her request. She had sent kind messages to me…. All her friends are greatly grieved & she had many for she was kind & good to all…. I sympathize with my colored friends in their afflictions & troubles & poor Maggy — she was to me a faithful servant whose care I needed.

August 3, 1873 - Today a very old servant woman named Ruth came to see me…. She belonged 20 years ago to Col. Jones. Mr. Robinson [her husband] owned some of her children — Louis & William. She is now with Louis. He lives on this Plantation. She is the mother of 20 children, fifteen she raised to be grown. How many is now living she does not know, for since they are free they have scattered. She is a healthy, sensible woman able to do any light work, can cook & work very good. She said her sight is not good. I gave her spectacles to enable her to sew. She [is] 108 years old.

Eight years after it ended, she reflected on the Civil War as well as on her favorite home — the Marion Plantation — which she had to leave after her husband died:

March 28, 1873 - The rememberence of my home at Marion Place comes to me like the sweet breath of the beautiful flowers that surrounded me there. It was all sunshine. But later years bring dark shadows of sorrows deep, & war with all its horrors, injuries & wrongs will long, long be remembered. Rest, rest, may it cure the broken spirit and a weary body.

The following was the last entry in my great-great-grandmother's diaries:

December 22, 1873 - I tried to prepare Christmas cheer today but have not succeeded as well as I wished. Jerry has fever, has slow fever.... At 4 o'clock he was chilly & then high fever all night. I sat by him till 12 o'clock at night then Peter came to take care of him. He sent for Dr. New. We expected him this morning. At three Mr. John Sullivan & Mrs. Garnat called on their way up the Bayou visiting.... Mr. Winset [?] went with them for the Dr. I hope he may come before night.
     Jerry is quite sick with slow fever.

Nancy Robinson died a week after writing these words. She was sixty-five years old. There is no indication in her journal of the cause of her death, but it is very likely that she died from illness. I know her son Jerry recovered, because he married in

1877, and his wife gave birth to my grandmother in 1882. Jerry Robinson died in 1905 at the age of sixty-nine.

I found the following diary entry to be especially interesting:

December 25, 1869 - Some freedmen came to see me & I was wearied by their stay, & their talk of Master Alfred made me sad. I do not regret that the slaves are free. No, I am glad. But the Southern people should be paid for the property they have been robbed of. Our broad lands & unplanted fields show the wants of the Southern people.

I deeply regret that my great-great-grandmother did not elaborate on her profound statement that she was glad the slaves were free. From what she did write in her diaries, it is clear that she was a sensitive person who was often troubled by the suffering of others. Her statement on Christmas day of 1869 suggests that she had come to feel uncomfortable with the harsh reality of slavery in spite of her obvious belief that black people were inferior.

I found the next entry both beautiful and profound:

May 8, 1870 - I feel humbled. Yes, & thankful for many blessings I may not desserve. I have written two letters this morning & [then I went] to visit our tenants, Mrs. Steward & Screws, for Mr. Screws has gone to Calhoun County. I walked to see the families. They were all well, but distressed at not hearing preaching. How could they be <u>saved</u>. They could not <u>read</u> the Bible & was out of reach of a preacher. How could they keep the Sabath. I told them I believed God was light & love, that he rested not on the 7th day, every day was holy. No wrong should be done. God's work never ceased. He grows corn, & trees & flowers every day. We are the children of God. Jesus said He is our Brother & they that live faithful lives are joint heirs with him; that punishment was the remorse of conscience; that we only need <u>salvation</u>

from ignorance, error, selfishness, bigotry, poverty, intemperance, & <u>unrighteousness</u>.

This statement offers a glimpse of some of my great-great-grandmother's spiritual beliefs near the end of her life. Throughout the years of her diaries, she was a Christian who went to church occasionally. During at least the last twenty years of her life, she was very interested in Spiritualism (as were many people at that time). A common belief of followers of Spiritualism was that "the dead communicate to the living through a medium."[68]

July 21, 1853 - I have been much interested in the spiritual influence, in raising a table to answer the inquiries made of spirits of your relatives, then just and true answers to many things we know. Sister Sarah <u>Posey</u> [her sister?] is a <u>medium</u> and through her <u>medium I conversed with the beloved spirits of my departed Parents, Brothers, Sisters, etc.</u> It is to happy a thought to believe that the spirits of the blest made perfect can wach over us here in our sinfull state and be our guardians.

In 1855 Nancy's husband had an interesting experience that must have reinforced her Spiritualist views.

March 15, 1855 - Mr. Robinson told me of dreaming of Mr. Sheapherd, of seeing him, their conversation and he bid him farewell. Mr. R. awoke, got up and looked at his watch, it was half past one o'clock. He was grieved for he believed Mr. Shepheard was dead.

March 18, 1855 - I rode to Dr. Fishers in the evening and heard of Mr. Sheapheards death. He died the hour Mr. Robinson dreamed Mr. Sheapheard bid him fairwell.

This entry was written on her sixty-fourth birthday, eleven months before her death:

November 27, 1872 - I do not dread the closing scenes of my earthly life, though my sun is nearing the western horizon. More than three score years have been numbered since the light dawned upon my existence. I rise each morning to do my duty with cheerfulness of heart & hope for the future each year. I feel more love & charity for others, more sacrifice for all. The many changes in life, of joy & sorrow, hath made my dear ones dearer to my heart. I love them for their causes, sorrows & trials.

The following poem was written 9½ months before her death:

March 15, 1873 -
Life is the torid day
Burned by the wind & sun
And death the calm, cool evening hour
When the weary day is done
(Nancy Robinson)

****

When I first read my great-great-grandmother's diaries, I was impressed with what a remarkable person she was. I was also surprised that she did not fit my stereotype of the cruel slave owner. I felt a connection with her in my heart, and sometimes tears came to my eyes as I read her most painful recollections. I imagined her supporting and inspiring me as I undertook the difficult and sometimes painful task of examining and writing about our family's racism.

Researching the subject of slavery was much harder emotionally than studying her diaries. I felt repulsion and sadness as I read firsthand accounts of the torture and humiliation American slaves were forced to endure for the pleasure and benefit of white plantation owners and the economic system of which they were a part. It pained me that Nancy Robinson and her family were participants in such a hideous institution. I also resented that my mother had taught me the myth that her parents had taught her: the myth of the romantic, benevolent southern plantation — a myth that gradually unraveled for me as my life unfolded and my awareness of my family's racism deepened.

Studying my great-great-grandmother's writings together with the history of slavery gave me a foundation for understanding my family's prejudices, including a prejudice against Northerners. I could see how entrenched attitudes about blacks became for many white Southerners during the years of slavery, the Civil War, and Reconstruction, and how those attitudes continued through the Jim Crow era (discussed in the next chapter) and even continue today.[vi] In many Southern families, these attitudes are passed down from generation to generation like a hereditary disease. This was certainly the case in my family.

A NOTE TO THE READER:

My website, www.healracism.com, contains three hundred excerpts from the slave narratives, organized by subjects, and 165 excerpts from my great-great-grandmother's diaries, the majority of which were not used in this book.

---

vi White supremacy and slavery in what is now the United States date back to colonial times, before the country was even founded. A number of early documents related to the colonies, and then the United States, supported slavery (and, therefore, white supremacy and "white privilege" - privileges whites had that were denied others). Some examples: (1) In 1669, a Virginia act prevented a slave owner or the owner's representative from being charged with a crime if a slave was killed while resisting him or her. (2) A Virginia act of 1705 stated that slaves were considered property that could be inherited by a slave owner's widow or heirs. (3) In 1787, the U. S. Constitution deemed all people who were not "free" or were in servitude for a set number of years to be three-fifths of a person (Art. 1, Sec. 2). The same document provided for the return of a runaway slave who escaped to another state (Art. IV, Sec. 2). (4) The Fugitive Slave Act of 1793 also allowed a slave owner to reclaim a slave who escaped to another state. (Source: *Slavery in America*, 398-404.)

CHAPTER 2

THE JIM CROW ERA
AND MY FAMILY [vii, viii]

During the Reconstruction years that followed the war, in spite of being under the control of the North, Southern states managed to pass laws, called Black Codes, which maintained white dominance over blacks. One only needed to have had one great-grandparent who was a "Negro" to have been considered a "Negro" and to have been subjected to these codes.[1] This led into the Jim Crow era, which began in 1877 when federal troops were withdrawn and Reconstruction ended.[ix]

Codes Mississippi adopted in 1865 made intermarriage between black and white people punishable by life in prison.[x] It was illegal for blacks and whites to associate on equal terms.[2]

Throughout the Deep South, some of these codes along with later laws essentially created a legalized extension of slavery. In Mississippi, orphaned black children could be forced to apprentice with a white person, and failure to pay certain fines resulted in blacks being forced to work for a white person selected by the sheriff.[3] Between the Civil War and World War II, tens of thousands of Southern black men were forced to do lengthy

---

vii Over twenty-five sources were studied for background information on the Jim Crow era. All of these are listed in the bibliography. Much of this chapter's information on Jim Crow consists of common knowledge, facts, or information that can be found in numerous references.

viii This chapter has a photograph of a lynching that might be upsetting to some readers.

ix The term "Jim Crow" was associated with a series of song-and-dance performances given by Thomas "Daddy" Rice, a white minstrel who imitated black people in the 1800s. Rice called his routine "Jump Jim Crow."

x In 1960, interracial marriage was illegal in thirty-one states. When the Supreme Court ruled against such restrictions in 1967, seventeen states still made such a marriage illegal. (Reference: Greene, *Henry Louis Gates, Jr.*, 49-50.)

terms of hard labor for farms, businesses, and governments due to phony charges or for offenses as trivial as vagrancy or not being able to pay a small fine.[xi] (When he was a Mississippi senator my great-grandfather, Lt. Col. W. H. FitzGerald, voted in favor of this convict leasing system.)[xii] The following statement, made in the late 1930s by a former slave, illustrates this phenomenon of forced labor for little or no reason:

> I gits into a picklement once years ago. I's 'rested on de street. I's not done a thing, jus' walkin' 'long de street with 'nother fellow and dey claim he stole somethin.' Did dey turn me a-loose? Dey turn me loose after six months on de chain gang. I works on the road three [of those] months with a ball and chain on de legs. — Zek Brown, an ex-slave from Warren County, Tennessee[4]

By 1890, a new set of laws and regulations were in place to maintain the system of white supremacy. More laws were added over the next few decades, and they remained in effect into the 1960s, when the civil rights movement forced an end to them.[xiii] In addition to laws or legal codes, there was also what social scientists and historians referred to as "racial etiquette." This included the many unwritten customs that protected white supremacy and oppressed blacks.[5]

During this dark period of Jim Crow, the notion of white superiority permeated everything and was reflected everywhere, keeping the black populace in its inferior position.[6] It was evident in the poverty of blacks as well as in their inferior homes, neighborhood locations, neighborhood facilities (such as streets and sanitation), schools, etc.[7] Most black workers knew that they

---

xi Douglas Blackmon's Pulitzer Prize-winning book *Slavery by Another Name: The Re-Enslavement of Black Americans from the Civil War to World War II* and a related PBS documentary titled *Slavery by Another Name* expose this horrible aspect of American history. These were the references used for this sentence.

xii "An Act to Provide for Leasing Out the Penitentiary and Convict Labor of the State," Mississippi Senate record, April 7, 1876, SB 262.

xiii It should be noted that some of the Jim Crow laws pertaining to blacks also applied to Asians and American Indians. (Reference: Osborne, *Miles to Go*, 3, 57) were doomed to take the worst jobs with the least pay. Those blacks who questioned their treatment or tried to advance economically and/or professionally were harassed or, in many cases, murdered. There are many examples of blacks being severely punished for owning what was considered an expensive car. Whites used "poll taxes" (a tax charged for voting), literacy tests, and other measures in order to keep blacks from qualifying to vote.

Education was one of the most damaging areas of discrimination. Blacks were denied adequate education in part as a way of keeping them in menial jobs and preventing them from being suited for public office and other positions.[8] There were separate schools for blacks and whites, and far more was spent to educate white pupils than black pupils. In 1910, for example, South Carolina's Beaufort County spent $5.95 to educate each black student and $40.68 for educating each white student.[9] Furthermore, student history books stressed the superiority of the white race.[10] A 1940 Mississippi law even made it illegal to keep textbooks for black students in the same warehouse as those for white students.[11]

Southern laws mandated segregated neighborhoods. Blacks also had separate hospitals, bathrooms, water fountains, eating areas, and so on. In some cases black people died because white hospitals would not accept them. At stores and doctors offices, they had to wait until all white people were served first. When taking public transportation, blacks were forced to sit in the back. A number of laws forbade blacks from living, working, or spending the night in certain towns.[12] Blacks were frequently harassed by white law enforcement officials.

In Johnson County, North Carolina, black witnesses and white witnesses were sworn in using different bibles.[13] In Washington, D.C., it was forbidden for blacks to bury their dogs in the areas of pet cemeteries used by white dog owners.[14] A 1915 South Carolina law and its amendments forbade all non-white textile workers from working in a room with whites, using exits and entrances while they were being used by whites, and even from looking out the same window out of which whites were looking.[15] (At one point the Alabama state government considered banning

"Colored" drinking fountain on the county courthouse lawn, Halifax, North Carolina, 1938 (Library of Congress).

the sale of Black and White Scotch, both because of its name and because the label pictured black and white dogs frolicking together.)[16]

It might not be in a legal code that a black man must remove his hat in the presence of white men and women, but failure to do so could result in severe punishment or even death for the black person. Black people had to refer to white adults as "Mr." or "Mrs.," but black adults were not given the same respect by white people. Whites would even reprimand or severely punish a black person that they observed addressing another member of the black race as "Mr." or "Mrs." It was a common requirement in the South that a black person who approached a white person

Segregated café, with left door labeled "white," right door "colored," in Durham, North Carolina, 1940. (Library of Congress).

on a sidewalk had to step into the street as the white person passed. Black people who owned cars were not allowed to pass cars driving in the same direction that were being driven by whites. White men could harass or even rape black women and get away with it, but black men could not even look at white women without the possibility of suffering severe reprisals. Furthermore, what could be considered offensive behavior by whites could relate to something as simple as a black person not showing what was considered enough politeness, humility, fear, or gratitude. What was deemed offensive to whites could relate to a black person's tone of voice, eye contact, or body language, including facial expression.

Segregated movie theater with black section in balcony, Belzoni, Mississippi, 1939. (Library of Congress).

A serious difficulty for black citizens during the Jim Crow era was the fact that laws and racial etiquette could vary from place to place. A black person could know how to behave in his or her home town but could get in serious trouble by not knowing the different expectations in a town being visited for the first time. They could also get in trouble for not knowing the layout of a new environment. Here is one such example, shared by a former slave when interviewed in the late 1930s:

> "I saw a strange niggah come to town once and didn't know where he was going and stepped in the door of a white hotel. When he saw all white faces, he was scared most to death. He didn't even turn around he just backed out and don't you know dem white folks kilt him for stepping inside a white man's hotel by mistake, yes they did." — Lulu Chambers, a former slave from Galatin County, Kentucky[17]

One hallmark of the Jim Crow South was the lynching of blacks. Lynching refers to murder without a legal trial at the hands of a violent mob, including the Ku Klux Klan. This was often done in the South by hanging. After years of research, the Equal Justice Initiative, published "Lynching in America: Confronting the Legacy of Racial Terror" in 2015. They documented 3,958 cases

Perpetrating hate, Ku Klux Klan christens eight week old baby, 1924. (Library of Congress).

of lynchings of Southern black men, women, and children between 1877 and 1950.[18] [xiv] (Hundreds of additional blacks were legally but unjustly executed by white judges and all-white juries during these years.) Blacks were lynched for such things as trying to vote, arguing with whites, and trying to sue a white person.[19] Many lynchings included sadistic torture. In general, lynching often took place because a black person behaved in a way that was considered insulting to whites or otherwise in disregard of the inferior position that had been assigned to blacks.[20] It could be assumed that the main reason behind lynchings was hatred of blacks.[21]

Lynching of MacManus, 1862. (Library of Congress).

Thomas Hall, born in 1856 on a plantation in Orange County, North Carolina, was interviewed at his home in Raleigh, North Carolina, in the late 1930s. He had this to say after a childhood under slavery and over seventy years under first the Black Codes and then the Jim Crow world of the South:

Conditions and rules were bad and the punishments were severe and barbarous [during slavery]. Some marsters acted like savages. In some instances slaves were burned at the stake. Families were torn apart by selling. Mothers were sold from their children. Children were sold from their mothers, and the father was not considered in anyway as a family part. These conditions were here

xiv Leon Litwack, in his excellent book *Trouble in Mind*, contends that from 1890 to 1917, two or three blacks were murdered every week in the South (284).

before the Civil War and the conditions in a changed sense have been here ever since. The whites have always held the slaves in part slavery and are still practicing the same things on them in a different manner. Whites lynch, burn, and persecute the Negro race in America yet; and there is little they are doing to help them in any way....

White folks are not going to do nothing for the Negroes except keep them down.[22]

By 1930, most Southern states had decreed that only one drop of black blood was needed to define a person as black. Since it was so hard to tell if some people had black ancestry, in a large part due to the raping of black women by slave owners and other whites, just *acting* as a black person was believed to act could be enough for a person to be treated under the law as a black person in some cases.[23]

It was dangerous, even for whites, to express sentiments opposed to segregation and the unfair treatment of blacks. A law passed in Mississippi in 1920, when my mother was a teenager, stated: "Any person...presenting for public acceptance or general information, arguments or suggestions in favor of social equality or of intermarriage between whites and Negroes, shall be guilty of a misdemeanor and subject to a fine not exceeding five hundred dollars or imprisonment not exceeding six months or both fine and imprisonment in the discretion of the court." (Using the consumer price index to calculate what $500 in 1920 would equate to in 2014, the amount would be $5,895.)[24]

White and black children learned the Jim Crow rules at an early age from their families, from experiences with society, and from interacting with those of another race.[25] For white children, this learning process prepared them to embrace and act on the myth of their superiority and to claim their supposed birthright. For black children, learning the written and unwritten rules of behavior was a matter of survival, of life or death.[xv] (Some of my own training in this regard is discussed in the next chapter.)

---

xv Jennifer Rittenhouse's *Growing Up Jim Crow: How Black and White Southern Children Learned Race*; Lillian Smith's *Killers of the Dream*; Sarah Patton Boyle's autobiography, *The Desegregated Heart*; and "The Ethics of Living Jim Crow: An Autobiographical Sketch" by Richard Wright discuss racial etiquette..

Sign at the Sojourner Truth homes, a new federal housing project in Detroit, Michigan. 1942. (Library of Congress).

Some black children were fortunate in that their families tried to shelter them from the harsh effects of Jim Crow and to instill in them a sense of self-worth that would help sustain them in a deeply unjust and racist world.[26]

It should be pointed out that racism clearly existed in the North, and several Northern states had their own laws that repressed blacks. A number of these regulations were just as oppressive as Southern laws.[27] However, while blacks in the North often experienced contempt, discrimination, segregation, and violence in the decades after Reconstruction, unlike in the South, an entire system of white supremacy did not evolve.[28]

Jerry Robinson, Nancy and Alfred's son, was my mother's grandfather on her maternal side. Jerry Robinson would consult an astrologer about the best times to sell his cotton, and he often did well following the advice he was given. He and his wife, Elizabeth Pattison Robinson, lived in Albin, Mississippi, and they were wealthy owners of family plantations. My mother recalled that her grandmother "was very independent and was the boss in her marriage." She was, according to my mother, "a real lady." Elizabeth had a black one-legged chauffeur named Watson and always had a new Buick. When she went to the bank, she would wait outside in the car while Watson went in and

Jerry Robinson (1836-1905), my mother's maternal grandfather

Elizabeth Pattison Robinson (1855-1924), wife of Jerry Robinson. When she married her husband, she was 22 and he was 41.

got a bank official to come out and wait on her.

Lt. Col. William Henry Fitz-Gerald was my mother's grandfather on her paternal side. He was a Civil War hero and the owner of at least one slave. Like Jerry Robinson, he lived to see the entrenchment of what became known as the Jim Crow era, characterized by a reassertion of the white supremacy that had existed during slavery. He was a Tallahatchie County supervisor, two-term Mississippi state senator (Democrat), and judge. He was first elected to the senate in 1875, during an infamous election that was fraught with violence and racism and which saw Republicans (who supported Reconstruction and black suffrage) murdered and blacks driven from the polls. The wording of a document he co-authored as a senator defended the 1875 elections. As a senator, he voted for the 1876 reorganization of Congressional districts in the state, a measure that had the intended effect of preventing Mississippi blacks from being elected to office. His efforts as a legislator helped lay the groundwork for the Jim Crow era.[xvi]

Their children, my mother's parents, were immersed in notions of white superiority from the time they were born. My mother's father was born in 1870, her mother in 1882. My mother and her two sisters, born between 1904 and 1922, were raised by their parents and their society to view white supremacy and segregation as completely natural.

The family, which lived in Clarksdale, Mississippi, during most of my mother's youth, had several servants, all of whom

---

xvi "Names of Slave Owners," Tallahatchie County, Mississippi, July 1860 (showing that William Henry FitzGerald owned one slave at the time); "Resolutions," Mississippi Senate record, January 6, 1876 (defense of 1875 election); and "Act to Reorganize the Congressional Districts of the State," Mississippi Senate record, 1876, SB 166.

Lt. Col. William Henry FitzGerald (1830-1904), a slave owner whose infantry division, the Tallahatchie Rifles (21st Mississippi Infantry, Company F), fought many battles as a part of Gen. Robert E. Lee's Army of Northern Virginia. On April 16, 1865, a few days before the war's end, he was captured during the Appomatox Campaign at Sayler's Creek. He is in the Tallahatchie County Hall of Fame. Of his seven children, Fletcher Poitevent FitzGerald was my maternal grandfather.

Frances Wilmoth Harvey FitzGerald (1843-1927), my mother's paternal grandmother, wife of Lt. Col. William H. FitzGerald. When she married her husband in 1862, she was nineteen and he was thirty-two.

Statue in honor of Lieutenant Colonel FitzGerald's regiment, the Tallahatchie Rifles (21ˢᵗ Mississippi Infantry, Company F), erected at the Tallahatchie County court house in Sumner, Mississippi, by the William FitzGerald Chapter Number 696, United Daughters of the Confederacy. Many town squares in the south have statues of this nature, upon which are listed the names of local Civil War soldiers. On such monuments that I have seen, if any black people are listed as having died for the South, they are generally listed separately from the names of white soldiers, under the heading "Colored." These monuments helped perpetuate the spirit of the Confederacy for many decades after the Civil War. To the right of the statue in this photograph are the American flag and the Mississippi state flag. The state flag, designed in 1894, includes within it, in the upper right corner, the battle flag of the Confederacy. This has been a subject of controversy in recent years, with some people opposing an image associated with the Civil War and the defense of slavery being part of the state flag. (Photograph taken by the author in 2002.)

were black — indeed, all black people who were actively involved in my mother's world were servants. Queenie (later replaced by Sara) was the cook, Tom was the house boy who cleaned, and Mattie washed clothes and performed other tasks. The family had at least one other servant, a man named George. In the style of the old Southern plantations, my mother and her older sister even had a black mammy, Margaret Williams, a former slave who helped raise them, perhaps even functioning as their surrogate mother. (Today, the concept of "nanny" is the closest we have to this old plantation tradition.) She was referred to simply as Mammy.

In her diaries, my great-great-grandmother wrote an entry that indicates the closeness of his mammy to her son (my mother's grandfather):

My mother, Wilmoth Harvey FitzGerald (left), her older sister Elizabeth, and their Mammy, Margaret Williams, a former slave. The picture was taken in October 1911, the month my mother turned five, at the family's home in Clarksdale, Mississippi.

Margaret Williams, who functioned as a "Mammy" to my mother and her older sister Elizabeth. This picture was taken around 1910.

November 17, 1858 — Jerry came home in the evening looking care worn and weary. Yes there was so greate a change in his appearance that Harriet [a slave] cried. She sayed it grieved her to see the child she had nursed so worn out and care worn, so young.

My mother and her mammy had the same degree of closeness. Even in her mid-nineties, my mother fondly recalled, "When I was a little girl, Mammy would hold my hand as I fell asleep. She was so sweet. She was a good nigra." When Mammy died, my mother went home from college for the funeral. The administrators of the college my mother attended thought my mother's leave of absence related to a member of her immediate family.

As my mother learned the "correct" relationship between the races, she learned the negative stereotypes and fears that whites associated with blacks. During their elementary school years, their servant George would drive my mother and her older sister to school in a buggy; Mammy always rode with them. After school George and Mammy would pick them up and take them home. The reason for Mammy's presence, my mother explained, was that "Daddy wouldn't let his little girls ride alone with a Negro man."

My mother's father often wore gloves, in part to protect himself from diseases that many white people assumed black people had, the most dreaded of which was syphilis. One of my mother's relatives told me that my mother, too, took such precautions, neurotically wiping off doorknobs in the family home after their servant, Tom, did the cleaning, a measure intended to prevent the family from getting syphilis. (It is not likely that my mother's fears were diminished when the family cook actually did contract the disease.)

I grew up in all-white neighborhoods in Norfolk, Virginia, went to an all-white church, was part of an all-white Boy Scout troop, and went to essentially all-white schools.

Two-thirds of my schooling before college was in all-white private schools. Had I attended public schools through eighth grade, they would have been all-white until 1959. Schools, like other institutions, were segregated in Virginia until the United States Supreme Court declared segregated schools unconstitutional with the *Brown v. Board of Education* decision in 1954; even after that, schools closed in several parts of the state rather than submit to forced integration. In September of 1958, six schools were closed in Norfolk. Granby High School, where I had practiced wrestling after my eighth grade classes at a nearby junior high during the 1959-1960 school year, was one of the schools. Yielding to pressure from the federal government and legal decisions, these schools reopened in early 1959.[29]

I clearly remember Bruce, a fellow member of the Children of the American Revolution (an offshoot of the Daughters of the American Revolution), telling me about Prince Edward County in Virginia closing its entire school system in an effort to keep the schools all-white. He was convinced that Prince Edward County had done the right thing. (Starting in 1959, Prince Edward County's schools were closed for five years. A foundation was established to create private schools for the education of the county's white children.)[30]

I also remember that in 1962 one of my cousins, a student at Ole Miss (the University of Mississippi), took his rifle back to school because a young black man (James Meredith) was trying to enroll as the first black student there. My cousin was willing to use violence to defend segregation.

In the junior high where I repeated the eighth grade during the 1959-1960 school year, after flunking out of my private academy, there was only one black student in the whole school. Her name was Geraldine. I rarely saw her and we had no interaction.

My childhood experiences were so segregated that the only black people I came in contact with were the men who worked for my grandfather and the women who cooked and cleaned for the family. Outside of those individuals, I rarely saw black people at all, since they were excluded from the places I frequented. I was so immersed in an all-white world that I did not even notice that it excluded black people. It was as if the black race was invisible to me. Growing up in a segregated society also made it virtually impossible for me to have positive experiences of black people that would have countered my belief that they were inferior to white people.[xvii]

My mother's influence on me was the most significant factor in my adopting racist beliefs. This will be discussed in the next chapter.

It is clear that throughout most of our nation's history white supremacy has done immeasurable harm to those Americans who happen to be black. The Jim Crow era alone, which lasted for over three-quarters of a century, affected generations of black Americans in the South. Several historians note that the race-related issues we face today, including racism and white privilege, evolved out of slavery and the Jim Crow period. In order to understand our present situation, achieve healing of racism, and create a fair and just society, it is imperative that we understand our past.[31]

---

xvii The Virginia constitution, approved in 1902, forbade integrated schools. (It also established a literacy test for voting eligibility and a poll tax.) During the first half of the twentieth century, Virginia laws were enacted which mandated that public transportation and places of public assembly be segregated and that neighborhoods be designated as "white" or "colored." Although these forms of segregation were successfully challenged in courts over the years, it was not until the Civil Rights Act of 1964 and the Voting Rights Act of 1965 that there were significant changes overall. (Reference: Wynes, "Evolution of Jim Crow Laws in Virginia.")

CHAPTER 3

MY MOTHER'S LEGACY

A NOTE TO THE READER: In this chapter, I endeavor to convey my mother's background that contributed to her beliefs and behavior and to show how I interpreted and responded to her influence. In addition, the chapter illustrates some of my mother's and my insecurities which contributed to the need to feel superior to black people and others (as further discussed in Chapter 10). My story of my mother and her family, subjective by necessity, is not intended to be critical even though it may seem critical or even self-righteous at times. See Chapter 8 for a different way I have come to see my mother.

More than anyone, my mother taught me racism through her influence on my beliefs, emotional make-up, and behavior. She often expressed how she viewed blacks as inferior to whites, and she modeled racist behavior in many ways. Because of my closeness to her, I emulated her and adopted her beliefs as my own.

My mother, Wilmoth FitzGerald Drake, raised me to be proud of my heritage. I grew up hearing myths about the South and slavery and stories about our "noble" ancestors. Because of what she had been taught as she was growing up, and perhaps because it was too much for her to admit to herself that our ancestors were involved in a practice that was cruel and destructive, she went to some lengths to justify slavery. She believed that the slaves were so well treated by our ancestors and other slave owners that they were better off as slaves than as free people. She told me the story

My mother, Wilmoth FitzGerald Drake, in the spring of 1964, near the time of my graduation from military high school.

about how the slaves had such a good life that, when my great-grandfather Lt. Col. William Henry FitzGerald began his service in the Civil War and freed his slave or slaves (he probably had one or two at the time), at least one slave voluntarily went to fight with him. (As I explained in Chapter 1, some slaves did go to war with their masters for a variety of reasons.) As a child, I was proud that our ancestors were Southern aristocrats and believed they were kind slave owners.

I remember a time, when I was about twelve, riding with my mother in her Ford through the streets of Norfolk, Virginia. We stopped at an intersection where Mom noticed two or three black men in the neighborhood. Immediately she locked all the car doors before continuing the drive.

She led me to believe that black people were not clean and were subject to unmentionable diseases. I came to think, as she did, that one should avoid touching black people if at all possible and that the prudent thing to do, if that was not possible, was to wash one's hands afterwards. I believed that black people had an offensive odor, and I would hold my breath when I walked past them.

Me, at age 3½, with our maid, Mary Finney. The photo was taken in January of 1949. Apparently we are on the street where Mary lived in her segregated neighborhood. My street had paved roads and nicer houses.

My mother had grown up with separate facilities for black people. In the home of my teenage years, we had a separate, less furnished bathroom located by the back door the two black maids used. I believe my mother would have been uncomfortable with them using the family's bathrooms.

Norfolk had the world's largest naval base, and our next door neighbors often hosted parties to welcome sailors from out of town. When my mother found out that some of the sailors they entertained were black, she expressed shock that our white neighbors let them into their home.

Her views about race were also evident when she would tell me during my childhood how unfairly my father was treated by his father. One example my mother gave was my grandfather's putting my dad in charge of "the boys" in the back of Drake Corporation. She considered it demeaning for him to have to supervise "colored" people. She would also point out that, before she became pregnant with my oldest brother in 1939, my grandfather paid my father only eighteen dollars a week, "the same as the colored boys."

When I was in my early teens, my mother told me, "Negroes today are disrespectful and stirring up trouble. They are not in their place like the good old Negroes I grew up with." (In the decades following Reconstruction, white Southerners often contrasted the "good old Negroes" who accepted the status quo with the new ones who had the gall to want equality.) More than once, during the Civil Rights years of the 1950s and 1960s, she stated that Martin Luther King was a Communist who was creating trouble, a rumor that was not substantiated by fact. (In his book *Strength to Love* King was very critical of Communism.)[1] When black people rioted in the Watts neighborhood of Los Angeles, August 11-16, 1965, my mother told me that King had given a speech there beforehand and encouraged the rioting, even though King's visit to the area actually began on August 17, in the riots' aftermath.[2] One day in the late 1950s, I was sitting in the small dining room next to our kitchen and heard Mom talking to to one of our maids. Mom said, "Mary, colored people don't really want to go to school with white children, do they?" Mary, who I assume was afraid of losing her job, had no choice but to respond, "No, ma'am, Mrs. Drake."

Occasionally she would use the word "darkies" to refer to blacks during my early years; she also used the words "Negroes" and "colored." With the exception of one time when she was in her 90s and was delirious, I am not aware of her using the word "nigger," although she did not seem to object to my father's frequent use of that word; her family in Mississippi used it regularly.

One time when my wife Joan and I were visiting my parents at their home in North Carolina, we were watching television with my mother, who was in her early 90s. My mother asked my wife if there was a show she would like to see. Joan asked if we could watch the Bill Cosby Show, a comedy program she enjoyed that featured a black family. Rather than watch black people on television, my mother turned off the TV.

A few weeks after my mother's ninety-fifth birthday, she became delusional and at times imagined she was experiencing some of her worst fears. She was staying in the skilled nursing facility of her retirement village when a group of high school students came to visit her and the other residents. One of the students, a black girl, helped my mother's caregiver adjust my mother's bedding. The next day my mother tried to have the caregiver fired, complaining that she had "put me in the basement with the niggers — the slaves — and now I'm covered with nits."

In my twenties, when I began to disagree with my mother's view that black people were inferior, she would say, "Son, you just don't understand." All of the teachings and experiences of her childhood and youth had firmly convinced her of her position and, as far as I could tell, she never examined or questioned it.

My mother had prejudices against other groups of people she saw as different from her, besides blacks. These prejudices were especially focused on Jews, Catholics, foreigners, and — because of the Civil War — Northerners. I adopted these prejudices as well. Although I did not fully understand the dislike for Northerners or "Yankees," I went so far as to apply that prejudice to sports. I always rooted for the Dodgers when the baseball team played against the New York Yankees in the World Series. (I did not realize at the time that the Brooklyn Dodgers were from New York too and thus were also a "Yankee" team!)

My mother was also prejudiced against people with less social status. When I failed the eighth grade at a private school,

I repeated it at a public school, where I started dating a girl. According to my mother, she was from a "lower class" family that lived "on the other side of the tracks." I myself did not think of her that way; to me she was just someone I liked who seemed to like me. My mother drove us on a couple of dates but told me she was very upset that I was going with a "lower class" girl and tried to discourage me from asking her out. "She is not our kind," she would say. I found my mother's attitude annoying and did not feel inclined to stop seeing my girlfriend. My mother was relieved that the relationship ended when I went away to military school the next school year.

Being a Southerner from Mississippi was a source of great pride for my mother, and she passed that pride on to me. The first word I remember her teaching me to spell was "Mississippi." She carefully went over each letter: M-I-S-S-I-S-S-I-P-P-I. She believed there was no finer state in the country. Had her marriage not taken her to Virginia, she would have been delighted to raise her children in the state where she had been born and raised.

The middle of three girls, my mother grew up in a well-to-do family. They experienced the advantages and privileges that were unavailable to most black people at that time and which had been achieved, at least in part, through their exploitation. She told me a number of times during my childhood that, at one point, her father, Fletcher Poitevent FitzGerald, whom she idolized, "was the biggest taxpayer in Mississippi." He owned five thousand acres in Arkansas and land in Mississippi, as well as several ferries that carried people and cars across the Mississippi River between the two states. (For some reason the man who had originally run the ferry across the river got mad at my grandfather and quit transporting him,

Fletcher Poitevent FitzGerald (1870-1945), my maternal grandfather and the son of William and Wilmoth FitzGerald.

Nancy Robinson FitzGerald (1882-1973), my maternal grandmother, wife of Fletcher Poitevent FitzGerald, and the daughter of Jerry and Elizabeth Robinson.

so my grandfather bought his own ferries.)

My grandfather was born in 1870. When he was twenty-five, he was elected the youngest sheriff Coahoma County, Mississippi, had ever had. In 1935, ten years before his death, an agricultural journal, which· my mother saved, mentioned that he had been planting cotton in Mississippi for twenty-five years. He held seats on the New York Cotton Exchange, the Chicago Board of Trade, and the New Orleans Cotton Exchange.

The family lived in the city of Clarksdale in an elegant two-story house, with large, high-ceilinged rooms. Each of the four bedrooms had a fireplace. Also on the property were a two-story house for the servants, a horse barn, a building for chickens, a rose garden, and a tennis court.

Sometimes my mother would visit her maternal grandmother at the family plantation at Albin. The huge two-story, four-bedroom house was built by my great-grandparents in the late 1800s. There were big magnolia and pecan trees in the yard and large fields of farmland nearby.

My maternal grandmothers' home at the Albin Plantation.

It was always a treat to visit my mother's family in Mississippi during my childhood. Mississippi was a land of mystery, full of unusual things and interesting people. It seemed much more colorful than where I lived near the east coast of Virginia.

Sometimes my Uncle GP, who was the county sheriff, took me fishing. First he would go to the jail and pick up a prisoner named Legs, an old black man, who had the job of piloting the boat for us. After our fishing expedition, Legs would go back to jail, and my uncle would make a great fish dinner.

Wide-eyed, I would watch the chain gang work on my aunt's and uncle's country property – the only time in my life I ever saw a chain gang, a work crew of criminals in striped suits guarded by men with rifles. For a little city boy from Virginia, that was exciting! (Mississippi state law mandated that prison populations be segregated, like everything else in the South. I believe that the chain gang I observed as a child consisted of black prisoners, but I am not completely sure of that.)

When in the 1950s my uncle lost his re-election bid for sheriff, it was my mother's family's belief that his opponent had paid black people to vote against him. In 1960, my uncle was appointed southeast regional commissioner for the U.S. Department of Immigration and Naturalization. When Uncle GP retired from that position, he was appointed a judge in Mississippi. My mother told me how fair he was to the black people who went before him, but by then I had rejected racism, and I was doubtful, since I knew he supported white supremacy.

All of my mother's birth family firmly believed in segregation. As I grew older, I felt more distant from them, and I rarely saw them. I no longer shared the same racist beliefs, and my world view had grown to be very different from theirs.

Having quality possessions that reflected her family's high social status seemed to relate to the image my mother wanted to present to others in order to be accepted and respected and to give validity to her misguided sense of self worth. She was proud of owning quality things, and they were part of her identity. Having a nice car was one of the things that was especially important to her. I remember our visiting Mississippi in my youth and her commenting on how impressed she was that a relative had the newest Lincoln Continental. In her later years, she took pride in owning a Cadillac.

When I was about thirteen years old, my mother confided in me that she realized she had an inferiority complex. Apparently one way my mother made herself feel less inferior was to focus on her aristocratic heritage. She often spoke to me of the importance of having "blue blood," the blood from an aristocratic ancestry, and, as I have mentioned, of her view that we were better than "lower class" people. During her life she was a proud member of at least nine different organizations centered around notable ancestry (Daughters of the American Revolution, United Daughters of the Confederacy, Order of the First Families of Mississippi, Order of the First Families of Virginia, National Society of Colonial Dames of the XVII Century, and several similar organizations).

My mother made a concerted effort to build up the self-confidence of her husband and three sons by constantly telling us how smart and wonderful we were and by complimenting us for even the most insignificant achievements. I cannot speak for my brothers and father, but for me, although her intention of instilling confidence was good, her efforts were so overdone that they drove me a little crazy. I got so many compliments that they did not mean anything and became irritating. They may have even caused me to feel more insecure about myself. After all, if my mother needed to try so hard to convince me I was a worthwhile person, maybe there really was something wrong with me.

My mother deeply loved her family and would always love us no matter what we did that she did not like. The negative side of that love, however, was her habit of sacrificing her needs for those of other family members in a way that went beyond altruism, as though she felt her needs were not as worthy as the needs of others. At least in part, this relates to the cultural conditioning of women at that time.

At times children misunderstand something they see or are told, which can result in their holding a mistaken belief, sometimes to their detriment. I remember one such experience with my mom during my early teenage years. She was driving me somewhere in our home town, and it occurred to me to ask her something. I had noticed that among the silent thoughts in my head were some that were like conversations with myself. For example, I might have thought, "William, you should not have done that," or "I should remember to call George when I get home." I wondered if everyone had thoughts of this nature. So I asked, "Mom, is it normal to talk to yourself?" Unfortunately, given my poor choice of words, my mother thought I was referring to people who appeared to manifest mental problems by carrying on a loud dialogue with themselves for everyone to hear while walking down the street. She responded, "No, William. People who talk to themselves are crazy." That was the full extent of the conversation, and I assumed her words expressed a truth about me and that therefore I was crazy. I cannot prove it, but I believe that the experience contributed to, or at least reinforced, the general insecurity I had as a child. The conversation left a deep impression on me, and it was not until years later that I realized that my mother and I had misunderstood each other.

My mother and me. I was in my early teens.

When she married my father, she believed that he was the perfect person for her and that she would live happily ever after. Unfortunately, their relationship was dysfunctional, and the idea of happiness quickly vanished for my mother. When we were little, my father's physical and verbal abuse of her, and my brothers and me, and his inability to give affection, almost caused her to have a nervous breakdown. The coldness of my father's parents also contributed to her distress. Her closest friends reminded her that if she were committed to an institution, my father's parents would get control of her three sons, and that reminder helped her to keep herself together. The most important thing in the world to my mother was her children. As she did with my brothers, she spent many hours driving me to Cub Scout and Boy Scout meetings, taking me to play with friends, giving me rides to tennis classes, watching all my junior high sports events, and so on. She even drove all the way across Virginia by herself to attend my college graduation. If my brothers and I knew anything about our mother, it was that she cared deeply about us and supported us in every way she could. Although I did not think about it a lot as a child, her active involvement in my life meant a great deal to me.

When I read my great-great-grandmothers diaries, I was intrigued to notice similarities between my mother and her. Like my mother, Nancy Robinson loved her children deeply, as this entry indicates:

> **April 20, 1873** - I arose this morning with renewed hope, for I saw some firmness of purpose in the Son I love, may he be able to keep it. I love both my children devotedly. They are my Treasures, yet they little know my troubles for them.

Nancy Robinson's love almost certainly helped her children survive the difficulties of their childhood, just as my mother's ever-present love helped my brothers and me in the same way.

CHAPTER 4

IN MY FATHER'S SHADOW

A NOTE TO THE READER: The main purpose of this chapter is to show how my development was influenced by my father. In it I also endeavor to give the reader an understanding of how my father might have been influenced by his parents. In addition, the chapter illustrates my father and his family's insecurities, which contributed to the need to feel superior to black people and others (as further discussed in Chapter 10). Another purpose of this chapter is to convey a sense of the prosperity and privilege my father and his birth family experienced, something that was almost impossible for black people. My story of my father, subjective by necessity, is not intended to be critical even though it may seem critical or even self-righteous at times. See Chapter 8 for a different way I have come to see my father.

As was the case with my mother's example and teachings, my father's example of deriding blacks contributed significantly to the development of my own racist views and behaviors. What I experienced as an oppressive childhood because of my father contributed to my doing things that were oppressive to black people. I learned how to oppress others by his example, and I had pent up anger that I displaced onto others.

My father, James Stoney Drake, Jr., was born in Lancaster, South Carolina, in 1909, and like my mother, he grew up in a family with racist beliefs in the middle of the Jim Crow era. At some point his family moved to Atlanta, Georgia, where he spent the rest of his childhood. His family had a huge home in Atlanta with a big yard that included two or three gardens and a fish pond.

My father, James Stoney Drake, Jr. (1909-2000).

My paternal grandparents' home in Atlanta, Georgia.

The house also had an elevator that was built to accommodate my grandmother's ill health and that particularly impressed me whenever my family drove down to Atlanta for a visit.

My father's family had several black employees, including a chauffeur, cook, and maid. His ancestors had been in the South for a number of generations, but I do not know if any of them were involved with slavery. I know very little about them except that two or three of them were Christian ministers.

James Stoney Drake, Sr. (1885-1963), my father's father.

My father's father, James Stoney Drake, Sr., whom my brothers and I called Buddy, lived in Atlanta as a young man. He started Drake Corporation in Norfolk, Virginia, in the 1920s. He was a brilliant man who began his working life in cotton mills; eventually he developed chemical formulas that helped the mills improve their products. He was also a strong-willed person who did what

Drake Corporation. It was in the family into the 1960s.

he wanted and took no "guff" from anyone. When my older brother Stoney worked for the family business, he visited some of the mills that our grandfather serviced. One mill executive told Stoney that, if my grandfather had wanted to, he would have "jumped up and pissed on the table."

During the 1950s, my grandfather gave ink blotters, mechanical pencils, tape measurers, and pocket knives to business people as a way of promoting his company. The ink blotters involved a rectangular piece of thin cardboard, one side of which was made of absorbent material that collected excess ink from the pens that were used at that time. The other side was printed with an advertisement or, in some cases, a cartoon. One such cartoon depicted a group of black men sitting around a table playing cards; they were dressed shoddily and were cheating at the game, passing cards to each other under the table. It was a racist characterization that portrayed the stereotype of blacks as worthless, ill-mannered, and dishonest, which was basically how both sides of my family viewed black people.

At some point before I was born, my grandfather built a huge house at Virginia Beach, perhaps an hour's drive from Norfolk. The house burned down, but, undaunted, he built another one just like it. Near the ocean, the house had four bedrooms (each with its own bath), two dining rooms, a large sunroom, a large living room with a marble fireplace, and servants' quarters. Over

House at Virginia Beach, Virginia, that my grandfather, James Stoney Drake, Sr., built.

a two-car garage were two additional bedrooms, one bath, and a kitchen. Also on the property was a beach house with showers and dressing rooms. One reason the house was so big was that my grandfather wanted to invite the heads of the big cotton mills up to visit. After hosting such visits for awhile, however, he stopped because he got tired of their expecting to be waited on all the time.

My father and me.

After my parents married, they lived in the Virginia Beach house with my grandfather. My grandmother, Lillian Gregory Drake, whom we called Mimi, spent most of her time in Atlanta but came up to Virginia Beach for extended visits, always bringing one of her maids and her cook with her. My brothers and I were born into that household between 1940 and 1945.

When I was six months old, my grandfather bought us a house in Norfolk and sold the Virginia

From the time I was 6 months old until about the time I became a teenager, we lived at this house in Norfolk, Virginia.

Beach house. He had an apartment over our garage and continued to go back and forth to Atlanta. After Mimi died in the 1950s, he sold their Atlanta home and bought a 2 ½-acre lot on the Lafayette River in Norfolk, where he built a one-story, four-bedroom house that we all moved into. The house was quite elegant: it had a cherry wood-paneled living room with a marble fireplace, a three-car garage with an adjoining workshop, a boat house, and a dog kennel, where my father kept championship show dogs (beagles) that he raised as a hobby. (My father also owned coonhounds for hunting,

Lillian Gregory Drake (1885-1953), my father's mother.

My favorite picture of me as a child. It was taken in April 1949, when I was 3½ years old. I do not know how old the teddy bear was.

¹ which a friend kept for him in the country.)

Both of my father's parents were verbally abusive and controlling toward my parents. When my newly-married parents moved into the Virginia Beach house, according to my mother, Mimi would read her mail to determine if she had married into the family for their money — even though my mother's own family was also quite prosperous. My mother told me this was the only time my father stood up for her against one of his parents. One time my mother was preparing dinner when Mimi called to ask what she was cooking. When Mom told her what she had in the oven, Mimi commanded, "You take that out! We're having something else for dinner."

Both my father and grandfather would pressure Mary, our maid, for information about the doings of my mother and us kids. Although Mary was put in an unfair position, my mother resented her for "informing" on us. She also resented her husband and father-in-law for asking Mary to inform.

My father worked for my grandfather at Drake Corporation. Once my brother Fletcher told me that, when he was a teenager, he was standing nearby when our grandfather walked up to our dad and slapped him across the face for doing something he did not like.

Mimi owned part interest in a lighting business. When my father was a young man, she offered to give him her share of the company if he quit smoking. He did quit smoking, but she gave her part of the business to her brother instead. Later in life my father resumed smoking, and though Mimi had died, he always kept his habit a secret from my grandfather.

My father had a younger brother named William, his only sibling, who died when my father was about seven years old. After his brother's death, my father's parents always made my father feel that they had loved his brother more than they loved him. In certain ways, the death of his brother signaled the end of my father's childhood as well; for example, the family never celebrated Christmas again.

My father, James Stoney Drake, Jr. (right), and his younger brother William (1913-1919).

In grade school my father was sent away to a military school in Chattanooga, Tennessee; he then went to Fishburne Military School, in Virginia, for high school. He attended a trade or business school for a year or two.

My grandfather lived for ten years after his wife's death, but I do not think he ever got over the loss. He always seemed lonely and broken-hearted. A few years after she died, he told me to turn off my record of Elvis Presley singing "Love Me Tender." He did not explain why, but I believe it was because it reminded him of Mimi. He died in 1963, when I was a junior in high school. My parents sold the Norfolk house around 1970.

Although my father never said a critical word to me about either of his parents, he gave away a portrait of his mother that my mother wanted to put in their new home after they moved from Norfolk. She was surprised that he did not want to keep it, but when she told me about this many years later, she indicated that my father did not remember his mother with fondness.

My father talked about black people with contempt. As I have said, he had no qualms about using words like "niggers," "jigaboos," "coons," and similar terms when black people were not around.

As was the case with my mother, his prejudice generalized to any group of people whom he considered different from himself, including foreigners, Jews, and Catholics. When my brother Stoney married a Catholic, my father refused to go to the wedding. (My mother went, although she, too, was very unhappy about the marriage. My grandfather was so furious that he threatened to take Stoney out of his will.)

My father's racism surfaced at every opportunity. Throughout my youth, whenever he saw black people on television, he referred to them in derogatory terms. (Blacks rarely appeared on television except for sporting events like boxing.) Once in the 1970s I was visiting my parents in Mississippi, and my father took my mother and me for a drive in his new Ford. As we drove along a levee on the Delta, we passed an older car parked by the water. Even though no one was in sight, my father said, "Look at that, some rich nigger on welfare with a fancy car, out fishing." By that time in my life, I found racism offensive, and I was annoyed by my father's words. At the same time, I knew that it would serve no constructive purpose for me to say anything, and so I was silent.

Once my father owned a pet store called the Leash and Collar Shop. One evening when I was about thirteen, he took me with him to visit Mrs. Strange, who worked for him in the store, and her husband. I remember the three of them sitting around the kitchen table discussing a newspaper story about an interracial marriage. My father and the Stranges were furious that a white person would marry a "nigger" and vice versa.

Perhaps because of a self-centered nature that resulted from his own painful childhood, my father did not seem to know how to give me the support and guidance that I would have liked. When I was growing up, he never attended any activity I was involved in or gave me rides to places I needed to go. When my mother went with me to my junior high wrestling matches, he would stay home and watch television. When, as a senior at military high school I was studying college brochures and filling out applications, I was stunned to notice that the fathers of my classmates traveled from faraway places to sit down with their boys and help them get into college. I had not realized fathers did those kinds of things, and my father's absence at that time was quite disturbing. When I was rejected by the first four of the five colleges I applied to, my father's only comment was, "Well, maybe it would be good for you to go into the army or dig ditches." He really did not care whether or not I went to college, and he chose to attend a Virginia Wildlife Federation conference instead of my college graduation. This was very painful to me.

During my childhood I exhibited clownish, immature behavior that was designed to get attention from my peers at school as well as excessive daydreaming both at school and at home. My father's lack of involvement in my life and his frequent criticism, which I reacted to by doubting my own self-worth, probably contributed to this behavior. In general, teachers did not seem to know how to be supportive of me. One teacher actually told my mother not to expect much from me because I had only a seventy IQ, a conversation that my mother shared with me, perhaps to the further detriment of my self image.

Often after school I would come home and lie listlessly on my bed for what seemed like hours, a behavior that I later realized indicated depression. A factor I believe contributed to my depression was my inability to be myself, even if I could not define what that was, and my difficulty in being who my parents wanted me to be. My father did not seem to want me to think about things deeply or question things, while my mother wanted me to adopt her strict moral values and beliefs about what she thought made one acceptable to other people and to society.

My father's behavior pushed me away from him and encouraged the closeness I felt with my mother, who was more protective and loving. When I was a child, he would tell me, "William, you are tied to your mother's apron strings." At times he would call me "Susie" to ridicule me for my connection to my mother.

He could be cruel in other ways as well. Like many fathers, ours made home movies when my brothers and I were little. One of his favorite movies records a time when Stoney was a baby sitting next to a Christmas tree in his high chair. Mesmerized by the brightly colored lights on the tree, Stoney repeatedly reached a hand out to touch one of them, got his fingers burned, jerked his hand back, and briefly cried. The film captured Stoney doing this for a long time. The movie was painful for my mother to see, but my father always laughed as he watched it.

I recall one Saturday morning when I was about twelve, my best friend George telephoned to see if we could get together to play. While George waited on the phone, I asked for my father's permission, which he gave. After we hung up, he said, "That's too bad, William. I was going to take you fishing today, but since you decided to play with George, I guess we won't be doing that." He rarely took me fishing, but he knew that fishing would have been my first choice if I had been given the option. The experience was very frustrating, both because I was denied an apparent fishing trip and because I was aware of my father's manipulation.

Me at about 12 or 13.

During grade school, I had a guaranteed whipping with his belt with every report card. My father thought that whippings would somehow help my grades improve, although that was never the case.

An important lesson I learned during those years was not to tell family secrets. When I was about twelve or thirteen, I told some schoolmates about the whippings. One Sunday our family was on one of our weekly drives in the country. We were somewhere far from home when my father said, "William, I understand you have been telling children at school that I whip you." I had a long time, the time it took to drive all the way home, to absorb the impact of that statement. Then he took me, as usual, to the bathroom that adjoined his bedroom. What was not usual, however, was that he left me there and walked away to get something from his closet. When he returned, he had a leather riding crop in his hand.[xviii] I have a vague memory of my horror as he walked toward me, but my memory of the whipping itself is repressed. It was many years before I told anyone else that my father whipped me.

My father sent me to all-white private schools for most of my school years. After attending the first three grades in an all-white public school, I was enrolled at the Norfolk Academy, "a country day school for [white] boys." Several of my friends at the Norfolk Academy often told jokes about blacks, Catholics, and Jews. I failed the eighth grade at the end of the 1958-1959 school year and was expelled. As I have indicated, I repeated the eighth grade at a public junior high school.

After I completed the eighth grade, my father sent me away to his old alma mater, Fishburne Military School, in Waynesboro, Virginia, for my high school years, as he had done with my two brothers before me. He was very active in the school's alumni association for a number of years, and I remember hearing a conversation he had with one of the school administrators in which they agreed that they would do their best to keep black students out of Fishburne.

My acceptance of my parents' belief in white superiority and my father's callousness toward blacks played a crucial role in the few acts of racism that I recall participating in during my youth. (Another major

Age 15, during my second year of military high school (1961-1962).

---

xviii A thick leather whip used in horseback riding.

factor in my participation, of course, was my own insecurity.) At the urging of some of my classmates, there were times I looked up black families in the phone book and called their homes to invite them to an imaginary National Association for the Advancement of Colored People (NAACP) meeting. It was easy to pick out phone listings for blacks since they lived in "Titus Town" and other all-black areas of Norfolk. I did my best to imitate the voice of a black person when someone answered the phone, but the recipients of my calls probably knew I was some white boy harassing them. They always went along with the "gag," perhaps because they were afraid to do otherwise. I did not even know what the NAACP was — I just repeated what my friends told me to say. I used the phone in my parents' bedroom, crouching near the floor behind the bed and speaking softly so Mary, our maid, would be less likely to hear me if she happened to come into the room. I was probably in the seventh or eighth grade.

Another act was more aggressive. One time when I was home from Fishburne, a friend and I drove my 1951 Plymouth through a black neighborhood. Imitating my father's language, we repeatedly yelled out words like "jigaboo" and "coon." After a quick drive through the area, we took off before anyone could try to retaliate. But just in case we got into trouble, I had a wooden club under my seat.

This incident was ironic since I was an insecure kid who tended to be introverted, nonaggressive, and basically kind to other people. My father, I believe, would not have disapproved of our behavior, although my mother would have because it was not "nice." Perhaps because of our family belief that blacks were not quite human, I was unaware that I was doing something very painful to other human beings.

I went away to college at Virginia Tech in Blacksburg after military school.[xix] By the end of my sophomore year, it had become clear to me how different my view of the world was from that of my father (and my mother). During our talks about Vietnam, he

xix At the time I was a student there, Virginia Tech was officially called Virginia Polytechnic Institute, or VPI. Later it was renamed Virginia Polytechnic Institute and State University.

expressed his support for the war because he believed America was stopping the spread of Communism. I, on the other hand, had come to believe that the war was immoral. After one or two arguments on the subject, I realized that our discussions did not serve any constructive purpose, and so most of the time I kept my views to myself. I also came to reject the idea of white supremacy, which was definitely a subject I kept to myself around my father. His belief that he was superior to blacks (and other groups) was a part of his self-perception. I believe that for me to question his basic premises about the matter would have been threatening to him and would have created a strong reaction. When I grew a beard and became a hippie a short time later, my relationship with my father took a turn for the worse. He was deeply offended by my appearance and would not speak to me, a silence that lasted for an entire year.

When I finished college, I moved to Cleveland and then to California. When I was in Cleveland, I did a weekend workshop at The Gestalt Institute, a training and workshop center related to psychotherapy. I had just visited my parents for Christmas and felt a lot of pain concerning my interactions with my father, which included disagreements about the war in Vietnam. The workshop leader had someone play the role of my father and had me tell "my father" three things I wanted from him. I started out with what I thought was the real issue, saying "I want you to understand how I feel about the war!" But after that I dropped to the heart of the matter and blurted out, "I want you to love me!" At that moment I broke down and sobbed. I realized it was not the differences in opinions that were the real issue, but my need to feel loved and accepted by him, just as I was. I think that he really did love me, but was unable to show it, and it was hard for me to see that his love was there.

The first week of January 1996, I received a phone call telling me that my fifty-three-year-old brother, Fletcher, had died of a massive heart attack. I was shocked. He had meditated regularly, had maintained a healthy diet...and was my brother.

Heavy snows on the East Coast caused the northern Virginia memorial service to be delayed, so I flew to North Carolina to comfort my parents before flying to Virginia. My mother and father were in their upper eighties and were not healthy enough to go to the service. When I was about to go to bed one night, my father said he wanted to give me money to help pay the expenses of my trip. I was very surprised because, except for the twenty dollar checks he always gave me for Christmas and birthdays, he had not given me any money since I was a teenager. He reached into his wallet, pulled out a ten dollar bill, and handed it to me. It was such a small amount, I was not able to feel grateful, but it appeared to be a big deal for him, and his face seemed to reflect a sense of pride.

A short time later, my parents and I stood in the lobby of their retirement village, waiting for my ride to the airport. Another resident approached my father and expressed her sympathy. My father responded, "Oh, Billie [my mother] is doing better. She'll get over it." He kept his own feelings to himself, as his father had trained him to do.

It always meant a great deal to my mother for me to visit, but at least in his last years, my father was not interested in seeing me. Their caregiver confided in me that whenever my parents discussed the possibility of my wife and me flying from California to see them in North Carolina, my mother had to really fight to get my father to agree to the idea. This was a painful revelation for me. It was not that he and I did not get along, at least superficially. Mainly he talked for hours as I listened, while trying not to show my boredom. Perhaps he was uncomfortable having someone in his environment with whom he did not have a good rapport.

In my opinion, my father never overcame the deep sense of inferiority with which he grew up; it affected his relationships with everyone and everything. (And, to a degree, I can see that all these things are true about me.) He never seemed to develop a conscious awareness of his life that would have enabled him to let it unfold in a more wholesome way than it did. He abused my mother, my brothers, and me as a result of the treatment he received from his mother and father. It is very likely that his parents were abusive toward him because of the way their parents treated them, as so often seems to be the case over many generations. I mention this not to excuse the abusive behavior but to share my understanding of it. But the pain of my childhood created a barrier between us that, regrettably, I could not overcome. Once I left home, I rarely went back to visit my parents.

I do not think my father was ever able to accept me the way I am. Before he died, however, I had a realization. I wanted him to accept me, yet ironically, I was not accepting him as he was — which seemed to include his apparent nonacceptance of me! I was not able to give him what I wanted him to give me.

I believe that my father did the best he knew how. For all his shortcomings, he was very kind to his grandchildren. He was also the repected executive secretary of the Virginia Wildlife Federation. Many people who knew him held him in high regard, and he was a good friend to those he was close to. Although they were infrequent, there have been times he took me hunting and fishing, and after my first year of college, he gave me his old car when he got a new one. To his credit, he did a better job of parenting than that done by his own parents, who were even more distant and repressive. Except for belittling my mother and getting angry at her, he was moderately congenial during the last years of his life.

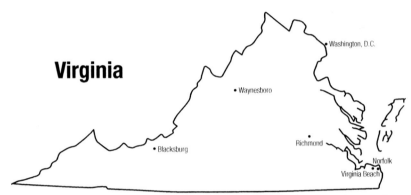

Virginia, my home state. My family lived in Virginia Beach when I was born and moved to Norfolk, where I grew up, when I was six months old. My brothers and I went to military high school in Waynesboro, and my brother Stoney and I attended college at Virginia Tech in Blacksburg.

CHAPTER 5

MY BROTHERS AND ME

Although I had two older brothers, James Stoney Drake, 3rd, and Fletcher FitzGerald Drake, throughout my childhood I always felt like an only child. I was five years younger than Stoney and three years younger than Fletcher, and the two of them spent much more time with each other than they did with me. Stoney and I never went to the same school at the same time, and Fletcher and I were schoolmates for only a year or two. Even then I rarely saw him at school.

Our father often criticized us boys as well as our mother. Because my brothers were considered overweight, he frequently ridiculed them for being "fat." His criticisms of us always bothered our mother, who would get upset and try to defend us. My parents argued a lot, and most of the time it seemed to be about us children.

Fletcher, who was very conscientious and sensitive, was the most studious of the three of us. While his sensitivity probably made him more susceptible to the pain of our father's abuse, it also made him an outstanding photographer during his early adulthood, and in his twenties he became one of the foremost theater photographers in Washington, D.C. Like me, he grew up with a desire to help others, and in college he went so far as to consider becoming a Christian missionary doctor. He was a very serious person — no doubt too serious.

One of the last times I talked to Fletcher before he died, he expressed appreciation for the fact that Stoney had looked after him during their childhood, defending him at times from bullies. Stoney was a very caring and protective big brother.

One thing I appreciated about Stoney was that he did not take little things too seriously. "Don't sweat the small stuff," he'd say. He offered me brotherly advice at times, and tried to discourage me from ever smoking cigarettes. He also shared his tips regarding relationships with girls.

Stoney was often generous with Fletcher and me. The greatest gift he ever gave me was his 1951 Plymouth, which he presented to

me in the early 1960s when I was sixteen or seventeen. It was painted with gray primer paint, and he had nicknamed it the "Gray Ghost." I had it painted shiny black for twenty or thirty dollars.

That car was a godsend. Before I had it, the only car I could use when I was home from military school was my mother's, for which I needed both my mother's and my father's permission.

My brother Stoney as a teenager.

My mother was always obliging, but my father was less predictable, and my fear of him made it hard to approach him for anything. With the Plymouth, I could take off whenever I wanted to as long as I was home by the time my father set. That car gave me an unbelievable feeling of freedom, even though at times it barely ran.

In the summer after my junior year in high school, Fletcher also gave me a great gift. Having just turned twenty-one, he took over an educational trust fund our grandfather had created for him when he was a child. (My grandfather had done the same for Stoney and me.) Fletcher immediately bought a brand new, burgundy Pontiac LeMans and asked me if I wanted to drive around the country with him for two months. It was a rare opportunity to spend time with my brother and to see wonderful new places, and I accepted with the greatest pleasure. Considering that he could have made the offer to one of his friends, I was touched by his kindness and his wish for us to spend time together.

My mother knew that we needed camping equipment, but she also realized that our father was too stingy to let us buy it. So she had Fletcher and me go to a store just before we left and charge the equipment we needed. Her willingness to face our father's anger over the bill, long after we departed, touched us. In any case, it was money well spent: Fletcher and I had a great time together. It was our first trip west of Mississippi, and we drove all the way to California. A highlight was spending a week backpacking in Yosemite National Park, walking through lush forest land and past emerald creeks and pools. I had never seen a place so beautiful.

Aside from that trip, though, I saw little of my brothers during my high school years. By the time I went to college, Stoney was working with my father at Drake Corporation.

My brother Fletcher (left) and me in June 1963, a month before my 18th birthday, as we are about to drive from our Virginia home to California.

When I came home to Norfolk on vacations, I enjoyed seeing him, his first wife Sandra, and their little girl Teresa.

During the late 1960s, my relationship with Fletcher and his first wife Renee became very important for me. I do not know how it happened, but at some point I realized that they also opposed the war in Vietnam. We attended several peace marches together, and we also shared a number of drug experiences (not all of which I look back on fondly). It meant a lot to me to have

Fletcher and Renee as close friends with whom to share that exciting and difficult period of time. And I always enjoyed seeing their young children, Jason and Lisa.

Fletcher, Renee, and I shared a deep belief in racial equality. Lisa, Fletcher's daughter, has the understanding that Fletcher grew up as I did, without questioning our family's racism. Apparently he came to question it when he was in college, perhaps due to the influence of a friend of ours named Bob Edwards (the subject of Chapter 6).[xx] Fletcher shared with Lisa his painful recollections of seeing black people forced to sit in the back of buses during his childhood. (Renee, who was from Iowa, also told Lisa about the segregation that she had observed as a young girl visiting her grandparents in Alabama. She had considered the idea of forcing black people to use facilities separate from whites' facilities ridiculous, and she would sneak drinks out of the "colored only" drinking fountains just to make fun of the system. She would have been severely rebuked for that had she been caught by any white adults.)

After Martin Luther King's assassination in April of 1968, Fletcher became a photographer for King's organization, the Southern Christian Leadership Conference (SCLC). That same year the SCLC sent him to Marks, Mississippi, a county considered the poorest in the nation, to photograph the incredible poverty of its black residents. The last time Martin Luther King was seen weeping was when he visited Marks and saw the people's living conditions. Marks is about twenty-five miles due north of one of my great-great-grandparents' plantations and about fifteen miles from my mother's hometown of Clarksdale.

Fletcher lived with some of the residents of Marks while he was working there. A few years after his death, his second wife Nancy told me he had recalled that experience several times during their marriage. "He told me how transformative it was. It deeply moved him," Nancy said. He told her how touched he was by the exceptional kindness and generosity of the poor people, both toward him and toward one another. It helped him realize that many black people had very meaningful values. He was also

---

xx Bob Edwards is not the person's real name.

struck by the contrast between their genuine goodness and our dysfunctional family's view that black people were inferior. He told his daughter that he had grown up with a lot of money but also a lot of misery, adding, "Lisa, I've been in some of the poorest homes in the United States and there was such joy and love there."

Not long after his Mississippi experience, Fletcher photographed the SCLC's Poor People's Campaign, which brought poor people from all over the country to Washington, D.C. Many arrived on foot or in horse-drawn wagon trains. From May 13 to June 24, 1968, they camped out in the rain and mud in what was called Resurrection City, along the mall in front of the White House, and demanded that the country's politicians take steps to end poverty. Fletcher spent a lot of time talking to and photographing them, and he was deeply impressed with their sincerity and commitment. I remember his telling me of one black family that came up from Mississippi in spite of their white landlord's promise to evict them if they joined the protest. To Fletcher these poor people — of all races — were real heroes, more so than some of the leaders of the campaign.

A number of Fletcher's photographs of the Poor People's Campaign and Marks, Mississippi, were published in a book the SCLC produced titled *The Poor People's Campaign.*[1]

When Fletcher worked for the SCLC, he made several black friends. I remember him taking me from his home in Alexandria, Virginia, into Washington, D.C., to visit a black family he had come to know. I do not remember the visit very well, but I do recall feeling self-conscious and uncomfortable, having been unaccustomed to experiencing black people as friends.

In the early 1970s, Fletcher became involved in a religious movement related to Guru Maharaj Ji, who had come to the United States from India. As is sometimes the case with new converts to a movement or cause, he tried to persuade me to become part of it. When it was clear that I was not interested, he broke off our friendship. He also broke off relations with our parents and Stoney at the same time. I could understand Fletcher's point of view, unlike everyone else in the family, because I, too, felt a deep sense of spiritual striving and had also been influenced by a religious teacher from the East. A year or two earlier I had spent a few weeks studying with a leader of the Sufi religion who had moved to this country from Ceylon and was living in Philadelphia. In spite of that, I considered Fletcher's break from the family unfortunate, and it was incredibly painful to lose my brother. I do not know how the experience was for Stoney, but I know it was very difficult for my parents.

In the late 1980s, although Fletcher still followed the same religious leader, he reestablished contact with family members. My wife and I enjoyed the times we visited Fletcher and Nancy after he renewed our relationship. Unfortunately, because we lived in California and they lived in Maryland, we had the pleasure of only a few visits before his death. It was terrible to lose him again, and I regretted that we had not had the time to redevelop the closeness that we had once had.

From left to right: my wife Joan Ramsey, me, my brother Stoney, my father, my brother Fletcher, and my mother. The photo was probably taken in the early 1990s.

Photographs by my brother Fletcher (c1968) on the following four pages were published in the Southern Christian Leadership's *The Poor People's Campaign*. (Permission to use photographs courtesy of Nancy Drake.)

A woman in Marks, Mississippi.

An old man in Marks, Mississippi.

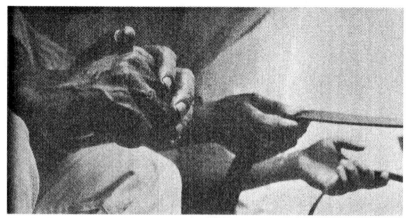

Hands of a wagon team driver, en route to Washington, D.C. to participate in the Poor People's Campaign.

A wagon en route to Washington, D.C., to participate in the Poor People's Campaign.

People in Washington, D.C. to protest poverty as part of the Poor People's Campaign.

People in Resurrection City, the encampment of the Poor People's Campaign, being tear-gassed by police, probably as part of an effort to evict them.

PART II

MY PERSONAL GROWTH
AND JOURNEY OUT OF RACISM

In this section I share many of the experiences and influences which have contributed to my journey out of racism and my current work of helping others unlearn prejudice. Some of the experiences described relate directly to prejudice and racism. Others taught me about human behavior and helped me to become more self-aware, open-minded, and open-hearted.

CHAPTER 6

A LIFE-CHANGING FRIENDSHIP

My first year at Virginia Tech in the small town of Blacksburg, Virginia, began in 1964. A typically conservative student, I dressed well, kept my hair short, and became president of my dormitory's house council system, a form of student government. In my sophomore year, I became president of the Civilian Interdormitory Council, which governed all of the individual dormitory's house councils. I was involved in a number of the university's committees and activities; and was likely to become president of the civilian student body. (The university had separate dormitories for military [Reserve Officers Training Corps] and civilian students.) By the time I graduated from Virginia Tech in 1969, I had become a hippie, a war protester, and an outspoken students' rights advocate. I also faced twenty to forty years in prison for possession of marijuana, but, in reality, probably more for my so-called radical politics. (This experience is addressed in Chapter 9.) The factor most responsible for this profound reorientation of my life was my friendship with Bob Edwards.[xxi]

I first met Bob when he accompanied my brothers and me to a wedding in New England. I was still in military high school at the time, and Bob and my brother Stoney were friends at Virginia Tech. From that trip, I remember Bob's keen mind and quick wit.

Bob subsequently decided he wanted to go in the army in a manner that would allow him to both avoid combat and return to college on the GI bill. He studied all the books on photography he could find in the college library, then dropped out of Tech to spend a year studying photography with Fletcher, who was

xxi Bob Edwards is not the person's real name.

then photo editor of the yearbook at Hampton Sydney College in Virginia. Bob learned what he needed to from Fletcher and then managed to get himself into the Army Exhibit Unit near Washington, D.C., creating displays that would help civilians appreciate the army's point of view. He landed what was essentially a civilian job. (Fletcher's beliefs changed so much under Bob's influence that he dropped out of Hampton Sydney, needing only a course or two to graduate. He also enlisted in the army to join Bob at the Army Exhibit Unit.) When Bob was discharged from the army at the start of my sophomore year, he came back to Virginia Tech on the GI bill.

When I heard that Bob was at Virginia Tech, I was excited to have the opportunity to get to know someone who had been so close to my brothers. My mother had trained me to have great respect for both of them, and I transferred this respect to Bob, approaching him with a sense of awe. I looked him up at his little white house in Blacksburg, and we began our friendship. During that year I visited him often, and with my complete permission, he took on the task of reorienting my view of the world.

One night he asked me if I wanted to smoke marijuana with him. I had never seen "pot" (slang for marijuana), which had been so absent from my family's awareness during my upbringing that my parents had never mentioned it specifically, although my mother had certainly decried the use of illegal drugs in general. So I took a day to think about Bob's offer and, because of my great respect for him, decided to give the drug a try in spite of my feelings of apprehension.

Later that year, after writing a fifty-page term paper on LSD for a sociology class, I felt comfortable enough to try that drug also. During that first LSD experience, I looked at some drawings a friend had made and told him how much I liked the colors he had used. He laughed and informed me that they were in black and white! I love that story because it shows how the drug allowed me to step outside of my usual way of looking at things and see them in a whole different way. Contemplating school and society in that light, I realized that what I and others perceived as important was often insignificant. I also gained valuable insights into my own behavior, realizing how much of it was ego-driven and related to my needs for love and acceptance. By my third year at Virginia Tech, it seemed like Bob and I smoked hashish (a derivative of the cannabis plant) together every night.

Overall, my drug experiences had an increasingly profound influence on me. They caused me to question the meaning of many of my other experiences and gave me a deeper awareness of a spiritual world. Realizing that a number of society's teachings about drugs were simply not true made it easier for me to question other things, such as the war in Vietnam.

This is not to say that all my drug experiences were positive. I recall once feeling terrified and suicidal on LSD. After taking it several times when I lived in New York City during the summer of 1967, I suffered daily states of depression when I returned to Blacksburg. I concluded that taking drugs was too unpredictable and uncontrollable for me to ever recommend it to someone else, and I had stopped using them by the time of my graduation.

Bob was living in Alexandria, Virginia, across the state from me, when I resumed school. A couple of our mutual friends suggested that I go talk to him about my depression to see if he had any helpful advice. I drove to his house, and we sat on the floor of his bedroom facing each other as I told him as much as I could of my experience while he simply listened. When I finished talking, I found myself looking into his eyes. We sat holding eye contact for a long time in complete silence until finally I felt a tremendous release inside myself, as if a heavy weight had been lifted from me. It was a feeling of lightness and well-being. Still in silence, we stood up and walked to the door of his room, where he looked at me and said, "Now do you believe in extrasensory perception?" My depression never occurred again.

This was not the first time I had experienced Bob's ability to go behind the scenes of what we usually think of as reality. More than once during his stay in Blacksburg, while I was living in the university dormitory, he showed up at my room at the same time I was feeling a strong desire to talk to him about something I was going through. When we went to the March on the Pentagon to protest the Vietnam War, Bob walked up to one of the members of the National Guard that surrounded the Pentagon and looked into his eyes for a long time. The soldier's commanding officer finally walked over and told Bob to leave his troops alone. I do not know what took place during Bob's silent communication with the soldier, but it was interesting that the man turned to his superior and said, "Sir, it's OK, he isn't hurting anybody."

Much more significant was Bob's persuading me to spend the summer of 1967 in a Puerto Rican ghetto on Delancey Street, on New York City's lower east side. He arranged for me to sublet a room from a member of the Socialist Workers' Party for thirty dollars a month. I had never before lived in a poor, or even nonwhite, neighborhood. I shared my small apartment with an occasional rat, and the view outside my window was of the massive and noisy Williamsburg Bridge. I attended "be-ins" (hippie gatherings, which I quite enjoyed) at Thompson Square Park, marched at anti-war rallies, and spent time with fellow hippies near Bleeker Street in Greenwich Village. I also went to a presentation given by the Socialist Workers' Party on the Arab-Israeli situation; I was surprised at how biased it was, and even more surprised at how much the audience seemed to like it. I also attended talks given by people who advocated violence against the government in order to champion the rights of poor people. I did not believe in violence, and such talks made me uncomfortable. But sometimes I went to wonderful concerts at Lincoln Center, among which I remember evenings with sitarist Ravi Shankar most fondly. My overall experience in New York was very rich, and I owe much to Bob for giving me a broader view of the world.

It took me a long time to assimilate the shift in my perception of the world that took place under Bob's tutelage, and my last couple of years of college as well as a few years that followed were marked by considerable confusion. I am certain that some of it resulted from a sense of having the rug pulled out from under me, and I have come to question if someone should have the power over another person that I allowed Bob to have over me.

I am grateful for Bob's influence, though, in spite of the insecurity that resulted. During our time together, Bob shared and reinforced my belief in racial equality, and thanks to him, I became more aware, open-minded, and inclined to question things.

CHAPTER 7
WAKING UP TO MY OWN RACISM

I have often been asked what inspired me to reject the concept of racism. Having been born into a family with deeply held racist views, I consider that rejection nothing short of monumental, and I attribute it principally to two pivotal experiences I had while I was still a teenager.

The first happened when I was seventeen years old, during the 1962-63 school year. A few months earlier, James Meredith had been escorted onto the University of Mississippi campus by federal marshals, becoming the university's first black student. (Rosa Parks' arrest for refusing to give up her seat on a Montgomery, Alabama, bus to a white man had occurred seven years earlier. That action prompted the Montgomery bus boycott, which earned Martin Luther King national recognition as a civil rights leader.) In the fall of 1962, one of my cousins came up from Mississippi to spend a year at Fishburne Military School, where I was in my high school junior year. During a school holiday, we took a bus together from Fishburne, in north-central Virginia, to my parents' home in Norfolk, on the East Coast. A black woman sat in front of my cousin, and during the entire duration of the trip, he kicked the back of that poor woman's seat.[xxii]

My mother raised me to think that blacks were inferior to whites, but she also taught me to be kind. I did not say anything

xxii An article published in the *Sacramento Bee* in 2001 sheds light on my cousin's behavior as well as my own and that of many young people. According to research studied by the American Psychological Association, professed racists do not commit most hate crimes. Most are committed by young people who normally obey the law and do not see much wrong with their behavior. Sometimes drugs and alcohol are involved, but the main factor seems to be a personal prejudice that affects judgment and keeps the aggressors from seeing the immorality of their actions. (Source: Mecoy, "Hate Crimes.")

to my cousin, but his cruel behavior, unprovoked by anything other than the color of the black woman's skin and her choice of a bus seat, was deeply shocking to me.

In spite of my mother's training, I had committed my own unkind acts toward black people, as I have described. But this time, on the bus, I was a little older and more mature; I was also the observer, which gave me a different perspective. I did not think a lot about the experience during the next months, but it worked on me almost unconscioiusly, softening and gently eroding my previously unquestioned belief that white people were superior to black people. Witnessing my cousin's senseless act was a catalyst that led me to begin to question racism and racist behavior.

In early May of 1964, I graduated from Fishburne. I was almost nineteen. A couple of weeks after graduation, I was riding in a car with Fletcher, who was in college at the time. As I have said, I respected Fletcher very much, and I decided to ask him a question. I looked over at him and said, "Fletcher, does it really make sense to look down on people because they're a different color from us?" Without hesitation Fletcher responded, "No," and the conversation ended.

The experience of my cousin's behavior on the bus had begun my questioning of racism, and this brief exchange with Fletcher marked the end. Short though it was, it was one of the most important conversations of my life, and from that moment on I rejected the concept of racism.

I say that I rejected the "concept" of racism, rather than racism itself, because I realize that I still have traces of conditioned racism within me. I think this is true of most Americans, whether or not they grew up in a family that expressed racist beliefs. Our country is dominated by, and favors, white people, as reflected in its corporate and political systems, its media and entertainment fields, its educational systems, and so on. It is inevitable that many Americans of all races, having grown up in such a society, would have some degree of conscious and/or unconscious racism.

Another important experience occurred one or two Christmases later when I was home from college visiting my family. By that time, my father was president of Drake Corporation. Several black men, who were probably in their seventies, had been working for the family before I was born. They worked in our yard at times, and I often saw them when I visited the family business. I experienced them as kind men and remember them with a sense of warmth. As children, my brothers and I knew them only by their first names or nicknames: Willie...Norman...Preacher...Rosie. One day I accompanied my father to a black section of Norfolk to deliver Christmas bonus checks to the men. We arrived at one of their homes, and the man came out to our car to receive the checks. We conversed briefly, and as we were leaving, my dad said, "You boys have a nice Christmas."

Although my father may have been using the word "boys" innocently as a term of familiarity (it was not unusual for white men to be called "boys," for example), because the word was used to demean black men in the South it hit me at the moment like a ton of bricks. For the first time in my life I realized that we had *always thought* of these older men — men who were older than my parents and decades older than my two brothers and me — as "boys." Even if the term was used innocently, we had not thought of them as men but as boys, boys who were inferior to the "real" men — the white men. The magnitude of my family racism began to dawn on me.

During my sophomore year in college, I took some extremely valuable psychology classes that gave me a deeper understanding of myself, my childhood conditioning, and the psychology of racism. I learned how much my parents and their child-rearing practices affected how I had come to view the world. It was a startling realization that gave me insight into my own behavior and the behavior of others, allowing me to think more for myself and mimic less of my family's thinking. I also came to understand that my insecurities and those of my dysfunctional family were a major factor in our need to look down on people of other races, religions, and nationalities.

From this time on, I was willing to disagree with my mother on the subject of race occasionally. Essentially, I would tell her that I supported equal rights for black people, and she would say that I did not understand that blacks were inferior. I did not argue with her or try to change her mind because I understood that she was too set in her beliefs to consider a different point of view. With my father, I avoided the subject entirely. I knew that any discussion we might have on the subject of race would just bring out his anger, causing him to withdraw and not speak to me for a period of time, as he had done when we disagreed on other matters.

CHAPTER 8

SIGNIFICANT EXPERIENCES ALONG THE WAY

In 1966, during the summer after my sophomore year at Virginia Tech, I worked in Franklin, Tennessee, as a door-to-door Bible salesperson. (This was the "Bible belt," where every family already had four or five Bibles, but somehow I was supposed to persuade them to buy one more!) I struck up an acquaintance with a black college student from Franklin. On one occasion, we joined a mutual white friend, whose aunt owned the boarding house where I stayed, to go to the movies. To prevent our black friend from getting harassed in his hometown for mixing with white people, we had to drive to nearby Nashville where he could be more anonymous. I remember sitting in the back seat of the car wanting so much to ask my black friend about racial matters but deciding not to because I was afraid of inadvertently saying something offensive.

(My boarding house owner's nephew had spoken on television in favor of civil rights. She worked for the county, and was told by supervisors that, if her nephew continued to speak publicly in favor of rights for blacks, she would be fired.)

By my junior year, I had become a hippie and an activist, very involved in the student rights movement and in protests against the Vietnam War. To some extent, I was carrying out a belated rebellion against my father and my military high school, but there was much more to it than that. I was also standing up for justice, freedom, and love, the values my mother had taught me (in spite of the double standard that came from her prejudices). I attended all of the big anti-war marches in New York and Washington, D.C. Although civil rights was not my primary focus at that time, it was always a concern of every march I joined.

Martin Luther King spoke during at least one of the protests I attended, although I was not able to hear his speech. It was on April 15, 1967, when three hundred thousand people marched to the UN building in New York City. King often pointed out the relationship of the Vietnam War to racism and poverty: a disproportionate number of blacks and poor people died in the war, the enormous financial cost took money away from programs that could end poverty, and the war itself had racial overtones (American soldiers often referred to North Vietnam soldiers as "gooks," a derogatory term for Asians).

Wearing a button that supported civil rights, I once attended a talk on campus by former Alabama governor George Wallace, who was famous for his stance against integration. Though thousands of students showed up to hear him speak, I was the only person in the audience with a beard, and he gestured to me on three occasions as he made irrelevant emotional appeals that vilified liberals. On one such occasion, he stated that "we should grab Washington's liberal politicians by their beards" and throw them out of Congress. Of course, the number of Washington's liberal politicians who had beards was close to zero, but such statements had emotional appeal, and it is unlikely that many Wallace supporters thought about how illogical they were. Wallace was a master of the psychology of persuasion. As far as I could tell, I was the only person who did not participate in the standing ovation he received at the end of his talk. I was shocked and disappointed that so many of my fellow university students were impressed by his presentation. (Admittedly, I had an advantage over others in the audience: my brief experience selling Bibles had taught me a lot about the psychology of sales, and, like Wallace, I had studied the psychology of persuasion.)

Wearing hippie clothes enabled me to experience prejudice and discrimination from "the other side" for a change. Once a college friend and I went into a truck stop near the Virginia-Tennessee border, where a Marine threatened to beat us up because of the way we dressed. In Washington, D.C., a restaurant

I had frequented in the past denied entrance to a friend and me because of my beard and our buckskin jackets. I also remember walking along a city street in Washington one day when a man, with what appeared to be his family in the car, began yelling profanities at me as he drove by (an experience that has reminded me of my own behavior driving through a black neighborhood only a few years before.)

Such experiences were always painful, and they left me feeling a little insecure and a little angry at the same time. While I valued the understanding that the experience of being the object of discrimination gave me, I also recognized that at any time I could shave my beard off, put on a "nice" shirt and slacks, and become an acceptable member of society again — unlike blacks and other visible minorities.

During the summer of 1967, when I lived on Delancey Street in New York City's lower east side, I often walked over to Greenwich Village, which was very popular with the hippies. I tried to organize some of them to collect toys from the suburbs for poor children, but I received a complete lack of response that initiated my growing feeling of disillusionment with the hippie movement. (A friend from Pennsylvania and I went ahead and did the project ourselves, using a borrowed Volkswagen bus.) I also became disturbed by all of the commercialism associated with the movement. Quite a few specialty stores made a fortune off hippies, and I knew that drug dealers were making money hand over fist while pretending to promote peace and love. I also recognized the irony of thousands of professed nonconformists wearing the same basic "uniform."

One evening during that summer in New York, I went to hear the black writer James Baldwin talk about the oppression of blacks. On another occasion, I heard H. Rap Brown, the famous black revolutionary who was a member of the radical Black Panther Party. I could understand the anger of people like Baldwin and Brown, but I felt confused and uncomfortable because, no matter what I ever thought or did, I was white and would probably always feel like I was the target of their anger.

Brown's violent approach made me especially uncomfortable, not only because I was white, but because using violence did not make sense to me, regardless of the situation.

This time of my life was one of confusion, insecurity, and naïveté. It was a time when I and some of my white friends felt guilty for being who we were — white — and sometimes wished we could be black, Native American, or another minority. We often looked at nonwhites with a sense of reverence, as if they were better than we were. I almost envied my white friend Jeff, who could easily create an Afro with his black curly hair.

Starting in the spring of 1967 and continuing throughout the following year, I was the target of an official investigation. My political activity appears to have been a factor in this, probably the principal reason. I know of the investigation because word got back to me in various ways. One of the university deans showed the father of a friend of mine a list of about ten students who were under investigation, and my name was on the list. Several of my friends were quizzed about my behavior by university officials. Neighbors warned me that men posing as insurance agents had been asking them personal questions about me. A friend told me of a student he knew who had been asked by a state trooper to try to buy drugs from me.

On May 25, 1968, four cars filled with Virginia State Police officers, two police dogs, and the director of Virginia Tech's campus security arrived at my house at two o'clock in the morning. After they had searched the premises for three hours, they arrested me for possession of marijuana. Virginia law placed marijuana in the same statutes as opium and heroin, and possession of a fraction of an ounce of marijuana carried a sentence of twenty to forty years in prison and a $5,000 fine.

The police confiscated marijuana and other evidence at my house that night. Most of the pot they found, which was a fair amount, I had recently purchased from a close friend for $200 so he and his family would have the money to move across the country to live in California. I did not really need or want the marijuana and had hidden it in a shed on the property until I could figure out what to do with it. Almost all of the rest of the evidence, including drug paraphernalia that was found in a suitcase an acquaintance had stored in my house and some hashish, I had never seen before. The hashish was left in my living room by a couple of friends who stopped by to visit after I had gone to sleep. The police arrived shortly after my two friends left. Ironically, by that time my experimenting with drugs had virtually run its course, and more significantly, I had never sold any drugs in my life (usually only dealers were arrested).

My arrest was considered big news; even though it took place in southwestern Virginia, TV stations in Washington, D.C. picked it up. When my parents found out about it, my mother was supportive but distraught, and my father did not speak to me for the next year. (As always, when I did something he did not like, he took it personally, as if it were a statement about him.) The raid occurred a week before final exams, and since I was in no shape to take the exams, I left it up to my professors to grade me without them. Those professors who were sympathetic to my situation gave me passing grades, while those who were not gave me Fs. Some of my country neighbors, and even some of my classmates, treated me with revulsion.

Once the apparent certainty of my going to prison sank in, I was devastated. The night of my indictment, my friends had a party for me and I got drunk, which was not my habit. Not only was the prospect of going to prison horrendous, but during the hearing, one of the investigators had testified that he had been meeting regularly with an informer and had prior knowledge of where some of the evidence would be located. Interestingly, the evidence he said he had prior knowledge of included the paraphernalia and hashish that I had not known was in my house. I was too depressed to feel like partying, and even a friend's idea of making buttons saying "Free Huey and Bill" did not amuse me. (The reference to Huey Newton was to an imprisoned Black Panther revolutionary.)

During the preceding couple of years, I had joined my friends in expressing outrage about politically related busts happening to people involved in civil rights and anti-war work, as reported in the "free press." But deep in my heart, I had not completely believed that such things really happened in America. My mother's teaching that the police and other authority figures were on the side of justice ran too deep. But when it became apparent to me that my own political involvement had been a factor in my being investigated and arrested, I realized that political imprisonment was a reality that happened to some people who stood up for what they believed and that some law enforcement officials did act without integrity.

In retrospect, I can see that my behavior of the late sixties helped bring on my legal situation. The university initiated the year of investigation after I made a speech at a student awards ceremony in the spring of 1967. I was the outgoing president of the student house council system and was the MC at the occasion. One of the university's deans had just given a speech in which he had proudly proclaimed that, in his seven years at Virginia Tech, he and his office had never interfered with student government, which, he said, was completely autonomous. After his speech, in front of the vice president of the university and other officials, I delivered an unscheduled talk that contradicted what the dean had just said, and while there was truth to my statement, it is understandable that I was immediately perceived as a threat to the university, or at least to some of its officials.

In addition, once the summer of 1967 had begun, I had started to wear hippie clothes and to actively protest the war, which made me stand out at my conservative university. It also had been obvious that I had some money, as I had bought a two-hundred-acre farm (for $16,000) and several vehicles with cash from the trust fund I had received when I turned twenty-one. All of this made me very conspicuous and suggested the possibility of drug involvement. (At the same time, a thorough investigation would have shown where my money came from and that I was not a drug dealer.)

After a year of trials, my case was dismissed due to an illegal search and seizure. The affidavit used to get the search warrant had contained wording that was vague, and my lawyer found a case that had been thrown out by the U. S. Supreme Court

The 200-acre farm I owned in southwest Virginia during the late 1960s.

because of a similarly worded affidavit. On the basis of that case, a local court ruled that the evidence found in my house could not be used against me, and later my whole case was dismissed. I was extremely fortunate, and to say I was relieved would be the understatement of the year.

That terrifying episode in my life gave me insight into how politics and bias can affect the justice system. I had the advantages of being white and being able to afford good legal representation. Even so, the powerlessness and hopelessness I felt before I learned that my case would be dismissed gave me empathy and compassion for minorities and the economically disadvantaged who get caught up in the legal system.

I graduated from Virginia Tech in 1969 and moved to Cleveland. After working for a year as a substitute teacher at a vocational high school, I started taking classes at Cleveland State University (CSU) to get a teaching credential. I was interested in the alternative schools movement that was popular at the time, recognizing that alternative schools could create an educational experience that was more humane and meaningful than the authoritarian and traditional education I had endured.

Student teaching was required to complete the CSU program, so I arranged to do it at the Cleveland Urban Learning Com-

This is a picture of me in my early 20s.

munity (CULC) in the fall of 1971. CULC was a "high school without walls" program. It was financed by private grants, and students did not pay tuition. The school offices were located in a downtown office building; seminars were held there, but the school encouraged students to find individuals and businesses in the surrounding area where they could apprentice within the context of specific courses. In group seminars related to subject areas, students shared what they were learning in the community so that the other students in the group could benefit. Students were required to set their own course goals, which were reviewed with staff members. Credit toward graduation was based on hours of work instead of grades. Staff members, the community mentors whom the students used, and the students themselves all took part in the process of student evaluation. The program emphasized "learning how to learn" over memorization of facts.

The setting of student goals, along with creating or finding a good structure or situation for learning, was particularly important. If the goals were too demanding and/or the structure for learning too rigid or confining, the potential for growth could be too restricted. On the other hand, if the goals were not demanding enough and/or the learning structure too "loose," the student might not be encouraged to stretch himself or herself. The goals and structure had to be tailored to each student in order to meet individual abilities and needs.

One tenet of the program was that students could learn from one another, especially when student diversity existed, and the student body was designed to reflect the population and diversity of the Cleveland area. Four-fifths of the school's eighty or ninety kids came from the city rather than the suburbs, and students were selected from each of Cleveland's twelve school districts.

The boy-girl ratio was one-to-one, and about 55 percent of the students were white while most of the remaining students were black. The school usually had six or seven staff members, almost half of whom were black. I served under two school directors (equivalent to principals), who were white. The year after I left, the director was black.

We did not consider CULC to be the perfect school for all students. Prospective students were interviewed by a small committee that included CULC students. The committee sought new students who were most likely to thrive in our program and could reject ones who were obviously ill-suited.

CULC was modeled after Philadelphia's Parkway Program. Parkway was known worldwide for its innovative approach to education. When my period of student teaching ended, I did an internship at Parkway in the spring of 1972, then returned to CULC to teach for the following two school years. During my time at Parkway, I lived with three other white staff members in a house on South Marvine Street in "South Philly." We were the only white residents in a lower income black neighborhood. At times, children from the neighborhood would come over to our house to visit and play. They were always intrigued with how I spoke, and one of the children once asked me, "How come you talk like us?" Unlike other white people they had met, I had a Southern accent and said "y'all," as did their families whose roots were also in the South.

I had never lived in a black neighborhood before, and it soon became apparent that my mother's teaching that all black people were dirty was a myth. After I had lived there for awhile, it was pointed out to me that our house was one of only two or three on the block that ever had trash in front of it. Almost everyone in the area took pride in keeping their homes and their outside environments clean, and some people were in front of their houses at eight o'clock every morning cleaning the sidewalk.

For the first time in my life, at both Parkway and CULC, I was involved in communities that included a lot of black people. My interaction with them was extremely educational for me, especially at CULC where I taught for a much longer time and where my experience was far more intense. As well as learning to see black people as human beings with positive and negative aspects just like any other people, I became more aware of the residues of racism that I still carried.

One of the black students I met at CULC was Chuck. The first time I saw him, I was observing another staff member's seminar in which he was taking part. I was quite impressed with how articulate and intelligent Chuck was. After I got to know him, he shared with me the subtleties of racism that tend to go unnoticed by us white folks. Walking Cleveland's streets together, he had me look carefully at the black mannequins in a department store window. To my surprise, I saw that they were white mannequins with stereotypic white features (narrow noses, thin lips and straight hair), painted black!

During the first year or two I was at CULC, the director was Father Tom Shea, a Jesuit priest who co-founded the school after convincing his Jesuit high school to award diplomas to CULC graduates. During a conversation Tom and I had about Martin Luther King, he pointed out that many people are either so focused on the "reality" before them that they do not have the vision to grow, or are so absorbed with their vision that they trip over the harsh reality in front of them. King, Tom said, had the amazing ability to: (1) be aware of the day-to-day reality for blacks on the streets of Birmingham, Alabama; (2) hold high ideals for blacks in America as well as for all other Americans (and for all human beings); and, significantly, (3) handle the gap between the two. That teaching has stayed with me all these years, and I have seen how it can be applied to one's day, one's life, social groups, institutions, and many other things. Often there is a gap between what we experience and what we would like to see. Being realistic about our experience, holding goals and ideals, *and* acknowledging and working with the gap between the two, allows for healthy growth and change.

My most painful but enlightening experiences at CULC centered around Sam, one of CULC's black staff members.[xxiii] At one of our staff meetings, four months into the 1972-73 school

---

[xxiii] Sam is not the person's real name.

year, he made the point that his white co-workers could not relate to the black students, reading negative quotes from anonymous black students about each white staff member. Although he acknowledged that he himself did not interact with white kids very much, his focus was on the white teachers as being the ones with a problem. It was clear to me that he considered us prejudiced, if not racist.

Like my white co-workers, I was shocked and confused by Sam's presentation. The student whose quote he shared about me said that I was testing black students and trying to figure out why they were interested in things I didn't think they should be interested in. Without knowing the student's name and the context of whatever remarks I may have said to him or her, I could not defend myself.

Later in the day, I noticed a black student in the hall who was obviously upset. I invited her to a local coffee shop to talk, and as we sat there drinking coffee, she started talking about Sam. She shared her view that Sam, who came from the Deep South and had worked only with black kids, expected to encounter white racism because of his past experiences. She said that Sam was encouraging black students to have the same expectation by asking them leading questions about white staff members (among other things). It seemed possible that Sam was stereotyping his white colleagues and creating a self-fulfilling prophecy of racial tension.

The conversation left me even more frustrated and confused than I had been. Over the next few days, I did some painful soul-searching. While I believed there was some truth in what the student had shared with me, I also wondered if there was some truth in Sam's concerns. Until his accusation, I had held the naïve view that I did not see people in racial terms and had overcome racism by that point in my life. Reflecting on the current situation, however, I came to realize that I did in fact have deep-seated racist conditioning related to my childhood. I realized, for example, that one reason I was so impressed with Chuck's articulateness and intelligence was because he was a *black* student. It also became apparent to me that most of the students I related to were white and that staff members in general tended to relate most easily to students of their own race. I reached the painful awareness that I would probably spend the rest of my life struggling with my conditioned racism.

Because I could not say that I was free of racism in the face of Sam's accusation, my insecurities as a liberal white person in a racist society — and especially my insecurities as a white liberal who had been raised with racist views and whose ancestors had owned slaves — were heightened. What should I say when a black person seemed to suggest that I was racist? What could I say that would not be misunderstood or make a bad situation worse? How responsible was I for the deeds of my ancestors or for the racism of our society? I discussed some of my feelings with a close friend and co-worker named Barbara, who reminded me that I should not feel guilty for how others have treated black people and helped me regain some perspective. She also expressed her belief that Sam was not consciously trying to hurt the white staff members and encouraged me not to respond to Sam in a way that would hurt him.

Barbara's efforts to be objective and fair were commendable, but unfortunately, for the next year and a half I allowed myself to be afraid of Sam. I found his forceful personality and his ability to wield power at the school intimidating and was concerned about his influence over black students. (Of course, my painful experiences of my father as well as my years at military high school also had a big effect on how I experienced someone with what could be considered authoritarian tendencies.)

As a staff, we tried to be fair to all of our students. When it became apparent that most of the students on the school's executive board were white, for example, we attempted to come up with an election process that would allow blacks and other minorities better representation. When our student population did not reflect the racial balance that we intended, we tried to remedy the situation.

After Sam's accusations, students and staff members spent more time getting to know those who were of a different race from their own. I was impressed when three black girls (who were close to Sam) went out of their way to initiate conversations with me. For a period of time I did not have an office space, and as a way to get to know my co-workers, especially the black staff, I spent several weeks sharing the office of each staff person, one at a time. On occasion, I made an extra effort to talk with black students and staff members, and Sam and I became a little closer.

In spite of such efforts, however, racial tensions continued. When conflicts arose that involved black and white students, there would usually be a number of black students, and sometimes one or two of the black staff members, who would see the situation in racial terms whether or not such a view was warranted. (It is probable that some white students took such a position at times, but I did not observe that.) On one occasion, for example, Stephanie, a white student, photographed students at CULC for a slide presentation a local TV station was going to air. When the program was broadcast, the students shown in the ten slides that were presented were all white. Understandably, this was of concern to a number of the members of the school community. At an executive board meeting, Stephanie tried to assure people that she had not intended her slides to be an all-white presentation, and that she had created a total of thirty slides picturing black as well as white students. My friend Barbara said that she had reviewed the slides after the conflict arose and felt that overall they were representative of all the students. It was also brought out that the TV station itself had selected the specific slides that were used for the show. (At this point, a white student insensitively suggested that the station might have picked slides with white students because "whites show up better in photographs." This did not help matters!) Barbara pleaded with the group to realize that, while the TV presentation was unfortunate, Stephanie had not done anything intentionally racist. In spite of her plea, a couple of black students walked out of the meeting in protest.

In May of 1974, when seniors met to plan their graduation ceremony, Stephanie and some other white students wanted the festivities to be held informally in a park, while some of the black students wanted a formal indoor ceremony. As the conflict escalated, some of the students began to perceive it in racial terms. At one point, two students got into a fist fight over the matter. The next day at a staff meeting, a black staff member was

also discussing the situation in racial terms. Sam had not spoken yet, but I was certain that he, too, would believe that the situation had racist implications. I felt very tense. When he joined Barbara in interpreting the conflict as one related to different values rather than to race per se, I was stunned and greatly relieved. They explained that Stephanie and her white friends' liberal values were reflected in their wanting a casual graduation, while some of

Me giving out diplomas at the Cleveland Urban Learning Community in the Spring of 1973.

the black students valued graduation as an extremely important event that warranted a formal occasion.

We agreed as a staff to do what we could to help the students on the different sides of the issue to understand one another, and within a few days tensions were diffused and the conflict resolved.

My experiences with Sam were challenging at times, but they gave me the gift of seeing some of my previously unconscious racism, and I came to respect him for his ability to broaden his own understandings and become an important peacemaker.

I moved to northern California in December of 1974 to live on some land owned by Ed, a college friend. Several years later, I got some friends together to start the Auburn Alliance for Nuclear Responsibility (AANR), a small, peace-oriented, anti-nuclear organization. As in the sixties, civil rights and peace issues seemed to go together, and the AANR participated in annual marches to honor civil rights and Martin Luther King. It was during this time that my understanding of the civil rights movement and Dr. King's work slowly began to deepen.

Having participated in civil disobedience while protesting against nuclear power, some of us in the AANR were asked to lead a training session in civil disobedience. I took on the task of discussing the history of the civil rights movement and its use of nonviolent civil disobedience for social change. Preparing for that presentation helped me appreciate the great lengths to which Dr. King and other black leaders had gone to discourage their followers from hating their opponents and adopting violence.

At the same time, I joined other AANR members in starting a group to study the writings of King, Gandhi, and other spiritual and nonviolent leaders. This endeavor also increased my exposure to King's books, speeches, and ideas.

Each year around the time of Martin Luther King Day, members of a local organization wrote letters to the editor for the *Auburn Journal* vilifying King, and I took it upon myself to research the contentions in these letters and send responses to the paper. Without exception, those attacking King used half-truths, lies, and/or irrelevant emotional appeals to make their cases, only rarely stating something factual. A typical example was a letter written in 1983 alleging that in one of King's own books, *Stride Toward Freedom*, he admitted preparing for his mission in life by studying Communism. I found that very hard to believe, so I went to the library and got the book to read for myself. Yes, King had studied Communism, but only in order to make an assessment of it — after which he became highly critical.

Once a local group supporting white supremacy circulated a flyer titled "The Beast As Saint: The Truth About Martin Luther King." It suggested, among other things, that William Sullivan, the former assistant director of the FBI, concluded that King was a Communist. I had a copy of Sullivan's autobiography (*The Bureau: My Thirty Years in Hoover's FBI*) and sent a letter to the editor pointing out that Sullivan had actually written that King was *not* a communist.[1]

After working for many years to overcome racism within myself, I felt an obligation to help overcome it in the world around me, and writing such letters to the editor was one way to do that. It also gave me an opportunity to learn more about King and the civil rights movement.

My most significant letter was published on January 19, 1998, Martin Luther King Day. It was a letter apologizing to black people, especially those who live in my hometown of Norfolk, for the racist actions of my youth. I had thought about writing such a letter for months and was grateful to have an opportunity to express regret for my past. The letter simultaneously appeared as a guest editorial in *The Virginian Pilot* in Norfolk, *The Union* in Grass Valley, California, and the *San Francisco Chronicle*.[2]

Dear Editor,

This is a letter of apology to the African-American community of Norfolk, Virginia.

I am a 52-year-old white male who grew up in Norfolk. My parents were from the Deep South, and my great-great-grandparents, on my mother's side, owned slave plantations on the Mississippi delta.

I wasn't a mean kid, but as a child I adopted the racist views of my family and the white community I grew up in. Such views, at least in my family, were passed on from generation to generation. I grew up hearing the adult black men who worked for my grandfather referred to as "niggers" behind their backs. When my mom and I drove downtown, if we saw black males, my mother locked the car doors out of concern for our safety, which led me to believe there was something to fear.

I learned from my family and peers to believe that blacks were naturally inferior to, and less intelligent than, whites. If I walked past a black person, I held my breath because I thought black people were supposed to smell bad. If I touched a black person, I would have wanted to wash my hands to avoid getting a disease. I did these things not to intentionally degrade blacks but because of what I had learned to believe about them. Living in a segregated world, with rules that regulated black and white relationships, I had no personal experiences to counteract the myths.

I deeply regret the racist attitudes I personally held in the past and which I have worked hard to overcome. Also, and more specifically, I offer my apology to African-Americans, especially those in Norfolk, for the misdeeds I committed as a teenager to gain approval from my peers and inflate a false sense of self-worth. On several occasions I telephoned black people's homes in Norfolk to try to imitate a "black voice" and invite blacks to an imaginary NAACP meeting. One evening a friend and I drove through a black neighborhood and shouted derogatory names. These misbehaviors added to the millions of other degrading experiences blacks and other minorities have experienced from fellow Americans.

Because my family had racist views did not mean that we were bad people. My parents were not prejudiced against blacks because they wanted to be cruel but because of deeply held beliefs that they were convinced were true.

A turning point came for me when I was 17, watching a white teenager on a bus kicking the back of a black woman's seat just to annoy her. Although I did not say anything, his action seemed senseless and cruel. About a year and a half later, out of the blue, I asked my older brother, "Fletcher, does it really make sense to look down on people because they are a different color from us?" His response was simply, "No." That was the entire conversation, but it changed my life, and during my college years I became a supporter of civil rights. My first relationships with African-Americans, as a teacher in Cleveland, completed the shattering of the myths I had learned.

Racist attitudes held by our family and others were tragic for many reasons. They perpetuated myths. They resulted in actions that caused other human beings pain, encouraged them to doubt their potential and self-worth, and denied them basic human rights. And, as Martin Luther King said, racism not only keeps the victims from being all they can be, it also keeps the perpetrators of racism from being all they can be. People with racist beliefs are not able to open their hearts to love all of God's children and to be a whole human being.

As human beings we tend to have prejudices and insecurities, and if we want to create a more loving, peaceful, and just world, those of us that have prejudices have to acknowledge them and work to overcome them. We also need to do our best to extend the healing power of love to all people, whether we like them and their beliefs and actions or not.

Racism still exists in the institutions and individuals of our society, but I hope that we are coming a little closer to realizing King's dream — that someday people will be judged by their character rather than their color and descendents of slaves and slave owners will be able to come together in friendship.

Bill Drake

In the mid-1980s, I began to write for a local social issues newspaper. Each time Martin Luther King Day came around, I wrote an article on King or the civil rights movement.

In January 1990, a broadcaster at the community radio station where I worked asked me to give a four-hour presentation on the civil rights movement as part of the station's Martin Luther King Day programming. The presentation caught the attention of the program director, and I was asked to contribute to future Martin Luther King Day broadcasts. Each year for the next eight years, I created a new program, often doing thirty or more hours of research and preparation for a one-hour presentation. I also directed or co-directed the day's programming for three years.

While writing for the social issues paper and preparing programs for radio, I collected and studied many books about the civil rights movement, and my understanding of King's philosophy as well as the role others played in the movement deepened. King's spiritual perspective and general philosophy were consistent with my own, but his speeches and writings gave me a greater understanding of the importance of loving those who utterly opposed equal rights for blacks and other minorities and the importance of bringing love to the act of protest. His considerable wisdom, courage, and compassion made him a role model for me.

As I discussed in the introduction to this book, a radio program that I created for Martin Luther King Day in 1996 included sharing excerpts from my great-great-grandmother's diaries and discussing my family's racism. To prepare for the project, I had to study photocopies of 1,350 pages of diary entries for the first time. The project was very laborious, especially because the handwriting was so hard to read, and I spent about 150 hours creating that particular show. I took it on, in part, because I wanted to go deeper into my family lineage and learn something about my ancestor whose husband owned between 136 and 200 slaves on the Mississippi Delta.

Much of what I found surprised me. I discovered that my great-great-grandmother was a remarkable and wonderful human being who also had deeply ingrained racist attitudes and who had, of course, participated in the horrible institution of slavery. I discovered how much my mother was like her great-grandmother, especially in terms of caring for others and being overly protective. Reading about the horrible effects of the Civil War and Reconstruction on the South and on my ancestors, and my ancestors' hatred of President Lincoln and the North that resulted, I realized why I had been raised to be prejudiced against Northerners.

During the mid-1990s, I joined members of different races in a race discussion group and briefly participated in a multi-racial committee called the Nevada County Citizens for Human Rights. Those of us who were members of the discussion group shared our experiences of racism and discussed different views of Martin Luther King's work. It was valuable for me to listen to the perspectives of the black participants. One of them, who had been involved in civil rights work on the East Coast, was very critical of King's allowing children to participate in marches that might have incurred white violence. He also lamented that the endeavors he was involved in got less support and attention because so much focus was on Dr. King.

The human rights committee assessed the problem of racism that existed in our county and took steps to mitigate it. Among other things, the group helped sponsor a successful workshop that focused on unlearning prejudice.

In 1993 I was attracted to a flyer that advertised a two-day men's retreat in my home town with an African shaman, Malidoma Somé. I was amazed that someone from Africa was offering a workshop in my community and decided to attend the event.

Malidoma is from the Dagara tribe of West Africa and was born in what is now Burkina Faso. The tribe and the surrounding region were colonized and exploited by the French from the early 1900s until the region gained independence in 1960. That very year, when he was four years old, Malidoma was taken from his village by a Jesuit priest and forced to attend a Catholic boarding school, where he remained for the next fifteen years. His experience was not unlike that of Native Americans who were torn away from their families and cultures and sent to government boarding schools. Like them, Malidoma was forbidden to speak his native language or otherwise identify with his own culture.

Malidoma's tribal elders were deeply concerned that the effects of French colonialism and the modern world were destroying their traditional values and way of life. As Malidoma's boarding school experience demonstrated, he and his people were pitted against the ethnocentric arrogance with which some Westerners view other races, religions and cultures. After he left the school and returned to his village, Malidoma's elders decided that he should be sent into the modern world to share the tribe's wisdom with others in hopes of bringing some sanity to Western countries that seemed to them to be so destructive and out of balance.

After earning three master's degrees and two doctorates, then teaching literature for three years at the University of Michigan, Malidoma moved to California where he began to lead workshops on building communities and creating spiritual rituals for adults. He also worked with teenage inner city gang members and other youths.

My first encounter with Malidoma, and his wife Sobonfu, who joined us for part of the weekend, left me impressed with their insights into our culture and their wisdom about life. I remember Malidoma's discussion of the sad fact that some young males in America's big cities seek initiation into manhood through their participation in drive-by shootings. Our young people suffer an enormous loss by not having elders from whom they can accept guidance. They also suffer by not having healthy initiations that allow initiates and their families and communities to honor and empower the initiates' stages of development.

I was impressed with the emphasis Malidoma's culture placed on the community instead of the individual. Sometimes our culture places too much emphasis on the individual and his or her "getting ahead." Relatively few people appreciate the idea of selflessly serving the community and helping everyone realize his or her potential. During the workshop, Malidoma and Sobonfu led some simple exercises in which we each acknowledged the other individuals in the group. I was left with a feeling of deeper kinship with the community we had created and a sense of being recognized by that community.

Over the next few years, I participated in additional workshops with Malidoma and Sobonfu. I also visited Malidoma on my own several times to seek his counsel about various aspects of my life. During these visits I always found his perspective refreshing, even when he talked about mundane things. His wisdom was far beyond that of all but a handful of Westerners I have known in my life.

One time when I was with Malidoma, I was struck by the thought that, if he and Sobonfu had lived in the American South in the mid-1800s, they almost certainly would have been slaves. The idea of their being forced to serve white masters was horribly repulsive, and I reflected on the incredible destructiveness of human bondage and racism. How ironic it was that I, a descendent of slave owners, who once believed that blacks were inferior to whites, had accepted a black person from Africa as one of my mentors.

After I began my work on this book, I went to Malidoma seeking a blessing for the endeavor. Since ancestors of his tribe had been forced into slavery and my own ancestors had owned slaves (perhaps even some from his village), it seemed fitting to bring together those two components of the history of racism and of the histories of our two cultures. He and I agreed that my book could help others to heal racism and contribute to the healing of the dysfunctional family lineage of which I am a part.

Through my work with Malidoma and Sobonfu, I learned to put aside my own cultural judgments and to look at another culture and see the beauty in its way of life and in its ways of relating to a spiritual world, no matter how different those were from that to which I was accustomed. I also gained a deeper appreciation for the wisdom of their culture and of indigenous cultures in general.

By early 2003, after months of work, this book was 98 percent finished. In March of that year, I put the book aside for several reasons, including the difficulty that I might face in getting published, the demands a publisher was likely to make on me in terms of promoting the book, and the quotations from other sources for which it was difficult to get permission to use. However, the main reason resulted from my doing a nine-day workshop that March with Byron Katie, author of *Loving What Is*.[3] (Katie's work is described in Chapter 11.) The workshop had a deep effect on how I view my world and changed how I would approach writing a book of this nature. The book I had almost finished was no longer the book that I would want to write.

One of the most profound and valuable effects of my work with Byron Katie was how it transformed the way I viewed my parents, helping me to be less judgmental and more accepting toward them.

A pivotal moment related to my judgment that my mother was "overly protective," which I saw as a form of control on her part. All of my adult life, I had deeply resented what I experienced as this aspect of my mom. While I could still make the case that my mother was overly protective *sometimes*, when I turned my judgment around to myself during the retreat, for the first time I realized that *I* can be overly protective and that there were ways *I* was overly protective of my mother! This realization took the wind out of my strong judgment of her. One thing that I realized was that never telling her about many of the experiences I had in the '60s (and '70s and '80s!) was a way of being overly protective of her. And while I always rationalized this behavior by thinking I did not want to hurt her, a deeper truth, which was revealed to me during the workshop, was that I was afraid of being judged by her and was acting out of my own self-interest. This was an amazing discovery that gave me considerable insight into myself as well as my relationship with my mother. (For twenty years I had not told my mother that I went to India in the 1970s with a Hindu teacher. Given what I thought were my mom's religious beliefs, I did not think she would handle the information well. Finally I told her about my trip and showed her some pictures I had taken. My mother seemed to enjoy what I was sharing and at one point said, "You know, I have always thought that other religions worshiped God also." I was stunned. I never expected her to react so positively.)

By looking at what I had viewed as my mother's controlling nature, I came to recognize how controlling I am of my own world. There are ways I try to control how I am perceived by others by "putting my best foot forward." I notice that there are times I slightly "spin" the truth of something I am saying, perhaps just subtly changing the inflection I might otherwise use on only one word or two as I am talking, in order to support the image of myself I want to project or to help justify myself in some way. I also take numerous steps to control my physical environment; for example, when I go camping or traveling, I take along everything I might possibly need in order to feel comfortable.

As an adult, I was frustrated that my mother never seemed to see me as someone who had grown up and was successful in his own right. When I have reflected on this perception of her, I have had to acknowledge that I never saw my mother as having grown up in the sense of overcoming the limited conditioning of her childhood. Fundamentally, her apparent perception of me was no different than my perception of her. I was not able to accept my mother as she was any more than she was able to do that for me.

I can also see that things I have admired in my mother are within me as well. She had a strong sense of loyalty to family and friends. I, too, have strong feelings of loyalty — to family, friends, and my workplace. I admired how accepting and loving my mother was with people she had a connection to, and I can see the same tendency in myself. And in spite of it being molded by racism, she had a strong sense of justice and integrity. During my life I have seen these attributes in myself as well.

Applying what I learned from Katie, I can see ways I have, or have had, the "negative" qualities I saw in my father. I considered him abusive, yet I have been abusive of him with mental stories and judgments I have told myself, as well as with stories I have told about him to others, countless times. By focusing on my "abusive childhood" during most of my adult life, I was not able to consider more positive sides of my relationship with my father, and I limited my own self-image by holding the story of my wounded childhood too tightly.

My judgments about my father's physical abuse toward me can also soften when I remember a time I was physically abusive toward someone else. When I was twenty, working at a summer camp in North Carolina, I was a counselor for a group of nine-year-old boys. One boy, Tommy, was a chronic bed wetter, and I resented changing his urine-soaked sheets every morning. At the end of the session, when it was time for the boys to pack and get ready to go home, Tommy refused to pack, behaving in a way that was more playful than disobedient. I lost patience with him, threw him over my knee, and began spanking him. I lost all self-control and spanked him for some time, unable to stop myself even though I wanted to at one point. I imagine I was releasing pent up anger, very little of which related to Tommy, and I was copying the behavior my father modeled, but it was very unfortunate that Tommy had that experience. It brings up sadness when I think of how I was physically abusive toward him.

When I think of my judgments of my father in light of my experience with Tommy, I am reminded of Christ's saying to those who would throw stones at a woman who committed adultery, "Let the person who has not sinned cast the first stone." Whether one believes in the concept of sin or not, this story contains a beautiful teaching.

I can also see in myself deep-seated fears of rejection as well as difficulty in being vulnerable and intimate in certain situations. Few people would realize these things about me, but I am well aware of them. I believe that these are qualities my father and I have shared.

I experienced my father as being very authoritarian, and I can see that in my 20s I had an authoritarian tendency, with a strong need to be "right." Although not so authoritarian any more, I can still exhibit a need to be right at times.

Another quality that I attributed to my father, which bothered me immensely, was what I saw as his self-centeredness. Yet, when I look at myself, I can see how I become self-absorbed at times. I can get focused on my own little world inside my head and "lost" in my thoughts. I can become so focused on tasks and projects that I neglect people who are around me. As for my father's preference in his later years that I not come to visit, which resulted in some pain as well as judgment of him, to be honest, I never looked forward to spending time with him. One criticism of my father relates to what I experienced as his tendency to talk compulsively (perhaps as an expression of his insecurity and as a way he could control his environment). I would not consider myself a "compulsive talker" in general, but

I am aware that, when I am with friends, sometimes I tend to talk more than I listen.

I believe my father saw his family as an extension of himself in a way that was unfortunate. If one of us children did something away from home that he thought was inappropriate, he took it personally, as if it was a reflection on him. When we were children, this might result in whippings, like when I told children at school that I got whipped at home. When we were older and did something he felt embarrassed about, like when I had a beard for a year and then later when I was "busted" for drugs, he withdrew from us. In the two examples I just gave, after each he would not speak to me for a year. I know that when I felt uncomfortable about a relationship with a girlfriend I had in my 20s, my approach was to withdraw from her, just as my father had done with me at times.

The qualities I have believed to be in my father and which I have come to see in myself do not relate just to things that bothered me. He loved nature and spent time in the woods whenever he could, usually hunting or fishing. I, too, love nature, and my wife and I love to visit the beautiful Southwest. In general, my father was a good friend to his friends, and he loved spending time with them. I can see in my own life that I am a good friend to those with whom I am close, and it means a lot to me to do things with them. My father developed many interests and hobbies throughout his life, reading and learning everything he could about each one. In my own life, I have had different interests, each of which I have delved into thoroughly.

I find it interesting that the older I get, the more I can see ways I am like the father of whom I had so much judgment.

In 2011, after having put aside my efforts to promote the healing of racism for several years, I was compelled to resume them in response to a racist incident in my community. After I published an article on racism in our local paper, the paper's editor, Jeff Ackerman, asked to read my book's manuscript. After reading it, he strongly encouraged me to publish it. A number of months later, my sister-in-law's father, a retired educator, read it and said that everyone should read it. Coming back to the work of helping others unlearn prejudice, along with this encouragement to finish my book, were the factors in my deciding to pick the book up again and make revisions that would allow it to be more in alignment with my new understanding.

CHAPTER 9

MY SPIRITUAL JOURNEY INTO GREATER AWARENESS

I have often thought of my life as a spiritual journey, and my attempts to overcome my racism have been a part of that journey. My exposure to American Indian spirituality and Buddhism has had a strong influence on how I perceive and approach my work related to racism and prejudice. They have taught me about the relatedness of all life and the importance of compassion.

My father never went to church or expressed an interest in anything religious, but my mother took my brothers and me to the Episcopal Church every Sunday when we lived in Norfolk. Our church, the Church of the Good Shepherd, was "low" Episcopal, meaning that it avoided ornate rituals. As a child, I took this church-going experience matter-of-factly. Like my brothers before me, I served as an acolyte on occasion, but I do not recall the services as in any way interesting or enlightening to me. Mostly, I remember the hard wooden seats.

At Fishburne Military School, I had to march to the Episcopal Church every Sunday. My chief recollection of that experience was how the minister, Reverend Frazier, greeted us cadets as we left the church. While he took his time with the other local parishioners, he treated the cadets as if we were part of an assembly line that needed to keep moving as quickly as possible. "Morning, Drake…morning, Johnson…morning, Hunt…morning, Conger," he would say as he grabbed each of our hands and quickly moved it, along with the rest of us, closer to the door.

In spite of my lackluster experiences in church, I had faith in God and Christ during my high school years. As captain of the wrestling team, I would pray before some of our matches that the wrestlers would do their best, and while it may have been only coincidence, those were the matches we tended to win.

During my trip with Fletcher to California, I had an experience that was of a religious nature for me. We had stopped somewhere, and as I got out of the car, I looked up at the sky and saw a cloud formation that looked like God sitting on a throne. I quickly ducked back into the car to get my camera, but when I looked back toward the sky, the formation was nowhere to be seen. This vision made me very happy, as though I had just received a "wink" from God.

When I started college, however, I went to church only on religious holidays. When one Easter I was irritated by the minister using guilt to maximize the congregation's donations, I stopped attending church altogether.

While I have always thought highly of Christ's teachings, the church never made God or Christ a living experience for me. It seemed to emphasize the idea of an external white male God who resided up in the sky, a concept that I eventually could not accept. As my religious thinking evolved, I came to think of God as synonymous with love and to perceive God's presence within me as well as all around me. I eventually rejected the idea that God had a particular gender.

My real spiritual journey began in the summer of 1964, when I was nineteen. I had just graduated from Fishburne and was working at Camp Sequoyah in western North Carolina, where my brothers and I had gone when we were children. As a counselor, I got involved in the camp's exceptional Indian lore department, making crafts and participating in Indian dances and Indian-like ceremonies. The following year, I worked at Camp Sequoyah again and directed the Indian lore department for the younger campers. The intention of the department was not to get white people to "become Indians" (all of the children appeared to be Caucasian) but to help them develop a deep respect for Native American cultures. I had had no exposure to anything related to Indians before, and my involvement in the Indian lore department triggered something very deep in me, as if I were awakening to something that had been a part of me forever. I was deeply moved by the Indian cultures and found solace in their deep spiritual traditions. For almost thirty years, Native American spirituality was my spiritual path.

Camp Sequoyah was located in the heart of the Cherokee homeland, and while I was there, I visited Cherokee craft stores and attended a play the Cherokee present each year that gives an overview of their history. I was very impressed with the story of the Cherokee and during the next years undertook an intense study of both Cherokee and Sioux (Lakota) history. I also became knowledgeable about the disastrous history of Indian-White relations, which inspired me to become a strong advocate for Indian rights, making financial contributions to Indian causes and educating others about issues affecting Indians.

In my freshman year at Virginia Tech, I attended a lecture on Vietnam by one of the army officers on campus. I felt that his remark that fighting the Vietnamese was not like "fighting a group of pesky Indians" so trivialized the near genocide of our country's first inhabitants that I almost walked out.

When I finished college and moved to Cleveland, my first job was substitute teaching at a vocational high school. While I was there, one of the history teachers let me give lectures on Native American history and politics to his students, an experience that helped me refine my knowledge of those areas.

When I taught at the Cleveland Urban Learning Community (CULC), my principal course was American Indian Culture, which became one of the most popular courses in the school. Our seminar group was offered the use of some land in the country outside Cleveland, and we often visited there on the weekends to build Indian structures and share experiences related to Indian spirituality and culture; for example, we put up a tipi, built a long house in the style of the northeastern Indians, and conducted sweat lodge ceremonies. We also met regularly with the director of the Cleveland Indian Center, who deepened our understanding of Indian politics in America.

We took a field trip to Minneapolis to observe the "Wounded Knee" trials involving American Indian Movement (AIM) leaders Dennis Banks and Russell Means, on trial for the Indian occupation of Wounded Knee, South Dakota, a few years earlier. Wounded Knee had been the scene of an infamous massacre of a group of Indians by the U.S. Cavalry in the late 1800s. William Kunstler and Mark Lane, both renowned trial lawyers, were defending Banks and Means. I was especially interested when Kunstler was cross-examining a rancher: using his delightful sense of humor, he asked the rancher a series of questions that easily exposed his racism. The students and I found the trial educational and entertaining. (Later the judge dismissed the case against the Indians, admonishing both the FBI and the U.S. government for presenting tainted evidence and botching the case in other ways.)

During that trip, we also spent an evening with a local Native American who shared with us some of his spiritual beliefs and experiences, and we attended a political rally that included Indian drumming. Both of those experiences were very moving for me, especially the remarks of the local Indian. He emphasized his tribe's connection to the earth and the belief that God, or the Great Spirit, is everywhere. These two aspects of Native American spirituality have always been significant to me, and his sharing helped deepen my own sense of spirituality.

In June 1974, I wrote the following prayer to Wakan Tanka (a Native American word for the Great Spirit or God):

The Prayers of a Seeker

Wakan Tanka
Grandfather
Keeper of the Holy Vigil
Breather of the Breath of Life
Hear the prayers of a seeker

Wakan Tanka
Grandfather
Lead me to Truth

Lead me to the Wisdom of the Holy
May my path be as straight as the arrow flies
May my path be as true as the stem of the Sacred Pipe

Wakan Tanka
Grandfather
Help me to remember my kinship with all things —
large and small
Help me to remember my kinship with all things
in the Universe
May my heart be as generous as the flames of
the Council Fire
May my heart be as warm as the bowl of the Holy Pipe
When passed around the Circle

Wakan Tanka
Grandfather
Hear the prayers of a seeker

During the summer between my two school years at CULC,
I drove from Cleveland to California and back with Jimmy, a
student who had graduated from CULC and had become a good
friend. On the way west, we visited Wounded Knee, where we
did not find much beyond a great feeling of desolation as we
contemplated the massacre that had taken place on that land.
After Wounded Knee, we drove through Custer, South Dakota.
Noticing a shoe store with a "going out of business sale" sign,
we went in to buy some shoes. When we asked the owner why
he was going out of business, he explained that he had been
a member of a local committee trying to improve relations
between whites and Indians. Many white people hated the
Indians, and the relationship between the races was strained.
Once he got involved with the committee, he was considered an
"Indian lover," his store was boycotted, and his life and the lives
of his employees were threatened.

We also visited a natural stone formation that a foreign sculptor
was carving into the image of Chief Crazy Horse. The sculptor
was attempting to create a monument to Native Americans as an

alternative to Mt. Rushmore's carvings of American presidents. At first we considered it a wonderful project that was desperately needed, but our perspective changed when we learned that many Indian people opposed the project because they believed carving up a natural feature of the land was an assault on nature. They preferred to keep the land formation just as it was.

From 1964-1991, Native American spirituality was the foundation for my life. During that time, I was fortunate enough to utilize Indian spiritual practices, both on my own and under the guidance of Native elders. I have been able to take part in Indian practices, often alongside Native people, but I realize that, while doing so, I always had the full privileges of being a white male in America. Unlike my Indian friends, I never had to worry about experiencing racism from agencies, institutions, and many of my fellow citizens. (In the past, some tribes were even prohibited from practicing their religion.) My exposure to the racism experienced by Indians strengthened my commitment to being an advocate for social justice.

In 1991, I developed a serious interest in Tibetan Buddhism, which became the next chief focus of my spiritual life. As I deepened my involvement with Tibetan Buddhism, I decreased my involvement with Native American spirituality. It had been a foundation for much of my life and had offered me great gifts, including a deeper sense of our relationship to the earth and a deeper view of the masculine and feminine nature of Spirit, but Tibetan Buddhism offered me more tools for day-to-day spiritual unfolding and for growing in compassion and awareness.

In April of that year, I covered the Dalai Lama's visits to the Bay Area for the *Community Endeavor*, a local social issues newspaper. I attended three events: a talk on "overcoming differences" at Grace Cathedral, a dinner and talk for the Himalayan Foundation, and a press conference at the Asian Art Museum on the opening of the "Wisdom and Compassion — The Sacred Art of Tibet" exhibit.

Three years later I was again able to cover the Dalai Lama's visit to the Bay Area for the same local newspaper, attending his press conference at Stanford University and his speech at the University of California at Berkeley. At Stanford, I was only a few feet from him, and I was moved by his presence and his sense of humor. But mainly the two visits left me deeply impressed with the Dalai Lama's compassion and wisdom — clearly he was, and is, a great spiritual person.

In June of 1997, I went to a week of teachings the Dalai Lama gave in Los Angeles. Later I attended a conference chaired by the Dalai Lama in San Francisco titled "Peacemaking: The Power of Nonviolence," as well as a retreat he led in Indiana. Those experiences exposed me to valuable Buddhist teachings on developing compassion, for which I remain deeply grateful.

After the first time I saw the Dalai Lama, I attended teachings given by several Tibetan lamas, and I also read a great deal about Tibetan Buddhism. What amazed me about it was its strong emphasis on compassion and selfless service; its numerous techniques for developing compassion and applying compassion to daily life; and its considerable awareness of the nature of the mind — developed over the many centuries of Tibet's isolation before the Chinese occupation. While I do not believe that Tibet was a perfect country, Tibetan Buddhists developed a religious system that reflects a profound degree of spiritual awareness.

During the early 1990s, I assisted my friend Joseph Guida with a radio program he did on Tibet. Eventually, at Joseph's initiative, we joined several friends in co-founding Sierra Friends of Tibet (SFOT), formed in response to the oppression that Tibetans have suffered at the hands of the Chinese government. Chinese soldiers invaded Tibet in the 1950s and have brutally occupied the country ever since. Those of us who worked with SFOT championed the Tibetan cause by educating our community about Tibetan issues, raising money for Tibetan refugees, and bringing Tibetan cultural and spiritual expressions to our area of northern California.

In the spring of 2000, I became involved with a local meditation group that worked with Pema Chodron's teachings (and those of her teacher, Chogyam Trungpa Rinpoche). I was privileged to attend some of her teachings when she came from Gampo Abbey, her center in Canada, to northern California, and I found her insights very valuable. In August of that year I also attended teachings by Alan Wallace, an author and former Buddhist monk who has studied with the Dalai Lama. His teachings deepened my connection to Buddhism.

Three years later a friend of ours loaned my wife a book by a teacher named Adyashanti, who came from a Zen Buddhist background. I saw the book in our home, picked it up, began reading it, and was unable to put it down until I finished it. My wife read it also, and the beauty and power of his writing impressed us deeply. At that point, we began an involvement with his "Zen-flavored" teachings and meditation retreats. Zen Buddhism tends to be a much simpler form of Buddhism than most of the Buddhism practiced in Tibet, and I came to appreciate the simplicity of Adyashanti's approach.

Another spiritual teacher I spent time with, after I met Adyashanti, was Gangaji, who had had a powerful "awakening" while visiting a teacher in India. One thing I found interesting about Gangaji was that she was from Clarksdale, Mississippi, my conservative mother's home town. She also went to college at the University of Mississippi, and while there, became more aware of the importance of civil rights. That was the same school attended by my cousin who had taken his rifle back to school with him in 1962 because of his concern that James Meredith had decided to enroll as the university's first black student.

Buddhism's emphasis on the practice of continually observing one's mind, or what goes on in one's mind, was instrumental in making me more aware of my own racist thoughts and tendencies. Pema Chodron's work reinforced my awareness that most or all of us have prejudices: we all have the same good and bad tendencies; we are all connected; and we all have "Buddha nature" (the closest Buddhist equivalent to "God within us").

Buddhist mindfulness has also made me more "real" — that is, more aware of how I feel, including awareness of feelings that are usually judged as less than desirable. In the past I used to "have a good day" most of the time, but I was out of touch with my deeper feelings. Now I still feel happy and content most of the time, but on days when I feel sad, upset, angry, or afraid, I am less likely to deny my feelings or judge myself for them.

During my involvement with both Native American spirituality and Buddhist meditation, there have been times I have had profound experiences of deep, unconditional love that I perceived as being everywhere. Some of these experiences have related to an indescribable perfection beneath the disturbing chaos we sometimes see in the world. Some have pointed to our being something much more than our stories about ourselves and others or our personal identities, although our strong identification with our stories can make it hard for us to see this. Some of my experience concerned the interrelatedness, or spiritual oneness, of all things. These have all had a strong impact on my view of the world and my approach to anti-prejudice work.

PART III

UNDERSTANDING AND HEALING PREJUDICE

In this section, some of the causes and effects of racism are examined, and concrete steps that readers can take to overcome prejudice both in themselves and society are presented. In some respects, this is the most important section of the book. It provides positive ways out of the morass of racism presented in Part I. It gives the reader options for action and personal growth. It offers hope.

CHAPER 10

SOME CAUSES AND EFFECTS OF RACISM AND OTHER FORMS OF PREJUDICE

The following definitions can be helpful in considering racism and other forms of prejudice:

Prejudice: (a) preconceived opinion that is not based on reason or actual experience... dislike, hostility, or unjust behavior formed on such a basis.[1]

Racism: a belief that some races are by nature superior to others; also: discrimination based on such belief.[2]

Conditioning (as used in this book): the influence brought to bear on our thoughts and behaviors by various factors. Such factors can include our family influences, cultural influences, social conditions we have experienced, places we have lived, our schooling, our friends, books we have read, and countless other factors.[3]

The American Anthropological Association has made the following statements about race:

Conventional geographic "racial" groupings differ from one another only in about 6% of their genes. This means that there is greater variation within "racial" groups than between them.... Throughout history whenever different groups have come into contact, they have interbred. The continued sharing of genetic materials has maintained all of humankind as a single species....

Historical research has shown that the idea of "race" has always carried more meanings than mere physical differences; indeed, physical variations in the human species have no meaning except the social ones that humans put on them....

"Race" thus evolved as a worldview, a body of prejudgments that distorts our ideas about human differences and group behavior. Racial beliefs constitute myths about the diversity in the human species and about the abilities and behavior of people homogenized into "racial" categories.... Racial myths bear no relationship to the reality of human capabilities or behavior....

...[W]e now understand that human cultural behavior is learned, conditioned into infants beginning at birth, and always subject to modification....

It is a basic tenet of anthropological knowledge that all normal human beings have the capacity to learn any cultural behavior....

How people have been accepted and treated within the context of a given society or culture has a direct impact on how they perform in that society. The "racial" worldview was invented to assign some groups to perpetual low status, while others were permitted access to privilege, power, and wealth. The tragedy in the United States has been that the policies and practices stemming from this worldview succeeded all too well in constructing unequal populations.[xxiv]

The American Anthropological Association (AAA) is deeply concerned by recent public discussions which imply that intelligence is biologically determined by race. Repeatedly challenged by scientists, nevertheless these ideas continue to be advanced....

...[D]ifferentiating species into biologically defined "races" has proven meaningless and unscientific as a way of explaining variation (whether in intelligence or other traits).[xxv]

---

xxiv Excerpts from the American Anthropological Association's "Statement on 'Race,'" May 17, 1998, http://www.aaanet.org/stmts/racepp.htm, accessed December 17, 2013, quoted with permission.

xxv Excerpts from the American Anthropological Association's "Statement on 'Race' and Intelligence," December 1994, http://www.aaanet.org/stmts/race.htm, accessed December 17, 2013, quoted with permission.

When we examine some of the reasons behind racism, it becomes clear that the person with racist beliefs has no ground to stand on and that his or her views are like a paper tiger, without substance or reality. The truth is that racism says more about the person who holds racist views than the person who is the object or target of racism.

In a 1997 letter to the editor, I explained why I thought some white people were so critical of Martin Luther King: "Most who vehemently attack King do so not because he might have been a communist or a 'beast' but because of what he most represents to them — the idea that white folks are not superior to everyone else on the planet. After all, prejudice, which we probably all have to some degree, is often based on fear and insecurity (the need to look down on others to feel a false sense of superiority and self-worth)."[4]

The negative effects of racism can be considerable. Racism can be crippling to both the target of racism and the person who acts on and/or has racist views. As long as someone is kept in a position of inferiority due to racism, the targeted person can suffer diminished self-esteem and may be denied his or her full potential. At the same time, the person with racist beliefs lives with a view of the world that is distorted by false beliefs about his or her race and the race of others, is likely to have unreasonable fears of others solely due to their race, and is not likely to be the kind, generous, loving person that he or she has the potential to be.[5] My great-great-grandmother's ownership of slaves kept her in bondage. Her family was inextricably bound to a system of immense suffering that diminished her ability to bring the principle of love, in which she so deeply believed, into all of her thoughts, words, and deeds. The fact that she wrote in her diary after the Civil War, "I do not regret that the slaves are free," suggests that she ultimately had a conflict about her family's owning slaves.

We are all connected. Martin Luther King echoed the view of Native Americans and some contemporary physicists that there is an inter-relatedness of all people, all life. From this perspective we are all part of a unity or whole. For one race to oppress another causes harm to both races.[6]

In *The Hidden Wound*, Wendell Berry, a white descendant of slave owners, offers some profound insights concerning the destructive effects of racism. He points out that it has a significant and damaging spiritual effect on society as well as its members. Only by ending the division between races can the possibility of wholeness arise.[7]

In addressing racism and other forms of prejudice, it is important to remember that they are often symptoms of deeper causes. While it can be necessary and important to work on individual symptoms at times (discrimination related to race, culture, sex, age, nationality, religion, sexual orientation, etc.), the more we can address the deeper causes, the more the symptoms are likely to diminish. The remainder of this chapter will focus on the following causes and effects of racism and other prejudices:

1. Learned Prejudice
2. Generalizing from Negative Experiences
3. Perceiving Others as "Different" Leading to Feelings of Fear and Separation
4. Low Self-Esteem in Both Targets and Perpetrators of Prejudice
5. Judging Faults We Perceive in Others That Are Unconscious Within Ourselves
6. Stereotyping
7. Scapegoating
8. Lack of Awareness of One's Racism That May Cause Unintentional Harm

1. Learned Prejudice

Prejudice is sometimes learned. My parents were taught by their parents to be prejudiced, not only against black people, but also Jews,

Catholics, foreigners, and Northerners. My mother also looked down on poor white people and servants of any kind. In short, they learned to be prejudiced against most groups of people who were perceived as "different" from them. Unfortunately, they did not question what they had been taught. And in my youth, neither did I.

My childhood conditioning was so thorough that I still have emotional reactions that are racist. The following poem was the result of such a reaction.

A Handshake

I wince
slightly,
ever so slightly,
and I feel
mixed feelings,
as I shake your hand.

My mind has broken
the chains
of my past,
and I know it's ok
to shake your hand.

But the emotional conditioning
of my childhood
sends some small part of my psyche
to the store
to look for disinfectant.

While once again
I feel the pain,
the lifelong pain,
the wretched pain,
from the
almost hereditary
teachings
of my southern
boyhood home.

Shortly before my fifty-third birthday in July of 1998 I wrote this poem. My wife and I were in a grocery store when I met a black acquaintance whom I had not seen in a few years. I enjoyed seeing someone I knew and liked, and it was nice to briefly catch up on the changes in our lives. But when we shook hands, I noticed a subtle emotional reaction, a very slight discomfort within myself at touching a black person. It was as if "some small part of my psyche [went] to the store to look for a disinfectant." The experience was very painful. I was saddened that such conditioning was still with me after all these years, and that it would probably always be with me to some degree. (Yet I also realized that I must do my best to accept and love myself as I am and not feel guilty about this part of myself, while continuing to work to overcome it.)

In a book on racism, a white author who was raised to not be prejudiced against black people, and who grew up with black friends, describes an experience on an airplane that shocked him. At one point he saw that the pilots of the plane were black. His immediate reaction was to wonder if they were capable pilots![8] To me, that is a beautiful story because it is so honest and revealing. Even those who were not overtly raised to be racist can have unconsciously conditioned racist attitudes from exposure to the culture and media that surrounds us. Because of my own conditioning, I believe I would have had the same initial reaction as the writer. But afterwards, unlike the author, while I might have felt dismayed, I would not have been shocked. I am aware that I have racist conditioning within me.

2. Generalizing from Negative Experiences

Prejudice does not have to be learned from the cradle. It can also develop from an emotional reaction due to trauma or a bad experience in a way that is beyond one's conscious control. A negative experience with one or more people who are part of a group can be generalized to all members of that group. During my intense study of my great-great-grandmother's diaries, I was deeply moved by the incredible pain she felt during and after the Civil War. Given her experience, her hatred toward those Northerners whom she perceived as causing her pain was understandable. Unfortunately, she applied her judgments to all Northerners. For the first time I really understood why my mother had taught me to be prejudiced against "Yankees."

While the diaries were still an active part of my psyche, my hometown hosted an annual Civil War reenactment. One evening my wife and I walked past a couple of men dressed in Union uniforms, and to my surprise, I sensed the words "Damn Yankees!" forming in my mind and felt my body tense as if among enemies. It was a bubble of prejudice, passed down from my ancesters, rising up from my unconscious.

My wife was very troubled during a 1968 visit to Italy when Italian men kept approaching her with unwanted physical advances. For awhile she experienced a negative emotional reaction generalized to all Italians, including women and children, in spite of her awareness that her reaction was irrational.

3. Perceiving Others as "Different" Leading to Feelings of Fear and Separation

Feelings of separation and fear between people who are of a different race, religion, political persuasion, sexual identity, etc., can lead to prejudice, especially against those who are visibly easiest to identify, such as those with different skin color or facial features. This may lead to an "us versus them" attitude, which then increases the feelings of separation.

This phenomenon of feeling separate, when combined with other factors, allows one ethnic or political group to commit atrocities against another. Sadly, our world is all too full of examples of this. It is evident in racism as well as in genocide, or what is sometimes referred to as "ethnic cleansing." It also can be a factor in such things as bullying in schools. When as a teenager I drove through a black neighborhood and yelled derogatory names, I did so, in part, because I felt separate and disconnected from the people I was abusing.

4. Low Self-Esteem in Both Targets and Perpetrators of Prejudice

During the Supreme Court's 1954 hearing of the case *Brown vs Board of Education*, which resulted in the ruling that school segregation was illegal, results of research by psychologist Kenneth Clark were presented. It was demonstrated that segregation was psychologically destructive to black children because it encouraged them to look at their own race as inferior and the white race as superior. Clark's tests showed that when black children were presented with black and white dolls, most of the children preferred the white ones. In addition, the majority of them described the black dolls as "bad" and the white ones as "nice."[9]

The white baseball player Babe Ruth held the lifetime record of 714 home runs when he retired from the sport. Black player Hank Aaron of the Atlanta Braves was the first person to break Ruth's record. During the days before his incredible achievement, Aaron was receiving as many as three thousand letters a day, most containing racist threats from angry white people. Ken Burns, producer of the documentary series *Baseball*, emphasized the point that this happened not during the time of Jim Crow but in 1974, a number of years after the laws of segregation had been dismantled. The idea of a black player breaking the record of a white player challenged the belief of some whites that they are superior to others.[10]

One reason for the belief in white superiority is our nation's history. For 244 years blacks in America existed in slavery, and then for another 100 years they were treated as inferior beings during Reconstruction and under the Jim Crow laws in the South and under racist policies that existed in the North. This history has influenced many generations of blacks and whites and affects our country today. (For this reason, at the end of Chapter 2, I said that in order to understand our present situation, achieve healing of racism, and create a fair and just society, it is imperative that we understand our past.)

Partly because of this history, over many decades our mainstream culture conveyed the message that blacks are inferior to whites. For years the Crayola crayon company had a crayon labeled "flesh" which was similar in color to Caucasian skin. Children all over the country, regardless of race, were being given the message that proper skin color was that of the white folks. Due to the crayon name's racist implications, the company finally changed it to "peach" in 1962.[11] They also had a dark red crayon labeled "Indian Red," which could have led children to believe that all Indians were supposed to have dark red skin color. That crayon's name was changed to "Chestnut" in 1999.[12] Throughout most of my life, the predominate color for Band Aids has resembled Caucasian skin color.

When I was growing up in the late 1940s through 1960s, advertisements, movies, and television shows were overwhelmingly dominated by whites. In a 2005 book of 1960s print advertisements that contains 253 mainstream ads, with the exception of two that appear to be oriented to black neighborhoods, only five of them include black people, some of whom are servants. Altogether, about 865 people in the book's ads can be generally identified by race. Two of them have Asian features. Eleven of them, or one in eighty, are black.[13] (According to the 1960 census, if the number of whites and the number of blacks were added together, the blacks made up about ten percent of the total. The remaining races in the census were grouped together, so the number of Asians is unknown.)[14] Clearly, counting ads and people in a book does not indicate a valid scientific study, but based on my experience, I believe the book's content gives a fair picture of 1960s advertisements.

A 1968 ad for American Airlines encouraged the viewers to think of a Caucasian stewardess as their mother. Did this not give a subtle negative message to children whose mothers were other than Caucasian? A 1961 American Airlines ad showed 38 women who were graduating from the airline's Stewardess College. Not one of them appears to be black.[15]

A strong message of white superiority has also come from text books. During my school days, the main characters in my American History books were almost exclusively white males. It was as if other races did not exist. Even in World History, the white race was given the most attention. (For a book that presents United States History for the point of view of the under-privileged, see Howard Zinn's *A People's History of the United States*.)

Bill, a black friend of mine in college, told me that some of his older relatives in Richmond, Virginia, would tell him that, as black people, they were inferior human beings. Sadly, these relatives had come to believe the racist messages that their environment constantly reflected to them, a phenomenon referred to as "internalized racism" or "internalized oppression." This affected their attitudes towards themselves and others and led to their feeling inferior to whites.

My parents, and my cousin from Mississippi who harassed the black woman on the bus, on the other hand, would say without hesitation that they were superior to black people and other groups. Considering oneself superior to others is often a compensation for unconsciously feeling insecure and inferior and creates a false sense of self-worth.

Both the blacks who were taught to believe they were inferior and the people who bolstered their self-esteem by believing themselves superior were mistaken. Ironically, both groups suffered from feelings of inferiority. In this area, they were more the same than different, even though they manifested their feelings differently: blacks by behaving as if they really were inferior and whites behaving as if they really were superior.

5. Judging Faults We Perceive in Others That Are Unconscious Within Ourselves

The undesirable thoughts, feelings, behaviors, and qualities one sees and judges in others are often partly — or entirely — one's own faults, past or present, that are seen as being only in the other and not in oneself. This phenomenon is often called "projection." These judgments can be directed toward entire groups of people, such as other races or cultures, as well as individuals. The more vehemently one reacts, the more likely the reaction is a reflection of a deeper issue within oneself.

Father Thomas Merton, a Catholic priest and writer, alluded to this when he wrote that when a deep self-hatred is too strong to face consciously, that which we hate is seen in others instead.[16] On the other hand, people who love and accept themselves are more likely to love and accept others.

Dr. Jeremy Taylor, who holds a doctorate of ministry and trains ministers and other spiritual leaders, teaches a stricter view than I am presenting. Nonetheless, it is an interesting perspective to consider. Whereas I am leaving it open as to whether or not a judgment one has of someone else applies to oneself, in Taylor's teachings to spiritual leaders, he emphasizes that whatever one is drawn to focus on in regards to another person is in some way a reflection of one's inner self. Among other things, this means that the long list of attributes which people with racist beliefs ascribe to blacks reflect the qualities that they themselves unconciously have, or can have at times. He also reminds us that because a quality seen in someone else can be found in oneself, it does not mean that the quality is not in the other person. It may or may not be.[17]

It is Taylor's belief that repressing undesired qualities into one's unconscious (which involves self-deception) combines with the tendency to project such qualities onto others to comprise a process that is the single most important psychological factor in allowing oppression to continue.[18]

6. Stereotyping

A stereotype is an unfounded belief about an entire group of people, such as another race. Stereotypes unfairly deny the uniqueness of individuals within the group. My mother, for example, was surprised to learn from my sister-in-law that there are black people who use computers, a fact that did not fit the stereotype that black people lack intelligence. Because General Colin Powell, Secretary of Defense under President George W. Bush, is black, my parents felt the need to rationalize his intelligence, so they told me that it must have come from a white ancestor that he had! How else, they wondered, could it be explained?

Unfortunately, such stereotyping of blacks is not confined to Southerners. Shortly after graduating from college, I was visiting a friend's parents in Cleveland. Her father, who was white, explained the wooden club he kept under the seat of his car with the words, "If I ever catch someone raping a woman, I'll beat that black SOB to a pulp!" Although I did not have the courage to say anything, I was amazed that he would assume that a rapist would be black, a common stereotype in the "old" South.

When I was impressed at a particular black student's considerable intelligence at the alternative school in Cleveland, it was because of a stereotype I learned from my parents. When I was surprised to see how clean black people kept the neighborhood where I lived in South Philadelphia, I had to face another stereotype I had held.

A common stereotype I have heard about blacks relates to their use of drugs, which is presumed to be much higher than that of whites. According to one website related to drug use cited in *Businessweek*, 90 percent of adults with drug or alcohol problems began using prior to their eighteenth birthday, and one-half began using before turning fifteen.[19] Consequently, drug use by our nation's teenagers is a good indicator of drug use in the United States by adults. In November 2011, the Archives of General Psychiatry published research pertaining to a survey of 72,561 young people, in every state in the country, from twelve to seventeen years old.[20] One intention of the study was to look at youth who had used drugs or alcohol within the previous year (27,705 of the young people studied or 38 percent of the entire study group) in light of their ethnic/cultural background. The percentages for each group that used substances in the previous twelve months were as follows: Native Americans 48 percent, whites 39 percent, Hispanics 37 percent, mixed-race 36 percent, blacks 32 percent, and Asians 24 percent.[21] Although the research project demonstrated that youth who were white, Native American, Hispanic, and of mixed race were more likely to use drugs and have a substance use disorder than blacks, for every white youth arrested for crimes related to drugs, ten black youths are arrested![22] This unfair rate of arrest, which could certainly relate to "racial profiling," or singling black people out because of their race, encourages a public perception (stereotype) of blacks as drug users.

A website related to shoplifting and loss prevention cites a poll indicating that 75 percent of black men have experienced being closely watched or followed in stores by white clerks. This is another example of racial profiling and stereotyping. In November 2013, a black teenager sued a New York department store because he was falsely arrested for theft. The item he was accused of stealing was an expensive belt. The fact that he produced a debit card and a receipt for his purchase of the belt was ignored by authorities who told him the belt was too expensive for him to have been able to afford. After the lawsuit was filed, a black woman came forward with a similar story related to the same store. According to the loss prevention website, statistics prove that the majority of shoplifters are actually white.[23]

Camp Sequoyah, where I worked during the summers of 1964 and 1965, was located in an area that used to belong to the Cherokee Indians. On a couple of occasions, I went to the community of Cherokee, North Carolina, where many Cherokees lived. I was dismayed to see some of them selling tourists figures of Indians wearing the feathered war bonnets that were worn by the Indians of the Plains; a few of the Cherokee were even wearing such headgear themselves. The feathered bonnets fit the stereotype many non-Indians had of Native Americans but were very different from what the Cherokee actually wore in the wooded areas of the East. I felt it was unfortunate that some of the people associated with this wonderful Indian nation were willing to encourage such a stereotype rather than promote their own unique heritage. (It is possible that, not knowing what their ancestors wore, they believed the stereotype themselves, but I think that unlikely.)

A number of years later, in the early 1980s, I was just as dismayed to notice a figure of the head of an Indian wearing a

Plains-style feathered bonnet on the side of a Jeep Cherokee. A major car manufacturer was perpetuating the same false stereotype. (Eventually, I understand, the image was removed because of pressure from Indian organizations).

In 1991, with support from the Director of Cultural Resources for the Tahoe National Forest, some friends and I founded an organization to protect Indian petroglyphs (rock carvings) and pictographs (rock paintings). We worked closely with various agencies, Indian groups, and others. When we became aware that an ancient petroglyph site was endangered by a proposed golf course, we began our involvement in the matter by showing the site to the chairperson of the local Indian Council and discussing with him what could be done about the situation. A few weeks later, I agreed to attend a meeting of the council to show slides of the rock art and discuss its protection. A new chairperson had taken over the group, and few of its members were aware of either the site or the issues. After the presentation, I was putting away my slides while talking with one of the Indians when he said, "I never met a white person who didn't try to screw us." The remark surprised and pained me. He seemed to be making a racist stereotype about all white people, including, of course, me. This certainly did not make him receptive to our working together to achieve our common goal.

Sexist stereotyping, like racist stereotyping, starts early and becomes very ingrained. I make it a habit to avoid sexist language, and I have no problem accepting women in what used to be traditionally male roles: one of my two principal doctors is a woman, and I know several very good female lawyers. However, if a person starts to tell me about his or her doctor or lawyer, without mentioning a sex or name, I am still inclined to ask, "Who is *he*?" During a conversation with a five-year-old friend of mine, it became apparent that she did not believe that female doctors and male nurses existed. "Boys are doctors and girls are nurses," she insisted.

As is the case with other stereotypes, a stereotype about women can be combined with discrimination. A female friend of mine loved geology and was seeking a major in that field at a well-known California university in the 1960s. The head of the department told her that this was a major for men, and that if she did not switch to another one, he would see that she flunked out. She changed majors.

Stereotypes have been embodied in, and perpetuated by, derogatory names such as: "nigger" for blacks; "redskin" for Indians; "greaser" and "spic" for Latinos; "jap," "chink," or "gook" for Asians; "kike" for Jews; "raghead" for Arabs, Sikhs, Muslims, etc. (some of whom wear turbans); "mick," "wop," and "pollock" for Irish, Italian, and Polish immigrants and their descendants, respectively; "retard" for the developmentally disabled; and "queer" and "faggot" for homosexuals. ("Retard," "queer," "faggot," and comments like "he's so gay" have also been used as insults toward others not actually developmentally disabled or homosexual.) The list goes on and on.

A label applied to a person whose beliefs and/or behavior we disagree with, such as "racist" or "redneck," also alludes to a stereotype. Any label can become a stereotype, denying the uniqueness of the individual. Applying stereotypes in this way builds walls and feelings of separation.

Sometimes believing in stereotypes encourages a self-fulfilling prophecy. (*The American Heritage Dictionary* defines "self-fulfilling" as "achieving fulfillment as a result of having been expected or foretold.")[24] When the dominant social group in a culture (e.g., white society) views another social group (e.g., black society) as inferior, some members of the nondominant group will tend to believe that they are indeed inferior and may behave in ways that express that belief.

Research on the self-fulfilling prophecy by psychologist Robert Rosenthal demonstrated that expectations teachers had of different students had a strong effect on those students' performances in spite of efforts to treat students equally.[25]

In her insightful book *Mindset*, Carol Dweck, one of the world's leading researchers in developmental psychology, offers some surprising information. She cites research by Claude Steele and Joshua Aronson showing that for some blacks to simply identify their race when required to do so on a test paper results in lower test scores than otherwise. The same effect was observed with some women who checked a box noting their sex when being tested in math and science, two subject areas women are stereotyped as being worse at than men. (This negative effect is more prone to happen to individuals who believe that their personal abilities are limited as opposed to individuals who believe that they can continuously grow and learn. One purpose of her book is to help people who have a fixed view of themselves to become aware of their potential for growth.)[26]

The article "Thin Ice: Stereotype Threat and Black College Students" (Claude M. Steele, Aug. 1999, *The Atlantic*) describes additional studies by Steele and his colleagues. The researchers concluded that black students' and female students' grades on tests they were given during the experiments were affected by whether or not the students could trust the fairness of the tests. Black students and female students did worse on tests that triggered the fear of being stereotyped. When the black students were assured that their race would not adversely affect test results (for example, when it was implied that a test was based on research done by blacks), their grades were noticeably higher than otherwise. Female students also did better when it was clear no threat of stereotyping was present. Researchers went on to create a simple, integrated program at the University of Michigan which helped black students feel more racially secure. This had a noticeable positive effect on their academic performance. The studies and the program have important implications for educational institutions.[xxvi]

Dweck also points out that their experience of being stereotyped encourages people to conclude that they are unable

xxvi To read the article in its entirety, see www.theatlantic.com/magazine/
archive/1999/08/thin-ice-stereotype-threat-and-black-college-students/304663/

to fit in with a group, institution, organization, etc. This has resulted, for example, in minority students quitting college.[27]

While our evaluations of others, including our stereotypes, may seem to be based on flawless logic and accurate perceptions and derived from a fully conscious process, psychologists have shown that they tend to be strongly influenced by mental processes of which we have no awareness. In fact, researchers at the University of Washington have produced evidence to bolster the view that our stereotyping of others is usually an unconscious phenomenon. And our unconscious beliefs are often an interpretation based on incomplete information.[28]

Stereotyping is never harmless, and sometimes it can be dangerous to the point of being lethal. Stereotypes about black people were responsible for creating and perpetuating slavery as well as for the humiliating Jim Crow laws in the segregated South.

Stereotypes and attitudes about Indians in the 1800s contributed to conscious efforts to exterminate the race. Indians, like blacks, were seen as subhuman, a perception that was convenient to white people during the California Gold Rush because it helped them to justify killing Indians and stealing their land. Since Indians were not considered human beings, it did not matter how they were treated. In 1855, Shasta City, California, paid five dollars for every Indian head turned in to the city.[29] The California legislature passed a law in 1850 that essentially legalized enslaving Indians under certain conditions and forbade the conviction of white people in courts of law on the basis of testimony from Indians.[30] Indians were blamed and punished for many crimes they did not commit.[31] California Indian settlements, whether they were friendly to white people or not, were vulnerable to attack by bands of whites. In some cases, the men were killed and the women and children captured and sold into slavery for fifty to two hundred dollars each. Between the enactment of the 1850 law and 1863, an estimated ten thousand California Indians were forced into servitude, prostitution, or slave labor.[32] One historian estimates that whites in California murdered at least 4,500 Indians from 1848 to 1880.[33]

7. Scapegoating

When an individual or group of people are unfairly blamed for an individual's or society's problems, it is called scapegoating. This phenomenon can include the unfair negative treatment of the targeted individual or group.

Chinese, who experienced racism in California from the time they immigrated to the state during the Gold Rush to work in the mines and build railroads, were scapegoated by union labor leaders starting in the 1870s. The leaders encouraged animosity toward them, blaming them for low wages and the scarcity of jobs for Caucasians. As a result, state and local restrictions were placed on the Chinese, and the federal government approved the Chinese Exclusion Act of 1882. This law prevented Chinese workers, with a few exceptions, from immigrating to the United States for ten years. It also barred Chinese who were already in the United States from obtaining naturalization.[34]

Latinos of Mexican descent have also been scapegoated. Starting in the late 1920s, they were blamed for stealing jobs from whites, and laws were enacted that prohibited their employment. Once unemployed, they were considered a burden on their communities, and in many cases they were deported to Mexico. Most of these Latinos were legal residents. In 2005 California enacted "The Apology Act for the 1930s Mexican Repatriation Program." The bill stated, "Between the years 1929 and 1944…it is estimated that two million people of Mexican ancestry were forcibly relocated to Mexico, approximately 1.2 million of whom had been born in the United States."[35]

A notorious example of scapegoating is the Holocaust, when Adolf Hitler ordered the herding of Jews into concentration camps, and over six million Jews were murdered. Hitler blamed

Jews for Germany's problems and advocated a "racially pure" Aryan state.[xxvii]

After the Japanese bombing of Pearl Harbor during World War II, Japanese immigrants and their descendents, most of whom were United States citizens, were rounded up and kept imprisoned in internment camps for the duration of the war. As a result of the fear and anger aroused by the attack on Pearl Harbor, Japanese Americans became the object of generalized prejudice, discrimination, and scapegoating.

Scapegoating has occurred after terrorist attacks in the United States. For example, when the Alfred P. Murrah federal building was bombed in Oklahoma City on April 19, 1995, some people automatically assumed that Arabs were responsible, and people who resembled the stereotypical appearance of Arabs became scapegoats. Even though American, Caucasian, Gulf War veteran Timothy McVeigh carried out the attack, between the time of the bombing and his arrest two days later, the Council on American Islamic Relations (CAIR) received over two hundred reports of harassment of Arab Americans or people who resembled Arabs.[36] Even after McVeigh was captured, the incidents of harassment went on for a number of weeks.[37]

In the aftermath of the tragic terrorist attacks on the World Trade Center and the Pentagon on September 11, 2001, once again there were Americans who blamed and took their anger out on innocent people based on their resemblance to the Arab stereotype. Three days after the attacks, the *Sacramento Bee* ran a front page story about the considerable scapegoating that was taking place. According to the paper, the situation was bad enough for President Bush to ask that revenge not be taken on innocent individuals.[38]

During the first five weeks after the September 11, 2001 attacks, CAIR received over nine hundred reports of anti-Muslim, anti-Arab incidents, ranging from verbal harassment to physical assaults, and including the firebombing or vandalizing of dozens of Islamic mosques. To put numbers of harassment

xxvii "Aryan" is defined as "(in Nazi ideology) a person of Caucasian race not of Jewish descent." *New Oxford Dictionary*, s.v. "Aryan."

reports in perspective, prior to the attacks on the Pentagon and World Trade Center, CAIR normally received between 350 and 900 reported incidents in any given year.[39] The day after the article, an American in Arizona murdered a member of the Sikh religion from India, mistaking him for an Arab.[40]

The scapegoating of others has been common in our human history, and, unfortunately, continues into the present.

8. Lack of Awareness of One's Racism That May Cause Unintentional Harm

Most people probably have some degree of racism or prejudice, yet many of them are not aware of it because it is unconscious. My friend Mary Lou grew up in Texas with strong racist conditioning. When she was eight, she and some of the other girls in her class were impressed with a hat one of their friends had. They were taking turns trying it on. One of those present was a black girl, and when it became her turn, with no intention of malice, Mary Lou said to the owner of the hat, "You are not going to let a nigger try it on, are you?" The friend whose hat it was took Mary Lou to task: "This is our friend, she is no different than the rest of us, she is not a 'nigger,' she is a person." Mary Lou was stunned. She had never questioned her racist beliefs, and having them brought to her attention caused her to avoid using the word "nigger" again and to eventually work to unlearn racism. Before that life-changing experience, she had not had the awareness to realize what she was doing. Learning the myths that black people were inferior and that they might have diseases that could contaminate clothing became beliefs she learned that seemed no different from any other fact about the world. "It was like learning that a tree is a tree," she explained to me. In this sense, while racist beliefs can have a personal impact on targets of racism when they are acted on or expressed, they are not necessarily personally related to the target. They can result from deep conditioning and be held by the believer in a way that reflects a degree of innocence or a lack of awareness for which the believer cannot be blamed. This, of course, does not diminish the destructiveness of such beliefs or the importance of helping the believers of them to see a different view.

When my teenage friend and I drove through a black neighborhood yelling derogatory names at the residents, I did not realize that my behavior was racist. I did not even realize that my behavior was hurting other human beings. I simply did not have the awareness to know what I was doing.

In military school, I had a Jewish friend whom I tried to compliment one day by saying, "Denny, you are really a good Jew." Since I clearly was not referring to his relationship to his religion, he was shocked and deeply hurt. I felt pain and confusion at having hurt my friend, but it took me a long time, perhaps several months, to realize why my words had been insulting. Rather than saying, "You are a really good person," I had essentially said, "You are a really good person, *for a Jew*," as if Jews in general were less good than other people. My prejudice toward Jews was so deeply ingrained as to be unconscious — so much so that I hurt someone I truly cared about.

When I worked at the alternative high school in Cleveland, I would stop my students when they used racially demeaning language. Once I heard a student refer to Brazil nuts as "nigger toes." When I told him why I found his words offensive, he felt sincere regret for having used such a phrase. He simply had been using a description his peers had used and was not conscious of what he was saying.

When well-meaning students in my Native American seminar teased their Chinese friend Wayman by calling him "Chink," a derogatory name for Chinese people, I would discuss how subtle, yet insidious, prejudice could be, even in the form of joking. Many years later I was visiting a former student who had been at that seminar. He mentioned my earlier teachings regarding the friendly name calling and told me that sometime after high school he had come to realize what I was talking about. He had been in the company of people who were telling

"Pollock" (Polish) jokes, and because his ancestors were from Poland, he experienced firsthand the offensiveness of such "harmless" jokes.

✳✳✳✳✳✳✳✳✳✳✳✳✳

Sometimes people cannot look at aspects of their family history honestly because doing so would be too painful. My mother was deeply proud of her Southern heritage. For her to acknowledge what a horrible institution slavery was would have meant admitting that her ancestors had done something horrible. She could not do that, so she believed the myth — which was encouraged by her white Southern culture — that the slaves were treated kindly and were better off as slaves because they were cared for. She once told me that she and my father did not have racist views and that I just did not understand the truth about the races. She really did not have the ability to recognize her racist beliefs for what they were. Instead, she saw her beliefs as universal truths.

Mama Don't Know

Mama don't know
that black folks
don't all have
unmentionable
diseases.

Mama don't know
that most black men
aren't muggers
and rapists.

Mama don't know
that General Powell's[xxviii]
intelligence
isn't
from some
white
ancestor.

Mama don't know
that black mammies
shoulda been home
with their own babies
from the get-go.

Mama don't know
that the kindest
of slave owners
wasn't kind.

Mama don't know
that her great-grandfather's
"Negro property"
of two hundred human beings
kept their owner
in bondage, too.

My Mama,
she got a bad memory.
She never learned
to forget
what her mama
thought she knew.

---

xxviii Gen. Colin Powell, an African-American, was Chairman of the Joint Chiefs of
Staff during the Desert Storm campaign against Iraq. In 2001 he became President
George W. Bush's Secretary of Defense. My parents attributed his intelligence to his
having a white ancestor.

CHAPTER 11

HEALING RACISM
AND PREJUDICE IN OURSELVES

If we want to heal society of racism and prejudice, the most important place to start is with ourselves, for we are the people we most have the ability to change. As we diminish our own prejudices and racism and become more accepting and loving people, we affect those around us in a more positive way, which in itself makes a powerful contribution to the world. As we grow to be more loving and less judgmental, our work to effect social change is likely to be more successful, and we are less likely to contribute anger and hatred to a world that is already too full of both. In the meantime, we need patience with ourselves and with others. Change often seems to take a long time. Even if we fail to see much change in our world, at least we can uphold our sense of integrity for its own sake and try not to be attached to the results.

When I was involved in the protests of the sixties, many protesters, including me, tended to have a feeling of "us versus them." We were the good people, and the government, university administration, military, and so forth, were the bad people. It is ironic that many of us decried the tendency of the United States to define its relationship with the Soviet Union and other countries with the same attitude of separateness.

When in 1974 I moved from Cleveland to rural northern California, I was unemployed or employed only part-time for two or three years. I spent a lot of that time praying, meditating, reading, and working on my inner growth. I developed the belief that the world's most critical human problems, those that had existed throughout time (such as war, rape, genocide, racism, and environmental destruction), were symptoms of two basic

202 · *Almost Hereditary*

causes: our lack of awareness of unconditional love and our lack of awareness that all life is interrelated, especially in terms of spiritual connectedness. When I love and accept myself (without egotism) and others unconditionally, and when I realize that all life is interconnected and all people are my brothers and sisters, I cannot permit myself to intentionally do anything that would harm another person or the environment. To do so would be to harm something which I am an integral part of; in essence, I would be performing a self-destructive act.

When I came to these beliefs, my whole view of social action and protest radically shifted. Although I had not yet studied his writings, I reached the same basic realizations that Martin Luther King had reached through his own spiritual search. I realized that I needed to do my best to love everyone whose actions I took a stand against. The real contribution to healing others and creating a more loving world was not the actions themselves, but whatever love was behind those actions, no matter how firm they needed to be. Victories might be won through actions fueled by anger and hatred, but the human cost of such emotions in terms of their effects on the psyche of both the "winners" and the "losers" would result in a greater loss in the long run.

I also came to believe that the true importance of whatever actions I took in life, whether related to work or otherwise, was in their providing an opportunity or excuse for me to give love to myself and others and to see the spiritual relatedness of all things.

Within my humanness, I don't live up to these ideals as much as I would like. But they are a sustaining guide for me when I consider such a daunting challenge as healing racism.

The remainder of this chapter addresses the following topics:

1. Broadening Our Understanding through Education and Life Experiences

2. Some Steps to Overcome Prejudice and Develop Compassion

3. Becoming Aware of and Examining Our Judgments and Stories about Others

4. Overcoming Self-Righteousness
5. Developing Self-Awareness
6. Accepting Ourselves
7. Overcoming Separateness by Seeing Our Sameness
8. Honoring Diversity
9. Understanding and Accepting Unintentional Racist Behavior
10. Love

1. Broadening Our Understanding through Education and Life Experiences

Learning about psychology and sociology, both sciences of human behavior, has served me well in my life. It has helped awaken me to a greater understanding of my own behavior as well as that of others. It has helped me, for example, to see how illogical and destructive racism is.

In college psychology classes, I learned how one's environment can condition one's attitudes and behavior. The environment that was created through generations of slavery and white supremacy, based on the assumption that blacks were inferior to whites, negatively conditioned many white and black people. Some blacks came to believe they *were* inferior and sometimes acted consistently with that belief. Many whites, like me as a child, grew up believing that they were superior, which helped justify destructive attitudes and behaviors toward blacks. Recognizing such conditioning and its effects has given me a greater degree of freedom to choose for myself how I will behave. Though deep-seated conditioning may never be fully overcome, becoming aware of it helps one see other human beings more clearly and choose to act more lovingly. One can then judge others by their character rather than their skin color, in accordance with the dream of Martin Luther King.

I learned a great deal from reading books, listening to speeches, and watching movies and documentaries related to black history, black writers, race, and racism. Studying books on the history of civil rights and Martin Luther King's speeches and writings left me with a deep appreciation for the civil rights struggle and deep respect for Dr. King and other civil rights activists. Listening to blues music from the Mississippi Delta helped me appreciate an expression of black culture that evolved near some of my ancestors' slave plantations. In my website's annotated bibliography I describe numerous resources that can be educational in regards to these subjects.

I have also gained a deeper understanding of the destructive effects of white privilege by participating in workshops related to racism. Workshops will be discussed further in this chapter's next section.

Sometimes life experiences can have significant educational value. When I was younger, common myths about homosexuals (as being perverted or different from heterosexuals) led me to be mildly prejudiced against them. Fortunately, when I was a child, my parents never said anything to me about homosexuals, or they would have been thrown into my mix of those to whom we believed we were superior (blacks, Jews, Catholics, foreigners, and Northerners). As I have grown older, I have come to know many people who were born to have a different sexual preference from mine. By realizing that fundamentally they are just like me and everyone else, my prejudices against them have melted. With many gay and lesbian people I have met, I would not have known they weren't heterosexual unless they told me. I came to realize that what people do in their private life is not my concern. One stereotype about gays is that they are prone to force their sexuality onto heterosexuals. I observed over time that "straight" males seem as likely, or more likely, to push their sexuality on others (i.e., women) than gay people are to bother straight people.

My wife's father was prejudiced against blacks for most of his life, believing that they should "stay in their place." When he was sixty-nine, he suffered severe depression and was hospitalized on a psychiatric ward for a period of time. The patient in the next bed was a black man who was healthier than he was and went out of his way to help him. When my father-in-law got out of the hospital, he exclaimed, "He was clean. They're just like us." While he missed the fact that, due to individual differences, some blacks are very clean and some are less so, just as is the case with whites and people of other races, he had had an experience that helped him see beyond the stereotypes that contributed to his racism and destroyed a myth he had held about blacks for decades.

My friend Neil, who taught English and creative writing for many years in a mostly white high school in the Cleveland area, helped his students in an all-white class have a valuable life experience regarding race. He made a connection with an English teacher at a mostly black high school who had an all-black class. They set up an exchange program which started with each white kid who was willing to participate being paired off with a black kid. After that, the pairs exchanged letters. Next, Neil's students spent a day at the other school, with each one being hosted by the black student with whom he or she had been partnered. In turn, the other teacher's participating students spent a day at Neil's school, where each was hosted by their partner from the other class. Following that, the students wrote about their experiences and shared their essays with their classmates. With the exception of one student who held strong racist views, everyone in Neil's class who was involved agreed that they learned and grew from the experience and gained a deeper appreciation for the other race. Some of his students said they came to realize that black kids were just like white kids in that there are some you can enjoy being with and others you do not find likable. As one student commented, "I thought they would be different, but they're just like us."

2. Some Steps to Overcome Prejudice and Develop Compassion

We can make a conscious effort to transform our emotional conditioning that relates to prejudice. A Native American friend of mine is aware enough to notice when she responds with such conditioning and takes steps to overcome it. For example, a number of years ago, even though she had black friends, she was aware that she felt uncomfortable around large numbers of blacks. To work through the unwanted emotional responses, she intentionally immersed herself in situations with larger groups of black people than usual. One of her black friends performed comedy at clubs. My friend made a point of going to the clubs, not only to see her friend, but also because everyone in the audience except her was black. The audience proved to be accepting of her presence, and after a few weeks her level of comfort was increased. If you try this approach, you might take gradual steps to overcome fears or prejudices, as trying to make too much progress at once could be overwhelming or counterproductive.

Workshops related to unlearning prejudice, which involve carefully designed exercises and opportunities to process the related experiences, can be very valuable. Both individuals who are often the targets of prejudice and discrimination as well as individuals who are generally not targets can benefit. Such situations offer opportunities for healing wounds created in the past, unlearning false beliefs about one's own race and other races, and making positive connections with people we might tend to have false beliefs about and be prejudiced against.

(Organizations offering trainings and workshops related to unlearning racism include the UNtraining [www.untraining.org], which offers workshops for both white people and people of color, including a workshop series titled "UNtraining White Liberal Racism." Currently they do workshops in the San Francisco area and the Midwest. The People's Institute for Survival and Beyond [www.pisab.org], based in New Orleans, offers trainings for undoing racism in individuals and communities.)

Some athletes do visualization exercises whereby they imagine themselves performing well in their sports, and there have been studies demonstrating that this approach can dramatically improve performance. In *Seeing With the Mind's Eye*, Mike and Nancy Samuels describe the use of visualization for overcoming fears, developing more compassion, and achieving greater success in various areas of daily life.[1] One could use visualization to help diminish or overcome conditioned prejudice. If a black person, for example, was concerned about feeling uncomfortable with white people because of their race, he or she might do a regular exercise during which he or she enters a relaxed state and then spends a few minutes imagining being at ease in situations with white people. There are a number of books on visualization that can help one use this technique effectively.

Some people use affirmations or statements repeated over and over to direct their unconscious toward some quality they want to develop in themselves or something they want to bring into their life. Examples of affirmation phrases are, "I am patient and kind," "I am unconditionally loving," "I am wealthy," "I am free of prejudice," and so on. To a limited degree they can appear to be effective, and people should use them if they are so inclined. However, having worked with them when I was younger, I see a problem with affirmations in the way they are often used to try to force the unconscious to accept something it does not believe is true.

In my opinion, a softer and more effective alternative to using affirmations for personal growth, including unlearning prejudice and developing compassion, is what is known in Buddhism as "Loving Kindness Meditation" or "Metta."

Loving Kindness (Metta) Meditation[xxix, xxx]

Metta is like a simple prayer or a statement of intention that can be easily remembered and recited mentally over and over during meditation, upon awakening or before sleep, or throughout your day while walking, waiting in line, etc.[2] Traditional teachers recommend focusing the meditation first on oneself, because if we do not have love for ourselves, our ability to give it to others is limited.[3] The practice begins with, "May I.... " and continues with any quality or experience you wish to grow or to free yourself from. You might say, "May I have compassion," "May I be free of prejudice," "May I have an open heart," "May I be free of fear," or any expression of your heartfelt desire regarding any area of your life. It is recommended that you focus on the same three or four statements once you are clear on what they should be.[4] You can coordinate the phrases with the rhythm of your breathing if you wish.[5] If this feels like just a mental exercise in the beginning, allow yourself to relax and drop your attention from your mind to your heart, feeling the intention behind the words in your heart, without forcing it.[6] If thoughts or feelings arise that distract you, just be aware of them and gently bring your attention back to repeating your phrases.[7]

The practice can also be used for others, e.g., "May Beth be safe," "May Beth have peace," or "May Beth be free from suffering," or "May black people be free from discrimination." You might also visualize the person

---

xxix This ancient meditation is taught by many teachers and many different sets of instructions can be found on the internet. This is my wife's version of the practice, with additions I have made from a variety of sources. For more information on Loving Kindness, Sharon Salzberg's book and CDs on the subject are recommended.

xxx In researching this practice on the internet, I came across a Christian version that might interest some readers. It is titled "A Christian Loving Kindness Meditation." As of August 2013, the web address was: http://jesusscribbles.wordpress.com/2012/10/03/a-christian-loving-kindness-meditation/.

or people.[8] It is important to focus on your intention, without expectations about the outcome.[9]

While it may be easy to use Metta for yourself or loved ones, compassion can be enhanced by focusing the practice on others with whom you have had difficulty or against whom you have prejudices. A traditional approach suggests a progression beginning with focus on oneself, followed by someone you respect or a benefactor for whom you feel appreciation, then a close friend or loved one, next a person toward whom you have neutral feelings, and finally a person or group toward whom you have negative feelings.[10] Some teachers add the additional focus of all beings.[11] With the difficult people, you can start with someone toward whom you have mildly negative feelings and, over time, go on to increasingly challenging ones.[12] (It is best to avoid focusing on anyone who triggers feelings of trauma.) Each step is to be practiced until it feels natural and heartfelt before progressing to the next level.

In the beginning you might devote five or ten minutes to the meditation, then increase the amount if desired.[13] If you use the statements that seem right to you but saying them does not feel sincere, it is likely you will eventually become more comfortable with them.[14]

(A simple guided version of the loving kindness meditation can be found on Tara Brach's excellent two-CD set *Mindfulness Meditation: Nine Guided Practices to Awaken Presence and Open Your Heart.*[xxxi] These CDs include guided meditations related to being present or mindful [acknowledging thoughts, sensations, and feelings without getting lost in them], opening your heart to yourself and others, dealing with fears, dealing with pain, forgiveness, and other subjects. Brach is a clinical psychologist

xxxi I especially like the following loving kindness statement that Brach suggests for oneself and others: "May I (/you) accept myself (/yourself) just as I am (/you are)."

and meditation teacher. Other resources of hers are described in my website's annotated bibliography [www.healracism.com]. A more traditional version of the loving kindness meditation, in the form of a guided meditation, is included in Sharon Salzberg's *Real Happiness: The Power of Meditation, A 28-Day Program,* a very good book and CD set. Salzberg is a well-known meditation instructor. The Center for Investigating Healthy Minds at the University of Wisconsin's Waisman Center offers their own version of the traditional Loving Kindness meditation which can be downloaded in written or audio form from their website, www.investigatinghealthyminds.org/compassion. Their research showed that doing the meditation for thirty minutes a day for two weeks can increase altruistic behavior and alter the brain's response to suffering.[xxxii] This has profound implications for personal growth.)

Another Buddhist exercise that can be very helpful in reducing prejudice and opening up more to love is called Tonglen. In Tibetan, the word Tonglen means "Giving and Receiving." It addresses the experience of suffering (your own or that of others) and can assist in the development of compassion, which can help reduce negative thoughts and feelings associated with prejudice. My use of this exercise has reduced mental agitation I have had at times and increased understanding and love for others. Pema Chodron has been instrumental in popularizing this ancient practice, but it has been taught by many others as well. I have included a variety of approaches, and I encourage you to experiment to see what method works best for you.

Giving and Receiving (Tonglen) Meditation

The practice begins by focusing on *opening the heart.* The sensation of an open heart may feel more like

---

xxxii "Compassion Training Alters Altruism and Neural Responses to Suffering," Helen Y. Weng et al, Association for Psychological Sciences, 24(7) 1171-1180, 2013.

expansiveness or warmth than affection. You could practice any of the following techniques until you can easily open your heart. (If you have difficulty experiencing it, just imagine it.)

— Think of someone or something you love unconditionally, such as a parent, child, or pet. You might visualize or imagine the person or animal as you experience a feeling of love radiating to your subject; a sensation of warmth and openness in your chest; or the image of a beam of light going from your heart to that being's heart.

— Recall an experience of feeling loved.

— Create an image of a sun in your heart, feeling its warmth as it sends out rays of light.

— Imagine or recall a scene in nature that touches your heart.

— Visualize a flower bud opening in your heart and sending out its divine fragrance.

The next step is to focus on *suffering and relief from suffering*. One approach is to imagine your body filling up with clear light with each inhale. On each exhale, imagine this healing light expanding out from your body.

— Once you have a sense of this, select a real person or group of people who suffer in some way (such as a family you know of who experienced racism or someone you know who experiences discrimination). Visualize or imagine the person or group as clearly as possible. Pause for a moment to really sense the suffering and allow yourself to feel a genuine wish for it to be relieved.

— As you inhale, focus on the healing light, and on the exhale, send that energy to the person or people you are concerned about.[15] As you do this, imagine the light giving relief from suffering.

You can practice this for yourself if you are feeling physical, emotional, or mental pain, or just resistance

212 • *Almost Hereditary*

about doing the exercise. For yourself, first feel or imagine healing energy expand within as you inhale, then as you breathe out, feel or imagine the healing energy releasing your suffering or discomfort.

Another approach is to breathe in the experience of suffering by feeling or imagining it as a harsh color, texture, temperature, and/or image (e.g., fire). These qualities might arise naturally as you carefully observe your experience while considering the suffering, or you can consciously create them. Allow the sensations and images to expand throughout your body.
— As if your heart transforms that energy, exhale relief from suffering in the form of a healing color, temperature, texture, and/or image (e.g., a waterfall). Feel or imagine the healing energy filling you and expanding outward from your body.[16]

You can be creative with this and use different images as you exhale, such as giving a friend who is in pain a bouquet of flowers or a warm cup of tea, or picturing a homeless person you have seen on television sleeping in a warm place.[17]

You can use whichever method you choose with each breath for as long as feels appropriate. Keep it simple. As much as possible, let go of any stories or judgments you may have about the suffering or expectations about results.[18] Just focus on the experience of the suffering itself with the intention of supporting rather than necessarily healing. Imagining that you are breathing in the suffering of another will not cause you harm.[19] To bring a balance to your meditation, do Tonglen for yourself as well as for others.

You can do Tonglen any time as you go about your day.[20] When you see someone suffering, imagine feeling their pain on the inhale and sending relief on the exhale. If you are experiencing a difficult person, you can do Tonglen for them. If you are feeling anguish or pain, spontaneously do the practice for yourself in that moment.

To nurture your compassion as well as your ability to embrace and cope with suffering as it arises, consider a daily practice of at least ten minutes while sitting with eyes open or closed. This exercise can be done by itself or included with a regular meditation practice.

One meditation practice involves focusing Tonglen first on people toward whom you have positive feelings, then on people who are neutral to you, and finally on people you have negative feelings about (for example, people who consider themselves white supremacists or other people you might be prejudiced against).[21] With this latter category, start with people you find mildly difficult and build up over time to those you find most difficult (while avoiding anyone with whom you have had a traumatic experience).[22]

After doing Tonglen for yourself or someone else who has a specific problem, such as being discriminated against, you can then do it for all those who suffer from the same problem. You can also do Tonglen for all people or beings everywhere.

This practice can be used to expand your compassion for others, including those toward whom you feel prejudice. Offering Tonglen for a person or group of people against whom you know you have prejudice (for example, so-called "racists," black people, white people, gays, lesbians, etc.) can help you feel a connection with, and open your heart to, the individual or group.

A variation of Tonglen can be used to address the suffering from one's own shame or guilt regarding actions that have harmed others:

— Begin by focusing on the harmful incident, taking full responsibility for the behavior and the desire to rectify it, while observing the accompanying emotions and body sensations. Imagining the heart expanding could assist in handling the pain.

— Imagine the situation being rectified, which might include apologizing, making amends, and/or being forgiven.

— Alternate between these two states as you breathe, focusing on the painful image or feeling on the inhale and on the healing image or feeling on the exhale.

— The exercise could conclude with doing Tonglen for all people who have shame, breathing in their shame and sending out healing.[23]

I used the above variation of Tonglen to help me deal with my shame and guilt regarding the following incident. While in a store, I found myself staring at a black man. I was aware that I was staring, but I had no conscious control over it, even after the person noticed my staring and, apparently because of it, appeared uncomfortable. It was not unusual for me to be around black people at that point in my life, and I had never had an experience of this nature previously, nor have I had one since. While I was not feeling animosity at the time — I just experienced it as staring — I wondered: was unconscious racism a factor? I have to be open to that possibility, but I really do not know. I just know that later I felt shame at having done something that might have been hurtful to someone else. I knew that, if I saw the person again, I would apologize and try to talk with him about it, but the likelihood of ever seeing him again was slim.

At home, with this person in mind, I did my best to feel the shame and regret as strongly as possible, without judging myself for having the feeling. Next, with each inhale I breathed into that shame, and on each exhale I breathed out a deeply felt apology to the person while visualizing him in front of me. At another time I did the same practice while focusing on black people toward whom I had exhibited racist behavior in my youth.[24] (Tara Brach's two-CD set *Radical Acceptance: Guided Meditations* includes two versions of the Tonglen meditation.)

3. Becoming Aware of and Examining Our Judgments and Stories about Others

Our prejudices relate to judgments or stories we have about others. One way to soften our prejudices is to see how our judgments of others can be true about ourselves. Our prejudices can also diminish when we question our prejudicial beliefs and discover that they are less true than we had thought. This section offers some tools for doing these things.

The psychiatrist Carl Jung wrote that we can come to understand ourselves better by examining whatever we find irritating about other people.[25] A "fault" we perceive may or may not exist - entirely or in part - in the other person; but it most likely exists, or has in the past, at least to some extent, in ourselves. The stronger our reaction, the higher is the probability that what we react to reflects something within.

Far from demeaning us, seeing our judgments of others as a possible mirror for our own shortcomings helps us to be humble and more tolerant of others with the same basic faults we have shared. It makes it easier for us to empathize with them and feel compassion. Putting the focus on ourselves rather than the other person also helps us gain insights into ourselves that further our personal growth.

There are many times that I have observed that a judgment I have of another person is true, at least to some degree, of myself (whether or not it is actually true of the other person). This has helped me soften my criticisms of others. For example, if I think of the racism my Mississippi cousins exhibited, or I am upset about someone's racist behavior in the present, I can remember the racism that I too demonstrated in my youth. As I recognize that even today I have prejudices and traces of racism, my judgments are weakened. (Examples related to the transformation of my judgments toward my parents have been given at the end of Chapter 8.)

During a talk on the subject of judgment, Donald Rothberg of the Buddhist Peace Fellowship explained that we can unconsciously use our judgments of others (and ourselves) to cover up a deep pain we have that is not apparent on the surface. A judgment we have about another person may validly relate to something about that person, and/or it may relate to a quality or experience of our own that affects our reaction to that person. Recognizing what is true or not true about a judgment can give us some helpful insight, and the emotional intensity behind a judgment can reveal an unconscious pain that we can also look at and from which we can learn.[26]

I might feel a strong judgment when seeing someone call a person of color a derogatory name, for example. If I explore the strength of the emotion accompanying my judgment, I might discover that, to some degree, it relates to my pain from having a father who called me derogatory names. I might find that it also relates to pain and self-judgment I have pertaining to my yelling racial slurs at black people when I was a teenager. My judgment in this case says something valid about the person I observed being abusive, but the intensity of my emotional energy relates, in part, to my own experiences. This awareness might help me respond to the situation with compassion rather than anger or hatred.[27]

It takes some degree of training and practice to be able to work with judgments in ways that arouse our personal emotions. The following sequence, recommended by Rothberg during his talk, is one of many that teaches such self-awareness. The practice begins with learning to observe, or be mindful of, one's thoughts, including one's judgments. This skill can be learned through practices such as "mindfulness" meditation. Once the ability to observe thoughts and feelings is developed, one can notice what triggers judgments and any emotional energy that attaches to them as well as any patterns that relate to them. One may begin to see previously unconscious pain behind one's judgments. Open, compassionate presence can transform what is painful and leave us with the insights related to our judgments. Thus, our judgments are softened and we are able to act more consciously and in a way that is born out of compassion and insight.[28] (If a person is not sure they are emotionally able to use such an approach, they might choose to work with a psychotherapist instead.)

Byron Katie teaches a process she calls "The Work," which includes four questions that help people examine their thoughts and beliefs that cause stressful feelings. The focus is often on judgments that others should be different than they are. The four questions are: 1) Is it true? 2) Can you absolutely know that it is true? 3) How do you react when you think that thought? 4) Who or what would you be without the thought?[xxxiii] [29] Follow-up questions asked by a facilitator can help the person explore these four questions in depth. After the questions, the person is encouraged to switch the belief around to look at ways it could be a reflection of something within himself or herself or to look for other possibilities that might be as true, or truer, than the original belief. For example, if I say, "John is prejudiced," I might explore possibilities such as: "I am prejudiced — at least against John," or "John is not prejudiced." I might realize that my reaction to what I see as John being prejudiced relates to my own previously unconscious prejudices. I might acknowledge that John is not really prejudiced, or he is sometimes prejudiced and sometimes not, which would soften my original judgment. It is important that this process be experienced on an emotional level in order for change to occur. If it is just a mental exercise, it is not likely to be very helpful.

When I returned to my job at a liberal organization after a retreat with Katie, I could often see when my reaction to others revealed something true about myself. Some of the people in my work environment were very critical of the more conservative elements of our community. At the same time, I imagined that

---

xxxiii In Chapter 8, I have described how my experience with Byron Katie softened my judgments and transformed my perception of my parents. Readers wishing to know more about her work can visit Byron Katie's web site, www.thework.org, and/ or read *Loving What Is*. For doing your own inquiry with Katie's questions, see *I Need Your Love — Is That True*, 16-25, or *Loving What Is*.

some of our area's more conservative citizens were critical of our liberal views. Even though I would be considered a liberal myself, being in a situation that seemed polarized at times was difficult for me. I experienced pain and sadness when I watched people separate from others due to differing beliefs. Interestingly, the moment a judgment would arise about someone in my work environment who was criticizing "conservatives," I could see how my mind was creating judgments of, and separation from, that person. In that moment I was being self-righteous and doing exactly what I was judging my co-worker for doing, and my own act of separation was painful.

Katie also helps workshop participants realize that if they look at criticisms others might have of them, they may find ways those criticisms are valid. While it has not always been easy, such explorations have given me useful insight. Interestingly, when I can find and accept the truth in others' judgments about me, the defensiveness that would normally arise tends to be less or nonexistent. This makes life a lot easier. (With a very painful experience, where I feel harshly or unfairly judged and deep childhood issues are tapped into, I can still react, and it can take me some time to work through the pain. But this is unusual for me.)

Part of Byron Katie's work helps us to unravel stories that are not, or might not be, absolutely true and to see how our stories can keep us from loving ourselves and others. The stories we tell of others are incomplete at best, and our story of someone might change as different details emerge or are emphasized. For example, when I was a substitute teacher in a trade school in Cleveland, I watched a social studies teacher read part of a newspaper article to his students. In the situation described, a young man was stealing a car battery when the owner of the car came out of his house and shot him dead. The class discussed the events, and some students felt that the car owner was wrong to take a life for a car battery. Then the teacher read another paragraph in the article. Next to the young man's body was a gun. At that point perceptions of the young man, the owner, and the situation shifted. Perhaps another detail would come forth. Maybe the thief was starting to run away and was shot in the back. Any number of additional details could lead to a different assessment of the situation and the characters, and it was not possible to know all of the possible details related to the two individuals and their lives and to the situation in which they found themselves.

While I might have one story about someone, a different story might be as true or truer. In recent years, my overall story of my father has placed less emphasis on what I perceived as his abusive nature and more emphasis on positive experiences I had with him. As a result of how my story changes, how I perceive him and how I perceive myself changes. For one thing, I have softened my story of myself as a "victim."

I have conveyed a negative impression of my cousin from Mississippi who harassed a black woman on a bus. Perhaps other people in his life would present a different, or more complete, picture of him. Since we have lived in different parts of the country, and long ago lost the personal connection we had as children, I have not seen him in over forty-five years, and it is possible that he has come to regret his racist actions. Maybe he still has racist views but devotes his life to helping people in need. Maybe he became a kind husband and father. Since I do not know these things, I try to avoid casting my impression of him in stone and believing that my perception is exactly the way he was, is, and always will be. I encourage readers to adopt the same openness when they read my critical descriptions of any of the people in this book.

Stories can be problematic because they are subjective. It has been suggested that we tend to see the world as we are rather than how it actually is.[30] Within their subjective nature, our stories are unique to us. My story of my father is different from my mother's story of him. It is different from his best friend's story. It differs from the stories his grandchildren have of him. It is different from the story he had of himself. As Buddhist teacher Alan Wallace has pointed out, each of these stories "dies" when the person who holds it dies, and none of them are who the person really is.[31] This does not mean our stories are not real to us or do not have meaning for us. Ira Progoff, student of psychologist Carl Jung, wrote in *At A Journal Workshop* that the real meaning of any of our experiences is not found in the experience itself but rather in how we relate to it within ourselves and how it moves us and changes us, perhaps even over time.[32]

Sometimes the biggest problem related to our stories is that they can hold a negative image of another person (or race) in a way that keeps us from opening our hearts. My story of my abusive childhood has made it harder for me to love my father during my adult life, and that saddens me. Katie often asks people to consider who they would be if they did not have their story. One might answer that question, as Katie does, with the simple word, "Love."

4. Overcoming Self-Righteousness

Self-righteousness — the belief we are better than others or that we are "right" and they are "wrong" — creates barriers between ourselves and them. Overcoming self-righteousness can help us break down those barriers.

When I think of the ridicule my father heaped on my mother, brothers, and me, I am prone to be less judgmental and self-righteous when I remember a time that I made fun of a boy in military school. He had large ears and a stutter. He was also new to the school, and I had seniority over him. One evening, I am sorry to say, I went into his room and commanded him to say a sentence that would shame him by inevitably forcing him to stutter. I humiliated him just as my father had humiliated me many times before.

Another example, less poignant but one that many people will relate to, involves driving. When another person's driving annoys me, I try to remember that when I am tired, off-center, or in a hurry, I, too, may exercise bad judgment, forget which car has the right-of-way, or otherwise unintentionally drive poorly or discourteously.

An awareness of the interdependency of all people can be applied to many situations and can have a profound effect on how we approach creating social change. It can diminish self-righteousness and our feeling of separateness, including the "us versus them" attitude. It can also encourage efforts to find compromise when we might otherwise have taken a rigid position.

In a radio interview, Buddhist scholar Alan Wallace once gave examples of how an awareness of our interdependence can be applied to protest. In protesting the logging of old growth trees, for example, I can keep in mind that I use paper and in my own way support that which I oppose. If I am protesting against a major gasoline company for behavior that has been environmentally destructive, I can remind myself that all of us who drive cars create the need for the big gas companies. Furthermore, the gas company has stockholders all over the country, which might include my uncle or distant cousin or even me. The model of "good versus evil" rarely works; conflicts are not that simple.[33]

If I am boycotting or demonstrating against a company that discriminates against black people (as civil rights workers often did in the late 1950s and 1960s), it is important for me to remember that I constantly have prejudices against various people and often feel my separateness from others that creates the feeling of "us versus them." This human tendency that I so often see in myself is not unrelated to what the company is doing when it discriminates against blacks. That which I oppose outside of myself can often be found within me. This realization inspires me to follow through on the protest, boycott, or whatever action I am taking with less self-righteousness and heightened compassion and honesty.

In his book, *The Dark Within the Light,* John Tarrant points out that our being aware of, and taking responsibility for, our own "darkness" decreases the burden we place on others.[34] We are less likely to dump our own "baggage" on them or overreact due to what is within ourselves. We are less likely to be self-righteous.

222 • *Almost Hereditary*

None of us has always acted purely in our lives and neither have all of our ancestors. This was brought forward in a multiracial forum on racial and ethnic tensions that I attended where people were encouraged to forgive those of other races. We are all human and we — along with our ancestors — have made mistakes, whether we are white, black, red, brown, or yellow. It is a fact that there are ancestors of every race who had the blood of slavery on their hands. In ancient times, the Persians, Romans, and others raided Africa for slaves.[35] Slavery was prevalent among many African tribes before any of them had European visitors. The first known Europeans to transport African slaves to Europe were the Portuguese in 1441. Many slaves who were transported to Europe and the New World were bought from Africans. (Once slaves were imported to the New World and Europe, however, slavery became much more brutal than it had been in Africa.)[36] It appears to be the case that during World War II, Japanese troops made sex slaves out of some two hundred thousand women.[37] In spite of the Geneva Convention, which defined rights of prisoners of war, the Japanese forced some World War II prisoners into slave labor.[38] A number of Native American tribes had slaves.[39]

My mother reminded me of some African tribes' participation in slavery as a way of justifying our white ancestors' involvement in the practice. But enslavement of human beings can never be justified, and the injustice committed by members of other races does not diminish the injustices committed by whites (or anyone else). The point is to try to avoid the self-righteous view that "I and my ancestors are pure, and you and your ancestors have to atone for your sins" or "I am the good nonracist (or victim of racism), and you are the evil racist(s)."

As psychologists like Carl Jung have pointed out, we all have positive and negative aspects to ourselves. Realizing this helps soften our view of people we consider enemies.

Whenever we see ourselves as "good" in a battle against "evil," whether we are individuals, nations, or other groups of people, not only do we become blind to our own human frailties, but we also discourage reconciliation and, when appropriate, forgiveness. Our attitude can undermine the possibility of finding common ground.

One approach that helps us to be less self-righteous is "putting ourselves in the other person's shoes." This will be explored more in the next chapter.

It is also important to realize that most people in the world probably have some form of prejudice. Many of us also have some degree of racism, which may be unconscious. It is common for us to compare ourselves to others and to place ourselves above or below them. It is also common for us to fear those who are different from ourselves. It is a rare person who does not prejudge others on the basis of appearance, occupation, or other criteria. The judgment may be due to someone wearing a police uniform, riding in a chauffeured limousine, or living under a bridge. I think it is almost impossible to grow up in our society and escape the effects of prejudicial advertising, racial stereotyping on television and in movies, institutionalized racism, and other harmful influences to which we are subjected almost daily. Realizing these things about ourselves and understanding the extent to which they are true for us helps prevent self-righteousness when we see racism or prejudice in others.

5. Developing Self-Awareness

The ability to observe one's thoughts and emotions is an important component of self-awareness. Some forms of meditation and psychotherapy can be helpful in developing the skill of self-observation. "Mindfulness" meditation is a simple form that is appropriate for anyone, as it is a practice that is free of any religious beliefs. Ideally, one should have a good, compatible meditation instructor to teach the techniques of a practice.

I have engaged in Buddhist meditation practices which have helped me become conscious of what I had been unaware of in myself. Among other things, meditation has taught me how to be more aware of the conditioned racism that still exists within me. Sometimes, for example, I can still hear in the back of my mind some of the racial epithets I heard so often as a youth, as though a part of myself might still feel inclined to use words like "nigger," were it not kept in balance by other parts of myself that are wiser and kinder.

With self-awareness, we are able to question our assumptions and beliefs, including our generalizations and stereotypes of other races. Watching my cousin kicking the seat of the black woman on a bus started that questioning process for me, which culminated in my asking my brother a year and a half later if it was right to look down on people because of their color.

For those of us who are white, becoming aware of our own unconscious racism can help us be more real and at ease in our relationships with people of color. This helps us to be more effective in working together as allies to heal racism and promote social justice.

Self-awareness also allows us to recognize when we project our faults onto others. It can decrease our feelings of fear and separation and increase the possibility that we can communicate well with people with whom we disagree. It makes it more possible for us to consciously choose when and how to respond to an emotionally charged situation, coming from a place of "action" rather than "reaction." It supports us in becoming more honest, loving, and effective. As psychiatrist Carl Jung pointed out, making the unconscious conscious helps us move toward wholeness.

(Good resources that can help people learn mindfulness meditation include: Jack Kornfield's *CD Meditation for Beginners;* Tara Brach's CD set *Mindfulness Meditation: Nine Guided Practices to Awaken Presence and Open Your Heart;* Sharon Salzberg's book and CD set *Real Happiness: The Power of Meditation, A 28-Day Program;* and Jon Kabat-Zinn's book *Mindfulness for Beginners: Reclaiming the Present Moment – and Your Life* and his CD sets *Mindfulness for Beginners,* which focuses on the basics, and *Guided Mindfulness Meditation, Series 1,* which is helpful in establishing a solid practice.)

6. Accepting Ourselves

We all feel guilt or regret at times. Two areas of guilt have come up for me as a white person: (1) guilt for racism or prejudice that arises within me in the present, or has arisen in the past, in thoughts, feelings, and/or actions for which I am responsible; (2) guilt for what I did not create, but have inherited as a white citizen (racist history/society, white privilege [i.e., the advantages of being white], etc.). Guilt can be useful if it is not excessive and if it encourages us to make amends and avoid repeating our mistakes. Negative prejudiced thoughts may arise — we are all human — but we can recognize and question them instead of acting on them. The healthiest response is to forgive ourselves when appropriate and put what we have learned to good use. (Shame — the belief that we are bad rather than that we have done something wrong — is never useful.)

Those of us who have unintentionally inherited, and benefit from, systems that have been oppressive or destructive in other ways can realize that these things are not our creation or our fault. As anti-racism activist Tim Wise has pointed out, we can look for ways to change them.

The feeling of shame can get in the way of seeing and functioning clearly and being a good ally to people of color. For example, it can cause us to hold back from doing something that could be helpful and positive. It can also cause us to interact with people of color in a way that is distorted or off balance because of our feeling uncomfortable. Shame can also eat away at us and have a negative effect on our well-being.

(Shame researcher Brené Brown's *I Thought It Was Just Me [But It Isn't]: Making the Journey from "What Will People Think?" To "I Am Enough"*, offers excellent suggestions for reducing the power of shame. Clinical psychologist Tara Brach has two good resources for working with shame that are influenced by Buddhism: the book *Radical Acceptance: Embracing Your Life with the Heart of a Buddha*, and a CD set, *Radical Self-Acceptance: A Buddhist Guide to Freeing Yourself from Shame.* One does not have to be a Buddhist to benefit from Brach's book or CDs.)

In looking at our own faults, it is best not to resist what is seen and not to judge it. Interestingly, the more we are able to accept parts of ourselves that we are inclined to dislike, gently and lovingly, the more likely they are to soften or dissipate. Such acceptance has to be genuine, or it can be resistance in disguise. In other words, if we pretend to accept a quality in ourselves with the hope that our false acceptance will make it go away, that is another form of resistance, and while the quality may seem to disappear in the short run, it is not likely to dissipate in the long run. Resisting or repressing something we find within ourselves makes it more likely to influence our behavior and to be projected onto others.

Our judgments tend to relate to past conditioning, insecurities, and other factors, and in a way, they can appear in our mind or show up as a thought without necessarily having been consciously invited. Seeing this can help us accept their presence while not taking them as seriously. As Byron Katie would say, seeing and accepting our judgments can cause them to eventually "lose their Velcro quality" — they stick to us less tenaciously or stay with us for a shorter time. It helps to observe the nature of the mind with openness and curiosity.

Just as there is great value in accepting our "negative" thoughts and qualities (without acting on them), there is considerable value in embracing an experience or emotion, such as when we feel anger or pain. Earlier in my life, I had to leave a very painful work situation. I was filled with anger, judgment, and blame. At a five-day meditation retreat, I decided to focus on my anger. In the library at the retreat center there were three books on anger, which I bought and read. When I woke up early one morning, I went into the meditation hall to practice an exercise in one of the books, *Anger* by Vietnamese Buddhist monk Thich Nhat Hanh. I focused on what I experienced as "pain." With one inhale-exhale I said to myself, "With this breath, I recognize this pain," keeping my awareness on the pain. With the next inhale-exhale I said to myself, "With this breath, I embrace this pain." Following the breath, these two expressions were repeated over and over in this manner, as I endeavored to embrace and accept the feeling more and more.

After sitting with this meditation for some time, the pain suddenly dissipated and revealed what was underneath it — a sense of love and of oneness with everything. Afterwards I wrote a letter to one of my supervisors. The letter was free of the judgment and blame I had directed towards him and, I like to think, helped create a bridge between us. There were still some experiences of anger that came up at times and that had to run their course, but this powerful exercise taught me a lot about acceptance. It was also one of a number of experiences I have had in my life which have shown me that mental and emotional states which appear to be very solid or fixed can actually be quite fluid.

Thich Nhat Hanh emphasizes the importance of embracing the experience or feeling — whatever it is you have chosen to work on, as if you are a mother holding her precious newborn baby. He advises that you hold your awareness on the meditation for as long as it takes for the experience or feeling to open up and be fully embraced. It is important to hold only the intention of acceptance, without expecting a particular outcome or trying to make something go away. You could do the exercise while walking or sitting. The words "with this breath, I recognize this pain" and "with this breath, I embrace this pain" could be shortened to "recognizing pain" and "embracing pain" if it makes the exercise easier to do. While I devote an inhale and exhale to each of the two phrases, Thich Nhat Hanh's approach is to say the acknowledging phrase on the inhale and the embracing phrase on the exhale.[40]

Dr. M. T. Morter, a chiropractor in Arkansas who developed Morter Health Systems, teaches four steps of forgiveness: (1) forgiving ourselves — at least for putting stress on our minds and bodies by harboring resentments toward someone; (2) forgiving the other person for whatever he or she did that we reacted to; (3) making room within ourselves for the other person to forgive us for whatever part we may have played in the situation; and (4) looking for a lesson to learn from the experience.[41] As Morter suggests, forgiveness can be applied to ourselves, perhaps in forgiving ourselves for our misdeeds, mistakes, and imperfections, including not being able to love someone whose behavior we detest (assuming one accepts the ideal of loving all people), or for having racist thoughts.

One could also work with difficult issues, or the uncomfortable experience of them, by using the "Loving Kindness" or "Giving and Receiving" practices described in this chapter.

Since what we perceive in others is often a reflection of what is within us, we can also possess the positive qualities we see in others. You might not realize that what you admire about Mother Theresa, for example, might be found somewhere within you.

Endeavor to accept yourself as you are, including your prejudices and other parts you would feel shame about. Self-acceptance does not mean acting on undesirable impulses or condoning racism or prejudice, nor does it preclude working toward overcoming some of your limitations. As I have said, when you deny or suppress aspects of yourself that you consider undesirable, they tend to become less conscious and can bear a greater influence on you. When you are aware of and accept them, they are more likely to be transformed, or at least to have a less destructive influence on you.

7. Overcoming Separateness
by Seeing Our Sameness

Native Americans and some contemporary physicists have expressed the view that there is an inter-relatedness of all people, all life.[42] From this perspective, our sense of separateness is an illusion when we look at the big picture. Martin Luther King and others have said that we are all children of God (or, as the Buddhists say, we all have "Buddha nature"), and that human life is sacred. King emphasized that, when we realize this sacredness, we will not be able to oppress others.[43] When we are able to see everyone as having the same divinity, we can see beyond our differences. A fact of birth or an aspect of God's creation we had no control over, such as our race, is inconsequential when compared to what I call our "sameness."[44]

King also believed that we have a responsibility for each other.[45] From a little different perspective, within our interrelatedness, to cause harm to another is also to cause harm to oneself. This is to say that we are all part of a whole.[46]

The Dalai Lama of Tibet makes the point of our commonality in his frequent references to the desire of people all over the world to be happy.

Physically, in spite of some differences between races, we are all far more alike than we are different, both in terms of obvious visible characteristics and in regards to the countless processes that keep each body alive. Psychologically, too, our basic human makeup is the same. While different people exhibit different outward behavior, we all tend to feel, to one degree or another, the same emotions: love, anger, lust, greed, fear, sadness, and so forth. Most of us have insecurities and the tendency to need an "enemy" or someone to judge, at least on occasion, so we can feel more worthy or more "right." We fall into the trap of comparing ourselves to others. Many of us tend to believe we are either worse or better than others, the latter often as a compensation for feeling inferior unconsciously. We all have unconscious material, and without realizing it, we sometimes tend to see a quality in other people because it is true about us.

Jamal Walker, who co-leads workshops on unlearning prejudice, points out that we all have suffered the experience of prejudice and at least the feeling of oppression, although certainly to varying degrees. If nothing else, we have had experiences of feeling oppressed as children or youth when we might have been treated unfairly at times by adults or resented their control over us. Some of us have been discriminated against because of race, religion, politics, economic "class," physical appearance, and so on. While the feeling of oppression experienced by those of us who are white may be insignificant alongside the suffering of many people of color, looking at our own experience of such feelings may help us, in a small way, increase our understanding of their experience.

Seeing how others are like ourselves can go a long way to helping us look beyond the apparent differences that keep us from being more open to love. Buddhism offers a number of practices for seeing our sameness and developing compassion. One traditional exercise of this nature is sometimes referred to as the "Equality Exercise" or the " 'Just Like Me' Exercise." It has several variations.[xxxiv][47]

"Just Like Me" Exercises

As you go about your daily life:

When around others, look directly at one person after another. As you look at each one, say to yourself one or more phrases which refers to your common human experience. Pick a quality you imagine, or have recognized, about yourself and say, "Just like me, this person ___ " (fill in the blank: has jealousy at times, can be insecure, wants to be happy, has anger sometimes, has a good heart, etc.). You could do this while sitting on a park bench, shopping, walking down the street, seeing other drivers on your way to work, etc. Try to feel each statement rather than just doing it as a habit. If you do it

---

xxxiv After referring to a version of this exercise in her book *The Courage to be Present*, psychotherapist Karen Kissel Wegela reminds readers not to use such practices as an attempt to avoid seeing human differences, suffering, racism, other forms of injustice, etc. (100). Honoring our differences is discussed elsewhere in this chapter.

often enough, gradually it can change your life.[48]

With a partner:

As you focus on the person in front of you, silently acknowledge things you have in common within the human experience, with statements such as those used in the preceding variation. In a group setting, a series of these equality statements might be read by a leader while the pairs of practitioners repeat each one to themselves as they contemplate it in relation to their partner. Next you might silently focus on positive wishes for your partner ("May you be happy," etc.).[49] The two people look into each other's eyes as they undertake this exercise.[50]

Traditional sitting meditation form:

Focus first on individual friends, then people who are neutral to you, and finally on people toward whom you have negative feelings. With each person you bring to mind, and perhaps visualize, say to yourself whatever words acknowledge that they want to have happiness and avoid suffering just as you do. Each time you say it, put as much feeling as you can behind your statement. With difficult people, you can start with someone toward whom you have mildly negative feelings and, over several sessions, go on to increasingly challenging people.[51] (Avoid focusing on anyone who triggers feelings of trauma.) Instead of a statement acknowledging a desire to have happiness and avoid suffering, you can use phrases such as those used in the two previous variations.[52]

"Without a Story" Exercise

This exercise, based on Byron Katie's teachings, can be done in a quiet space with a focus on someone with whom you have challenging issues. (Do not start with someone with whom you have had a traumatic experience.)

> First see the person in your mind's eye while you remain aware of your story about him or her. Observe how you react as you do this. What do you feel? How does your body respond? Take a moment to clear your head of your story, your feelings, and the person's image. Then imagine seeing the person again, but without any story about who he or she is. See how the person appears to you, how that feels, and what you observe in yourself.[53]

Our "sameness" as human beings is far greater than the "differentness" that contributes to our feeling separate from others.

8. Honoring Diversity

While our "sameness" transcends, and is always greater than, our "differentness," and seeing how we are all alike can diminish the barriers between ourselves and others, it is very important to respect the unique cultures and experiences pertaining to people of other races and cultures. To not see differences at all, through what could be called "colorblindness," could even be a form of racism which denies, for example, a black person's experience of being black.[54] Jamal has told me how important it is to him that people see him as black. He comes from a cultural background that he wants others to appreciate, and he wants others to understand the challenges he has faced as a black person in America, especially in terms of the privileges afforded the white race. With this in mind, I see a value in holding a balance between seeing "sameness" and seeing "differentness." (And, when I am with Jamal, I just see a friend named Jamal. I am not thinking "he's black, he's black, he's black." In this sense, there is a "colorblindness," but at the same time, if it comes to mind, I am fully aware that Jamal *is* black, and that the culture he grew up in, his negative experience of white privilege, and so on, have influenced his life considerably.)

Learning to appreciate the richness of different people and different cultures fosters more respect and tolerance for people who are different. It breaks down barriers between ourselves and others and helps dispel destructive myths about other groups while enriching our own lives.

In my youth, the segregated world I lived in prevented me from these possibilities and kept the myths I learned about others in place. Since my ancestors had slaves on the Mississippi Delta, I wanted to deepen my appreciation of the black culture that evolved in that area. As I indicated earlier in this chapter, immersing myself in the blues music that had its roots in the Delta helped me connect with, and appreciate, one aspect of that culture. Over the years I have read black literature and done other things to help me appreciate black culture.

It can be valuable for people of all races and ethnic groups to take pride in their heritage and history. The key element in honoring our own heritage is to avoid doing it in a way that is ethnocentric, in other words, that makes us feel that our race, ethnic group, country, or whatever else, is better than everyone else's.

9. Understanding and Accepting Unintentional Racist Behavior

As much as possible, of course, we need to be sensitive to the feelings of others and do our best to avoid words or behaviors that might be considered racist. At the same time, we also need to be accepting when interacting with others who use words or actions that are unintentionally offensive. Furthermore, we should try to avoid assuming something is racist when we do not know all the facts that are involved.

In November 2001, a white citizen addressed the city council of Sacramento, California, regarding his objection to cameras that photograph drivers who run red traffic lights. At one point, referring to something he thought was obvious, he used the common phrase, "call a spade a spade." At that point, a black council member stated that the remark was racially offensive. The citizen, according to an article in the *Sacramento Bee*, was very upset. He did not consider his words offensive and, according to the newspaper, felt that he was being viewed as someone who either had racist views or was insensitive to racism.[55] Like him, I never would have imagined that the words "call a spade a spade" had a racist connotation in the context in which they were used. I have always understood the phrase to mean to speak precisely or to "tell it like it is."

The article noted that one's intention is an important factor in determining the phrase's meaning, as it can mean different things to different people. According to many language experts, the word "spade" originated as a reference to a garden tool, although it has also been used, as the newspaper story pointed out, to refer to a black person with dark skin.[56] I remember my father using the words "black as the ace of spades" as a demeaning reference to blacks. This meaning of the word makes the word offensive to many black people, even when it is used in the context of speaking precisely. (The Sacramento city council member later apologized to the citizen. While maintaining that she had a right to be offended by the word "spade" and the phrase it was used in, she said that she realized the term was not meant to have a racial connotation.)[57]

The episode reminds me of times in my past when I have been afraid to speak openly with a black person for fear of saying something unintentionally offensive. Sometimes I have felt that I was walking through a mine field, not sure of where I could safely step. Failing to speak candidly for fear of offending someone is not ideal, but I would have found it easier to communicate had I believed that the person I was talking with would have been patient with any of my missteps. My friend Jamal has a good attitude in this regard. He knows that as human beings we will make mistakes, and that is something we need to accept about ourselves and others.

For Martin Luther King Day in 2011, I wrote a front page article for my local newspaper. It discussed my family history, the racism that was present during my childhood, the causes of racism, and the healing of racism. It also had pictures of some of my ancestors and a couple of my great-great-grandparents' slave receipts.[58] As I have indicated, I believe it is ideal for those of us of different races to be able to talk freely about issues pertaining to race, and one day I showed a black acquaintance the article with its pictures and mentioned that my ancestors had owned slaves. To my surprise, she burst into tears. She explained that a factor in her reaction was her belief that she had been turned down for housing that day because she was black. As well as being concerned about her apparent experience of discrimination, I was concerned that my discussion of the article had upset her and sincerely apologized for it. She said she knew I was "a good person" and that I did not mean any harm. I am grateful that she was forgiving and understanding. And I realize I was very naïve and insensitive in touching on a subject — or in how I approached a subject — that could be, and was, disturbing for her. It is important for people of different races to be able to discuss race, but sometimes using discretion in approaching the subject is just as important.

When a person's unintentional racist behavior is pointed out by others, it is ideal if the person can listen to the observation or criticism without getting defensive, reflect on the truth of it, and offer an apology if appropriate. This approach maximizes the opportunity for the person to learn from the harmful behavior, and facilitates understanding and communication between him or her and whoever is sharing their concern.

10. Love

The 13th Century mystical poet Rumi suggests meeting another person at a place that is beyond the concept of right and wrong.[59]

During part of my adult life I have worked in food cooperatives. At one such store, every Saturday morning, Jack would come in and sell us eggs. Through the co-op I had interacted with Jack for years and was always glad to see him. One Saturday as I was paying him for his eggs, he shocked me by casually mentioning that he was a member of a particularly conservative organization, several of whose members had written letters to the editor of our local paper vilifying Martin Luther King. After my initial reaction, I had to acknowledge to myself that I loved Jack anyway and that my feeling for him need not change. Compared to that love, the differences in our personal beliefs were insignificant.

Some years earlier, when I was still dressing as a hippie and wearing a beard, I was traveling across Virginia with some friends on the way to the 1967 March on the Pentagon to protest against the Vietnam War. En route, feeling self-righteous, I took my friends by my all-white military high school in Waynesboro so we could make fun of the place. As I stood in the parking lot, I noticed my former math teacher standing nearby. I reacted with pleasure because I had always liked and admired him. At that moment I just saw someone I cared for, and I completely forgot that we were wearing different "uniforms" and held diametrically opposed beliefs. I ran over to him to say hello and was shocked and hurt when he responded by saying something sarcastic and walking away. For me, my love for him transcended our differences.

On another occasion during my protest days, I was walking through an airport when I saw a line of men in military uniform. Normally I would have felt tension because I associated them with a war that I believed to be immoral. On that occasion, however, for some reason I saw only a group of human beings who were playing a certain role in life, just as I was. I remembered that I had friends in the service (some in Vietnam) and acknowledged that it might have been me in one of those uniforms. I knew that many of these soldiers believed in what they were doing, just as I believed in protesting the war, and I realized that these individual human beings were not what I opposed. On the contrary, I felt compassion for these brothers of mine who faced great challenges, and even though I continued to protest, my attitude toward the soldiers who fought in it was different from that point on. When we start to love others, our experience of them improves.[60]

I have always loved Christ's instruction to "Love your neighbor as yourself."[61] Notably, in commanding people to love their neighbor, Christ did not make distinctions between races, religions, and so on. The love he manifested and encouraged in others was for everyone, without exception. He even advised people to "love your enemies."[62]

Martin Luther King was very clear that you can dislike someone but still love them.[63] You can dislike certain qualities, beliefs, or behaviors while loving the person. Love, King pointed out, can turn an acrimonious relationship into a friendship.[64] He also stressed the importance of love in overcoming the world's problems and expressed his belief that power used appropriately incorporates love as well as justice.[65]

The word "love" has many different meanings in our culture. It is often used to refer to romantic love and the affection and attachment between family members and friends. Such expressions, while meaningful and not something to be discounted, tend to be conditional or limited in that only certain people in our lives receive its blessing. When others fall out of our favor, we may stop loving them, as with some bitter divorces.

Greek philosophers referred to a more profound expression of love, called "agape" (pronounced "ah-gah-pay"). This type of love, which, for some people, is synonymous with what could be called "God," is unconditional and is experienced for everyone, not just a select few. By everyone, I include people who do horrible things we do not like, including acts that relate to such things as racism and genocide. It does not discriminate. Christ was a model of this love.

In my experience, this deep love is so powerful that it can negate any sense of a need for forgiveness, and any notion of forgiveness as an issue. I once had an experience where I felt terribly wronged by someone, which triggered my feeling of righteousness. As we talked about the situation, without any effort on my part, I was overcome with a sense of deep unconditional love. In that moment, there was nothing to forgive and it no longer mattered who was right or wrong. There have been several times in my life, sometimes in the middle of a personal crisis, where I have found myself enveloped in Agape, with unconditional love for everyone.

When aware of this incredible love, it can appear as if all acts of bullying, racism, unkindness, etc., are acts done in innocence, as with little children who do not know any better. When aware of this love, in my experience, one is not able to harm anyone. There is just love for oneself and all others, and through that love everyone seems connected.

As long as it is genuine, any form of love can have great healing power, but this deeper form of love, Agape, has the greatest healing power. Prayer and other forms of spiritual expression, as well as exercises such as those I have given, can help move us toward this deep compassion.

I have come to believe that we all have the possibility of knowing and expressing this love. In 1975 I wrote the following poem, addressed to my fellow human beings:

The Purpose

It often gets lost in my games
And hidden in my stories,
But the purpose of my life
Is to love you.

CHAPTER 12

HEALING RACISM AND PREJUDICE IN OUR COMMUNITIES AND THE WORLD

Some of us are naturally drawn to care about social justice, fairness, and creating a better world for all people. Some of us act out of having awakened to unconditional love, love not as an idea but as a reality that is lived, or perhaps, "lives you." When this love is present, and not distorted by our thoughts, beliefs, and other feelings, it naturally moves toward kindness and away from prejudice and doing harm. Martin Luther King spoke of this love. But even if we do not yet know this love, are not attracted to social justice, or do not think social justice matters, working to end prejudice in ourselves and our society personally benefits us. It helps us be more whole, make connections with others, and be more able to give and receive love. It adds meaning to our lives and makes them more rewarding in the long run. Most of us have many years left on the planet. As long as we are here, why not make our time more rewarding?

This chapter addresses the following topics:

1. Reducing Our Prejudices by Connecting with People Different from Ourselves

2. Becoming Aware of White Privilege

3. Breaking Down Barriers Between Ourselves and Those Whose Beliefs and Actions We Oppose

4. Acting Effectively Against Prejudice and Discrimination

5. Examining Our Motives

1. Reducing Our Prejudices by Connecting with People Different from Ourselves

My friend Jamal Walker believes that black people should have white people in their lives and white people should have black people in their lives in order to learn to appreciate each other and break down any barriers that might exist. In my own experience, having Jamal as my first close black friend has helped me learn more about what it means to be black in America and what it means to be white in America. It has also helped me to be more comfortable in discussing issues related to race with a black person. In part, because of my connection with Jamal and his family, his telling me how painful it was to try to help his ten-year-old son make sense out of being treated as "different" by white classmates deeply touched me. This, in turn, strengthened my resolve to further the unlearning of prejudice, especially in young people. These experiences have further softened the racist emotional conditioning that has been with me since my childhood.

As my experience with Jamal suggests, one way to counter prejudice and discrimination is to help people who are on both sides of an issue to make a heart connection. One's own prejudices can be diminished by connecting with the people against whom the prejudices would be directed. This is evident in terms of the growing acceptance of gay marriage in California over the past several decades. Field Poll surveys have shown that when heterosexuals are aware of knowing gay and lesbian people, the heterosexuals are more likely to have a positive view of them and to support gay marriage. This is because the issues become less abstract and more personalized.[1]

According to psychological research, if we come to realize that we have an unconscious bias against people who have an identity different from ours and we have the intention of transcending that prejudice, we can do so by getting to know some of those individuals against whom we have been biased.[2] Research has also shown that when people from potentially opposing groups have to work together for their common benefit, such as to overcome challenges they all face, unconscious discrimination diminishes.[3]

The more interactions we have with people who are different from us in some way, the more we will be able to overcome our biases and stereotypes. This not only improves our relationship with fellow members of the human race but also contributes to our personal growth.

2. Becoming Aware of White Privilege

As a white person, "white privilege" (i.e., having the advantages of being white) can be hard to see because it is so much a part of my life…yet, if I look, it is everywhere — throughout my life and throughout the society and world. Many of the advantages I have had in my life have been because of my whiteness, and my advantages existed because of others' disadvantages.

As I have written, my Uncle GP, a grandson of a slave owner and a firm believer in segregation, served in the 1960s as Director of Immigration and Naturalization for the southeast United States.[xxxv] After serving in that capacity for a few years, he postponed his retirement for a year or two so that a black person would not be promoted to his job. My mother approved of Uncle GP's decision, and as she related the story to me, the issue was not the black person's qualifications but his race. My uncle was not willing to share power with black people.

When Barack Obama ran for President in 2008, I was not sure Americans were ready to elect a person of mixed race who had black skin color. After all, only white people, and white males at that, had ever held the presidency. In a way, his election was an amazing milestone. Before he was elected, his March 8, 2008 speech focused on race ("A More Perfect Union," Constitution

---

[xxxv] "Names of Slave Owners," Tallahatchie County, Mississippi, July 1860 (showing that Greek P. Rice [Sr.], my Uncle GP's grandfather, owned one slave at the time).

Hall, Philadelphia), but in general, during his campaign he did not discuss white privilege. Had he done so, I do not believe he would have gotten the white votes he needed to win. (In an Associated Press poll conducted in late 2012, 51 percent of Americans expressed anti-black sentiments. When statements that implied a negative view of blacks were taken into account, the number of Americans with anti-black sentiments increased to 56 percent. In a 2011 survey, almost identical percentages were noted in terms of non-Latino whites' views of Latinos.)[4]

In his excellent book, *Racial Healing*, Harlon Dalton states that true racial equality can happen only when white people are willing to give up their position of privilege, and the distribution of power is altered.[5] My privileges as a white person were built into social systems, businesses, and institutions. And because my privileges have been a part of my everyday life, they have been mostly unconscious. Thanks to a race relations workshop I participated in, I was able to gain considerable insight into what Dalton meant when he wrote about white privilege. The facilitator had all participants stand side by side in a line, holding hands. Then we were told to step forward or backward in response to various commands. For example, take two steps backward if you grew up in poverty; take one step backward if you did not graduate from high school; take two steps forward if you graduated from college; take two steps forward if you are a white male; take two steps backward if you are a person of color. At the end of the exercise we were all quite scattered, but white folks were clearly at the head of the room, while "minority" people were way at the back. A white woman cried when she and a close friend of hers, who was black, reached the point of being too many steps apart to continue holding hands.

In 2011, I joined forces with Jamal to work on the underlying causes of racism and prejudice in our county in Northern California. As we began our endeavor, it was clear that he wanted me to know about white privilege in general and to deeply understand how I had benefited from it. This was not so he could "rub my nose in it." Such an understanding was essential for me to grasp his experiences as a black person and his view of the world and for us to have an honest friendship and working relationship. It was also essential when undertaking an endeavor such as ours related to helping others overcome prejudice and oppression. He directed me to the work of Tim Wise, and from there I discovered two important books on this subject, *Understanding White Privilege* by Frances Kendall, and *White Privilege: Essential Readings on the Other Side of Racism* edited by Paula Rosenberg.[xxxvi]

To further my understanding, I made a list of ways I have actually benefited by being white as well as some ways I could have benefited by my whiteness. Doing this gave me important insight. Here are some items from that list:

- When I visited relatives in Mississippi during my childhood, white people treated me with a respect that would not have been given to black people. (This is an extreme understatement.)

- I lived in nice homes as a child, homes that would have been less available to many blacks due to discrimination and their lack of economic opportunity.

- During most of my pre-college education I went to all-white private schools which black students would not have been allowed into and which offered a better education than schools available to most black students.

- During my youth, I was given summer jobs that included all-white co-workers and that I do not believe would have been available to children of color.

- At least one or two jobs I was given after college would not have been given to a person of color.

- Throughout my life, I have been in many white-owned stores where my presence was welcomed and the presence of a person of color would probably have been less welcomed.

xxxvi Tim Wise's *White Like Me* and his speeches and speech clips on YouTube are a good starting point for learning about white privilege. Another interesting resource, which can take one deeper into the subject, is The White Privilege Conference [www.whiteprivilegeconference.org] which holds annual conferences. Their WPC University offers learning experiences for high school, undergraduate, and graduate students. They also feature the Diversity University, a traveling one-day conference focusing on young adults and educational professionals, which addresses forms of oppression and privilege.

- It is extremely likely that there were times white police officers treated me more favorably than they would have treated a person of color.

- The parents of the white girlfriend I had after college would not have accepted me had I been other than white. My girlfriend's father had connections that allowed me to get a teaching job I would not have gotten had I been a person of color.

- I received inheritances earlier in my life that would have been less, or nonexistent, were it not for the fact that my ancestors, because they were white, had a greater chance to gain wealth than people of color.

- Financial security at times in my life has come from inheritances that, to some degree, related to exploitation of black people.

- There are many situations today in which I would be favored over a black person, a lesbian, a Muslim, a Native American, an Hispanic, etc.

Being white has allowed me a greater possibility of having a positive self-image than if I were a person of color. One factor is my not having been discriminated against in areas I have visited, places where I have sought housing, jobs I have applied for, stores I have shopped in, etc. In addition, almost all of the heroes and role models in my school text books, and on the television programs and movies I watched growing up, were white folks. Furthermore, when people of color were in the movies or TV programs I saw, in a number of cases, they were shown in a less positive light than the whites. In many such incidences, negative stereotypes were encouraged. (The stupid way Native Americans talked to the white heroes in most of the Westerns of my childhood is one of many examples.) All or almost all store manikins I have seen, including ones painted black, depicted people with Caucasian features. During most of my life, most mainstream advertising presented to me depicted white people. And on and on. All such things have a bearing on people's self-images.

One thing I came across during my research on this subject was a film on YouTube. It was a copy of the program *True Colors*, broadcast on ABC's Primetime on September 26, 1991. The program ABC created, hosted by Diane Sawyer, involved a black male and a white male, both from Ivy League colleges, "clean cut," well dressed, and about the same age. Over two-and-one-half weeks, the individuals took turns approaching the same places in St. Louis, Missouri, to shop, look for work, buy a car, rent an apartment, etc. The difference in how they were treated was shocking. There were times the black man was treated well, but every day he had experiences of discrimination. At one point, when the same car salesman offered each of them the same car (at different times), the amount needed for a down payment and the overall price for the black customer were both higher. At one point, when the black man was walking through a white area, a white man drove by and paused to tell him he did not belong in that part of town. When they were walking on a downtown sidewalk one night, with the white man ahead of the black man, a police car approached the black man from behind, slowed down to look him over, then drove past the white guy at normal speed. In the final experiment, each of them walked along the street near the ABC offices in New York, with the white man a little ahead, and they each tried to hail the same cab. The cab passed the black guy and stopped to pick up the white guy.[6]

In his excellent book, *Affirmative Action: Racial Preference in Black and White*, Tim Wise makes a very significant point. The debate on affirmative action tends to focus on whether or not people of color should be granted racial preferences. The real focus should be on whether or not white people should be allowed to have their numerous white privileges![7]

Looking at white privilege as a white person is not about blame. After all, "we" are not responsible for having developed this system that has its roots in our country in Colonial times. As Tim Wise points out, it is about awareness and accepting responsibility for a system we have inherited so we can seek ways to change it and create more equity and fairness.[8] It is about helping others, who have been unfairly treated, have more opportunities.

Not surprisingly, some white people feel uncomfortable when this subject is discussed, perhaps because of fear of giving up one's unearned advantages and/or guilt for having them. I have to admit that the idea of giving up whatever I have gained in life due to privilege is an uncomfortable thought for me. It is hard to imagine what results doing so might have. Perhaps it would mean that I would have a lower standard of living and a less comfortable job, or I would have no job at all, or I would not have a car, or that I would be homeless.

For minorities to have more privilege in our society, white people will necessarily have less. Fewer white people will be running corporations, fewer white people will be governing the country, fewer white people will control financial institutions, fewer white people will control law enforcement and the legal system.

Harlon Dalton suggests that white people will give up power only when they realize that it is in their own best interests. One benefit for white folks is that they will be relieved of the burdens of trying to rationalize and hold together a system of oppression. In addition, a significant percentage of our population — those who have been oppressed — will finally have the opportunity to realize their potential and contribute what they can to our country, for the benefit of us all. Dalton suggests that a way to break through the fears white people might have related to releasing their grasp on power is for them to have positive experiences with minorities that are based on equality. Such experiences, of course, would have to occur outside of the traditional structures of power where whites are in control.[9]

Examining the personal cost of racism and white privilege can encourage whites to oppose the system of white privilege. *Combined Destinies: Whites Sharing Grief About Racism*, edited by psychotherapists Caroline Haskell and Ann Todd Jealous, includes powerful stories by fifty-three white people who have reached this point. Some of the stories relate to whites who grew up with black servants with whom they had loving relationships but were not allowed to experience as equals. It has chapters that address such issues as shame, guilt, and being silent in the face of racism. The book encourages the reader to reflect on the reader's own experiences in light of white privilege. A premise of the book is that healing takes place in our society when hearts as well as minds are opened.[10]

Because of his position on issues like white privilege, Tim Wise has been called a traitor to the white race, as well as being called much worse things by some white people. Perhaps it is more appropriate to say that when we whites willingly and actively support the system of white privilege, *we* are a traitor to both the white race and the human race, since everyone loses.

Having equal privilege for all allows for a just society. It creates a fair system where everyone has a chance to contribute according to his or her talents and to be compensated appropriately. It opens up opportunities related to jobs, education, housing, and so on, that are not currently available to people of color and others who are currently discriminated against and, in many cases because of prejudice, mired in poverty. It encourages people who are now oppressed to have higher self-esteem, or to at least not feel inferior, because they would be valued. It can allow white people who are now privileged to develop a more honest sense of self-worth that is not based on a false sense of superiority and external factors associated with privilege. It takes a society that is now wounded and divided due to oppression and inequity and moves it towards healing and wholeness. It is to the benefit of everyone.

3. Breaking Down Barriers Between Ourselves and Those Whose Beliefs and Actions We Oppose

Martin Luther King was very clear about opposing injustice itself, not the perpetrators of injustice.[11] When I wrote letters to the editor in response to those who vilified King, I tried to adhere to this philosophy. I opposed the ideas of the other letter writers, but not the letter writers themselves. (Unfortunately, not all of those who debated me responded in kind.) Attacking the character of an opponent is a negative approach called "character assassination," which is sometimes done because one's arguments are weak. When people cannot win by arguing with another person's opinions, they may attack the person expressing them. The usual effect of this approach is to build barriers that destroy any hope of finding common ground.

I have already mentioned that my judgment of people who have racist beliefs is softened when I remember times I have had such beliefs, and the fact that as human beings we are all more alike than different. There are many other perspectives we can use to look at people whose beliefs or actions we oppose in order to break down barriers that might exist between us.

An effort to understand those people whom we consider to be perpetrators of injustice can contribute greatly to breaking down the barriers between us and increase the possibility of a healthy dialogue. It helps if we can comprehend some possible reasons for why they think and act as they do, such as their life experiences and the people and cultural surroundings to which they have been exposed that have influenced them.

In a speech on peacemaking, Thich Nhat Hahn suggests that, if he had grown up on the coast of Thailand with an alcoholic father and a neglectful young mother, with ruffians for friends and no one to teach him about love, he might well have become a sea pirate who raped and murdered instead of a Buddhist monk.[12] Rubin "Hurricane" Carter, a black prizefighter who spent almost twenty years in prison for murders he did not commit, points out in *Eye of the Hurricane: My Path from Darkness to Freedom* that we have no control over a number of significant influences on our lives. Such things as our race, the social class we are born into, our birthplace, who our parents were, and so on, are pure "accidents" we did not create.[13] These views expressed by Nhat Hanh and Carter remind me of the popular saying, "There but for the grace of God go I."

In a way, I think of many of the events of our lives as "simple twists of fate." Just one little variable unleashes an infinite chain of developments as it shifts things in a very different direction than otherwise. If my parents had not met, I would not exist as the person I seem to be. If, in July 2011, I had not read a newspaper article about a racist incident, I would not be publishing this book — at least at this time. If I had not worked at a particular food co-op over twenty-five years ago, I would not have known the people who connected me to my wife and, consequently, I might never have met her. If I had asked someone other than my brother Fletcher if we should look down on others due to their race and gotten an answer different from than the one I received, I might have held onto racist views for much longer.

Clearly, there are many things that influence our lives and cause them to appear as they do at a given moment. While perhaps we have "free will" in a limited sense, it is my opinion that, for the most part, most of us do not have total free will that is completely independent of all of our conditioning. This would mean freedom from all conditioning related to family influences, cultural influences, social conditions we have experienced, places where we have lived, our schooling, all of the friends we have had, books we have read, things we have seen in our lives, white privilege, and countless other things. In other words, for the most part we do not make decisions completely free of all the influences of life.[14] Albert Einstein, one of the most brilliant thinkers of the last century, noted that our actions, thoughts, and feelings are not at all free but are bound to causes just as the stars are bound by their own motions.[15] I know that most or all of my own beliefs are heavily conditioned or affected by all I have experienced over the past seventy years. If a number of those experiences had been completely different, it is a safe bet that some of my beliefs would be different from what they are today.

Furthermore, many of us seek media that reinforces what we already believe rather than media that might change our beliefs. If I am a conservative, I might listen to a conservative talk show host on the radio and read conservative newspapers. If I am a liberal, I am likely to seek out liberal programming and read liberal publications. An article printed in the *Sacramento Bee* on January 21, 2012, made this point about voters. The article, titled "Voters Seek Own Spin," stated that, according to numerous studies, liberals and conservatives tend to only take in information that is compatible with the views they already hold.[16] In this sense, whether I had white supremacist beliefs or believed in racial equality, I would tend to find sufficient "facts" in print or broadcast media or books to "prove" I was right and to reinforce my beliefs. And I would hold my beliefs no less sincerely than someone with opposing views.

When I consider the things I have done that I regret in my life, who am I to judge anyone? I can work to counter someone's racist actions at the same time as I try to see the person's humanness and how it reflects my own humanness. This is not easy for me, but I can do my best as I hold it as an ideal. It is important for me to remember that opening my heart is more important to me than being right (and perhaps self-righteous and arrogant).

When we start to love others, our experience of them improves.[17] The people may not change, but our experience of them does. This can apply to people we may have formerly detested, which might include so-called "racists."

As we oppose injustice, it is sometimes impossible to avoid triggering negative reactions in those on the other side of the issue. Our social action could increase the barriers put up by those who perceive us as threatening or wrong. But the more we can feel a sense of connection with those we oppose, the more we see beyond our stories of who we think they are, the easier it will be for us to act in a kind and nonconfrontive manner. At least we will not be contributing our own angry energy to the barriers that might exist. When we can do this, we are more likely to diminish prejudice than to reinforce it. And in the process of opening our hearts and building bridges, our own lives will have been enriched.

4. Acting Effectively Against Prejudice and Discrimination

Prejudice and discrimination (including racism) are interwoven throughout many of our society's institutions, be they educational, economic, governmental, judicial, or any other type. Discrimination and prejudice can be addressed on many levels, beginning with ourselves and moving out to our community's and our society's institutions. If we can afford to make financial investments, we can choose to invest only in companies that have fair hiring and employment practices. Opposition might also take the form of a boycott, a picket line, or civil disobedience. It can include making our views known through letters to the editor, and it can be as simple as stopping someone as he or she launches into an ethnic or racist joke. (I would advise against entering a situation in which you would not feel physically safe or that would be too much for you to handle emotionally.)

As I indicated in the previous section, it is preferable to act against discrimination or prejudice in others in a way that diminishes barriers between people and prevents defensiveness. For example, angrily confronting business owners for racist policies might not be the most effective approach. My friend Jamal suggests that a white person might interrupt white people using racist language by "speaking from his or her soul" and using words like, "Excuse me, but I have friends who are black and it hurts me to hear you talking about black people that way. I would appreciate your not doing that in my presence."

Dr. Marshall Rosenberg is a psychotherapist and educator who created a form of communicating called Nonviolent Communication (NVC). He teaches an effective way to communicate with others, and Rosenberg has used it to help opposing factions communicate with each other in other parts of the world (bringing together, for example, Israeli Jews and Palestinians). In general, the four components of NVC include: 1) observing a situation that is affecting you without coloring it with an evaluation or judgment, and articulating that nonjudgmental observation; 2) expressing how you feel when you observe the situation; 3) expressing what needs you have that relate to your feelings; and 4) making a specific request of the other person.[18] (His method takes some work to master. In order to learn more about it, it is best to study his book, *Nonviolent Communication: A Language of Life*, or, even better, take a workshop related to the process as well as read the book. In my community, there have been a number of study and practice groups that teach NVC skills.)

In his book, Rosenberg discusses an incident in which he found himself in a cab with a man who made a derogatory comment about Jews. Rosenberg contained the anger he felt and endeavored to connect with the person and show his empathy for what was underneath the man's comment. In doing this, he looked for the humanness that was behind the other passenger's remark. He asked the man questions that allowed the man to elaborate on his experiences, which included frustration and sadness, and to feel that he was being heard. Only after that did Rosenberg tell the man how his comment affected him and how he had had positive experiences with Jewish people. He did this *without an element of blame*. Rosenberg makes it very clear in his book that if other people feel blamed, they will not open up to hearing about our pain, and true communication will be blocked. In addition, the more we listen to them, the more they are likely to listen to us. Rosenberg's approach to the situation in the cab, which required skill and time to unfold, had much more potential for broadening the other man's view than would have been the case if Rosenberg had initiated a direct confrontation.[19]

Another excellent book on communicating with others is *Difficult Conversations: How to Discuss What Matters Most*, by Stone, Patton, and Heen. Paul Kivel's *Uprooting Racism: How White People Can Work for Racial Justice*, discusses ways white people can be allies to people of color and offers a variety of suggestions and tools for opposing institutional racism and creating social change. In Chapter 7 of *The Story Factor: Inspiration, Influence, and Persuasion Through the Art of Storytelling*, Annette Simmons discusses the importance of finding common ground (similar desires, ideals, etc.) with someone you want to influence. The chapter offers valuable insights for social activists who want to create positive change by motivating or influencing others. Chapter 8 of her book stresses the importance of listening to people we want to change.

5. Examining Our Motives

If one has taken on the goal of diminishing prejudice in the world, it is useful to examine one's motives. It took me many years to look back on my most active protest days and realize how much anger and self-righteousness I had. As I have said, I also came to realize that my opposition to authority figures through social and environmental action related to my having oppressive authority figures in my youth. To a degree, I was rebelling against my father and the rigidness of my military high school, even though I had left home and high school years before. This is not to discount my motive of wanting to contribute to the world, but to acknowledge that my motivation was not quite so simple.

Jeremy Taylor sees the phenomenon of self-deception among many liberals who want to "help" targets of racism. A person who endeavors to help victims may have repressed his or her own conditioned racism and projected it onto people judged as racist. In addition, the unacknowledged racism in the individual gets in the way of his or her being a good ally for targets of racism because the person cannot come from a clear place. (Taylor's internet article, "Education to Counter Oppression at Starr King," has some interesting and insightful writing about judgments and their relationship to racism.)[20]

The more self-awareness one has, the less likely one is to dump their baggage onto someone whose behavior they would like to change, a subject addressed in the previous chapter.

6. Addressing Prejudice in Educational Settings

Three colleagues and I have led workshops and discussions at schools, sharing our personal experiences of racism, giving students a broader understanding of the issues, helping oppressed students feel supported, offering exercises that provide direct experiences related to unlearning prejudice, and helping students develop tools for dealing with prejudice in themselves and others. At one high school where we have been involved, a group of students formed an official school club related to social justice. Fortunately for them, there are members of the school administration and faculty who are very supportive of their intention. There are also members of the county school system who appreciate what the students are doing. I like the common advice to "think globally but act locally," and one thing they might decide to focus on is finding ways to counter prejudice on campus, since prejudice is a big contributor to social injustice (as well as such things as bullying in schools).

During their meetings that we have attended, we have encouraged them to become aware of their own prejudices and to develop tools to diminish prejudice in themselves as well as others. The importance of self-knowledge for any group or individual wanting to reduce prejudice in the world (and/or foster social justice) cannot be overemphasized. As I stressed earlier, we have to start with ourselves. One reason for this is the tendency to project our own prejudices (and other undesirable qualities) onto others, whether they exist in others or not, which in turn can weaken our efforts at social change and even cause us to become self-righteous. If we only see the problem in "them," we can create resentment in them and even do harm. Another reason is to understand the human experience in others by understanding it in ourselves (including the tendency to be prejudiced), which makes us more compassionate, better able to communicate, and more likely to be effective.

It is also important for white students who are opposing prejudice to explore what might be their relationship to shame and guilt due to having privileges not available to people of color.

As I discuss elsewhere, shame and excessive guilt can get in the way of effective communication and action. (See Appendix 4.)

Ideally, schools should have a multi-faceted approach to prejudice, preferably involving students, teachers, and administrators. If prejudice at a school is pervasive, the approach to remedying it should be pervasive. There are many things that can be done. For example, the school can develop a policy that prohibits certain behavior and encourages acceptance and diversity appreciation; the school can host cultural exchanges, perhaps with other schools; the school's library can highlight books that encourage acceptance of others; there can be assemblies with panel discussions; workshops on unlearning prejudice can be offered; curriculum materials can be utilized; students can learn positive ways to interrupt conversations involving slurs against gays, students of color, and others; students can undertake projects related to art, music and other areas to help educate other students and celebrate diversity; and so on.

In trying to change prejudice on a high school or college campus, one has to be careful about singling out specific students or groups of students who are considered the problem, as it could create resistance and ill will. Just addressing prejudice on campus, without targeting anyone in particular, can, of course, create a backlash of resistance on the part of students with strong prejudices. This is not necessarily bad. When Martin Luther King was accused of creating or increasing racism with his protests, he responded that the nonviolent protests did not create or increase racism but rather brought it to the surface so it could be dealt with and healed.[21] Students who are endeavoring to diminish prejudice on campus, who are facing a charged situation, should have support from their administration and may need to call on outside consultants or other resources.

When trying to address prejudice at a school, it is important to accept that there will probably be some students who are not able or ready to change their racist or prejudicial beliefs. As much as possible, they need to be respected as individuals who are doing the best they can with what they have been taught or have experienced. If you are fortunate, some seeds will be planted that may bear fruit in them in later years. Of course, any overt negative behavior should be addressed in an appropriate manner by the school.

While racist or prejudicial beliefs can be a problem with a percentage of a student population, there may also be teachers who, unconsciously or otherwise, encourage racism or prejudice because of their own beliefs. In this situation, it would be ideal for students and teachers seeking change to have sympathetic administrators they can work with to find positive solutions.

Students working to effect change should do their best to include students from different grade levels among their ranks. I have seen situations whereby the main students in a group were graduating seniors. When they left school, the group was weakened.

Students, teachers, and administrators wishing to make positive changes at their school can study what has been tried and accomplished at other schools and look for allies and resources such as like-minded student groups, organizations, websites, and books. For example, black students at Harvard created a project entitled "I, Too, Am Harvard" in which they shared their experiences of racism at the university through a play, a photo display, and a video which was placed on You Tube. Inspired by the Harvard project, minority students at Bethesda-Chevy Chase High School in Maryland produced a powerful six-minute You Tube video called "I, Too, Am B-CC." In it they share painful school experiences related to their skin color. It has stimulated awareness and open discussion in classrooms and among school administrators.

At the time of this writing, the Southern Poverty Law Center (SPLC) offers PDF downloads of "Speak Up — Responding to Everyday Bigotry," "Speak Up at School: How to Respond to Everyday Prejudice, Bias and Stereotypes," and "Responding to Hate and Bias at School, a Guide for Administrators, Counselors and Teachers." These publications discuss how to take a stand against prejudice, including the use of language that targets blacks, LGBTs (people who are lesbian, gay, bisexual, transgender), and others. They also offer "Teaching Tolerance" curriculum material for schools and many other valuable resources to counter prejudice. See www.tolerance.org for more information. (Note that the SPLC uses the term "tolerance" in labeling some of its material. I don't consider it to be the best choice of words in that it can have the connotation that that which is "tolerated" is something negative that one endures. In one workshop I co-led for high school students, I had a student tell me how offensive that word was to students who face discrimination. I prefer the word "acceptance.") Another organization that provides educational programs to combat prejudice is Facing History and Ourselves. Their website is www.facinghistory.org.

I would encourage students wanting to address prejudice on their campus to consider the other topics discussed in this and the previous two chapters, perhaps in group discussions.

Whatever can be done to counter prejudice at a school is good, even if there are only a few students doing several projects a year. Even though there are a lot of things a group can do, it is important that it take on projects that are manageable and do them well rather than weaken its efforts by trying to do too much. If only a few students who are concerned about the problem learn tools to unlearn some of their own prejudices, and tools to help others unlearn prejudice, something significant will still have been achieved. Those students will be better off because of it and will go on to positively affect many, many others during the rest of their lives. (This will be discussed in more detail in the next section of this chapter.)

7. Not Overlooking the Trees for the Forest

A common saying in our culture is, "Don't miss the forest for the trees." In other words, do not get so lost in the little picture that you miss seeing the big picture or the overall view. While this perspective has value, it is also important not to become discouraged or overwhelmed by the big-picture task of creating a world full of love and absent of prejudice and discrimination.

These negative feelings can keep us from doing the small but important things that are possible (the individual "trees"), which would contribute toward achieving that dream (a healthy "forest").

It is easy to look at the news, or what seems to be the state of the world, and feel overwhelmed or hopeless. (For the moment, let's put aside the fact that news tends to focus on negative events and ignore positive ones and is not at all an objective picture.) But it is a mistake to think our small, positive efforts are inconsequential due to the big picture that can seem so negative.

Each step we take toward creating a less prejudiced world — and, especially, each step we take toward overcoming our own prejudices, making connections with others, and being more open-hearted — has enormous consequences over time, if not in the short run. Fifty years ago I realized racism and prejudice were wrong. Because of shifts in my understanding and my taking steps to overcome some of my prejudices, over the past decades I have directly and indirectly affected the lives of thousands of people. This is not to boast, but to give you a real life example. As I grew and changed, how I related to people changed, and I had a more positive effect on others. This involved connecting with many people through several mediums (writing, personal interactions, radio programs, etc.). Many of the people I affected positively then went on to affect many people in their lives more positively. In this way, many, many people were affected. Just as this has been the case in my life, it can be case in your life as well. The little things in our daily lives have enormous effects in the world, like a small pebble thrown into a still pond sends out countless ripples. In their own way the little things change the world. But it is important to see that fundamentally this change begins within each of us. As we change ourselves, we make contributions to others and to the world, in more ways than we can ever know.

Instead of getting lost in what you think is the big picture (the "forest"), especially if it seems overwhelming or hopeless, focus more on what is in front of you, especially on the work you can do on yourself (the "trees" that contribute to a healthy "forest").

And find ways to nourish yourself and stay positive. Learn from the successes of others and find individuals or organizations that share your goals and can help you keep a healthy perspective. Do not overlook the big picture of creating a more loving world, but find little ways in your daily lives and in your local community to work toward achieving it.[xxxvii]

* * * * * * * * * * * * *

It has been 180 years since my great-great-grandparents began their life together as plantation and slave owners. The racism that allowed them and other Southerners to participate in human bondage continued for one-hundred-years after the end of slavery, during Reconstruction and the form of the Jim Crow era. This was a period of white supremacy that my ancestors helped to initiate and perpetuate. Although federal laws mandated the end of Jim Crow in the 1950s and 1960s, the racism that was its foundation continues to exist in our society.

Shortly before my nineteenth birthday, in 1964, I rejected the idea of white supremacy that I grew up with. In the five decades since that decision, using some of the approaches described in this chapter and the previous one, I have worked to overcome the remnants of my family's racism that have remained within me.

---

xxxvii The following books, described in my website's annotated bibliography, offer insights in avoiding despair and making a positive contribution to the world: *Active Hope*, by Johnstone and Macy; *Coming Back to Life*, by Brown and Macy; *The Engaged Spiritual Life*, by Rothberg; and *World As Lover — World as Self*, by Macy.

PART IV

THE JOURNEY CONTINUES

This fourth section covers one of the results of my journey out of racism, the co-founding of an organization to help others unlearn prejudice.

CHAPTER 13

THE JOURNEY CONTINUES

In January 2011, on Martin Luther King Day, an article I wrote about my family history and healing racism was published in *The Union*, the local newspaper.[1] Shortly after its publication, Jamal Walker, who was a co-worker at the food co-op where I work, expressed an interest in talking about my article in relation to some of his experiences as a black person. I did not follow up on his suggestion until the July 4th weekend.

What prompted me to finally meet with him was an incident described in a newspaper article I had read during the holiday. The incident involved a Hispanic family that had been the object of racist behavior at a local park.[2] After reading the article, I visited Jamal to discuss his experiences as well as my concerns related to the article. During our meeting, we committed ourselves to forming a group that would help those in our area unlearn prejudice. For me, it was not so much that I made a decision but more like I felt an energy within me that responded to the situation, and I had no choice but to move in that direction. It was a movement of the heart, not the mind.

Within a short time, after honestly sharing many of our experiences and thoughts related to prejudice, as well as our lives in general, Jamal and I became good friends. And it is evident to me that our friendship has further softened some of the elements of racist emotional conditioning within me. For example, today I might be a little less likely to write the poem *A Handshake*, which I shared in Chapter 10.

For Jamal, it was like he had been waiting for a meeting such as ours so he could resume work he had done earlier in his life — work he had found personally transformative. When he was a young man, he was involved in a workshop program that focused on unlearning prejudices and dismantling oppression. It was called New Bridges, and it helped young people from different backgrounds bridge their differences, share their feelings, and become allies for each other. New Bridges grew out of the work of a therapist named Ricky Sherover-Marcuse.[3] Jamal's mom, Isoke Femi, was very involved in this work and became a skillful workshop leader.[4] Jamal went from being a participant in such workshops to helping lead them, and he developed considerable skill in working with others.

Jamal considers work on unlearning prejudice to be "soul work," and he brings a lot of heart to it. He has good ideas and knows a number of great exercises to help people become aware of their prejudices. He is also skillful at helping people develop tools to both overcome their own prejudices and help others unlearn prejudice. He and I agree that it is important to focus on the underlying causes rather than the symptoms of discrimination and prejudice (including racism).

Jamal and Me   (Photo courtesy of Chris Harada)

One person who responded to a newspaper article Jamal and I wrote together was Reverend Lew Powell, a local Episcopal minister who attended a group meeting we had scheduled.[5] Lew is a couple of years older than I. It did not surprise me that Lew was black (as well as having other identities, including that of being Native American). What surprised me was that he grew up in a rural region of Portsmouth, Virginia, about ten miles from where I was growing up at the same time. As a black kid, he lived in the other half of the world I lived in as a white kid with racist beliefs. While I was able to go to any white school I wanted, he had to go past four white high schools to get to his own "colored" one. Fortunately for Lew, his father was a minister who taught him the power of love and forgiveness and to not hate those who oppressed him. Here we were in Northern California, three thousand miles from our boyhood homes, drawn together to help others unlearn racism and prejudice!

Lew, Jamal, and I became a team, and we began to work together to help address the deeper causes of prejudice in our area. In his capacity as a minister, Lew was already involved with church-sponsored workshops related to racism and prejudice. Our first project was to participate in the Martin Luther King Day programming at our local community radio station, KVMR FM, in January of 2012. After that, we participated in a panel discussion at our local library related to the novel (and movie) *The Help*. The book, by Kathryn Stockett, focuses on the experience of black women working in white households in Jackson, Mississippi in the early 1960s. It had been selected for reading by a county program called Nevada County Reads. In addition, we began to work with local schools to facilitate unlearning prejudice.

During the summer of 2012, Cindy Santa Cruz-Reed joined our core group. She has a Masters in Human Development and Social Justice and has been trained by the Nonviolence in the Lives of Children Project. Cindy has been a classroom teacher and has helped facilitate youth camps. Currently she teaches human development at a community college in Northern California. Among other things, her skills relating to group activities and discussions have been very valuable, and her insights and ideas make a significant contribution to our group.

Near the end of 2013, Lew had to drop out of our group due to other time commitments. Cindy, Jamal, and I have formed an organization called Creating Communities Beyond Bias (CCBB). We give workshops on unlearning prejudice for students and adults. We also have joined forces with members of our area's Quaker community, who share our concerns about white privilege and prejudice. As of this writing (January 2015), we are focusing on bringing together local civic leaders, church representatives, educators, students, members of law enforcement, and others in order to devise ways to diminish prejudice in our region. Our first step as a group will be to examine our own prejudices.

Since the original edition of this book, I have been increasingly involved in public speaking. A presentation I gave on Martin Luther King Day, January 19, 2015, is now on You Tube.

****

In closing....

Part of my life's work revolves around healing racism in myself and in the world. This focus relates to how painful it is for me to see the effect prejudice and discrimination have on people who are its targets. It also relates to the pain I have when I see other people and institutions act out of prejudice in a way that causes harm, and it also relates to seeing how my own prejudices have adversely affected myself and others. I have a strong impulse to bring more love, fairness, and justice into our world and — due to my personal and my family's past — a personal connection to the human problem of prejudice. In part, I see this work as redeeming the considerable harm I and my birth lineage have caused other human beings (while harming ourselves in the process).

I wish you, the reader, well in coming to terms with prejudices you might have and encourage you to be patient and compassionate with yourself and others.

My own journey of healing racism continues.

Through These Eyes

Nancy Robinson,
Sweet sister,
whose name I carry,
I have seen the world
through your eyes,
…seen your illusions,
and your truth,
…your joy,
and your sadness,
…your pain,
and
your incredible love.

If only you could
see through mine
humankind's
delightful diversity
and the wonder
of our oneness.

…And maybe you can.

William Robinson Drake

Visit Bill Drake's website

www.healracism.com

- Links to:

  - You Tube videos of talks by Bill Drake

  - Audio recordings of radio programs with Bill Drake and others

  - Facebook page

  - Blog

- Additional excerpts from the interviews of former slaves and Bill's great-great-grandmother's diaries

- Annotated bibliography

- New information and links as the journey continues

EPILOGUE

MISSISSIPPI REVISITED

Reflections on my last visit to Mississippi.

MISSISSIPPI REVISITED

Most of the reflections in this epilogue were written on an airplane enroute to my California home after my brother Stoney, his son, and I visited the Mississippi Delta in February 2002. During my time in the Deep South, for the first time in forty years, I walked on farmland that was part of my great-great-grandparents' slave plantations. The visit took place because some of that land was being passed down to my brother, the children of our deceased brother Fletcher, and me after my ninety-five-year-old mother's death the preceding Christmas day.

In Mississippi, I visited several cousins whom I had never met and became acquainted with a number of other white residents as I embarked on matters related to the property. Each of these individuals was kind, generous, and likable.

Those who spoke of such things believed that the history of race-related beatings, tortures, and murders in Mississippi and the rest of the South was despicable.

Attitudes on race, however, varied among those I met. Although the term "black" was commonly used in private conversation, in contrast to the more frequent use of the word "nigger" by other Mississippi relatives I visited several decades ago, I did hear the "N word" on occasion during my visit. While some whites did not seem to prejudge people on the basis of skin color, others did. Most of the white people I met expressed some discomfort about living in areas where blacks comprised as much as 80 percent of the population.

I am not sure what it would be like for me today if I were to find myself living in an area where the vast majority of residents were of a different color and/or economic situation than I. In my youth, my conditioned prejudices would have made it difficult, although later I comfortably lived in a poor section of New York City's Lower East Side and in an almost all-black neighborhood in Philadelphia.

In order to avoid an unconstructive confrontation with most of the whites who befriended me, I kept my perspective on race and prejudice to myself, but I felt uncomfortable with the prejudice that was apparent to me, even though I could understand it as a human experience.

During my time in Mississippi, I reflected on how different people respond to the presence of black people in their lives. My nephew, who was from South Carolina, had positive experiences of blacks as a child and later as a college student and was able to avoid the effects of the racist beliefs that so crippled my own family. (He also had a home environment that discouraged prejudice.) One of my cousins told me she had served the cause of civil rights by driving people to civil rights meetings at night, sometimes with the headlights off to avoid detection. I had no idea I had a Mississippi relative who took such a stand. Regrettably, time did not permit further discussion. Former President Jimmy Carter's wonderful book, *An Hour Before Daybreak*, makes it clear that his positive experiences of the poor blacks in his rural Georgia childhood environment helped him avoid developing racist views.[1] The Mississippi relatives whom I knew as a child, because of conditioning, insecurity, negative experiences, and/or other factors, held deeply racist attitudes.

In some respects, my time at my ancestral homeland resulted in contributions to this book. Two of my cousins gave me pictures of my mother's paternal grandparents, Lt. Col. William Henry FitzGerald and his wife Frances Wilmoth Harvey FitzGerald, which can be found in Chapter 2. I also learned some details related to my family history.

To a degree, my trip made the publication of this writing much more painful and difficult. It reminded me that some of my relatives in Mississippi and perhaps elsewhere will be disturbed that I have written this book. Some may be troubled by its position on racism, as well as my observations about the racist side of our family history, a discussion I have considered to be essential for the telling of my story.

While I may pay a personal price for it, the potential contribution this book can make to my fellow human beings far outweighs any cost to me.

APPENDICES

APPENDIX 1

THE CAMPAIGN TO DISCREDIT MARTIN LUTHER KING

by Bill Drake

A version of this article appeared in the *Community Endeavor*, Nevada City, California, in 1990. Permission to use the original article was granted by Su Lukasha.

Some folks who fear racial integration are delighted to see Martin Luther King Day come around every January. Why? It gives them another chance to decry King as a villain and a "commie." Where does much of the so-called proof for their accusations come from? U.S. Senate committee hearings which investigated the FBI's involvement with Dr. King give us a good idea.[1]

During the 1975 hearings, several committee members were allowed to review FBI files, and the committee received testimonies from the Assistant Deputy Director of the FBI and other FBI representatives.

The committee's final report stated: "From December 1963 until his death in 1968, Martin Luther King, Jr. was the target of an intensive campaign by the Federal Bureau of Investigation to 'neutralize' him as an effective civil rights leader. In the words of the man in charge of the FBI's 'war' against Dr. King: 'No holds were barred. We have used [similar] techniques against Soviet agents.' The FBI collected information about Dr. King's plans and activities through an extensive surveillance program.... Congressional leaders were warned 'off the record' about alleged dangers posed by Reverend King.... The FBI's program... entailed attempts to discredit [King] with churches, universities, and the press.... The FBI campaign to discredit and destroy Dr. King was marked by extreme personal vindictiveness."[2]

William Sullivan, who oversaw FBI Director J. Edgar Hoover's domestic intelligence branch and supervised Hoover's campaign against King, told the committee, "I think behind it all was the racial bias, the dislike of Negroes, the dislike of the civil rights movement.... I do not think [Hoover] could rise above that."[3]

The report goes on to state, "The FBI now agrees that its efforts to discredit Dr. King were unjustified. [FBI agent Adams], the present Deputy Associate Director testified: 'There were approximately twenty-five incidents of actions taken [to discredit Dr. King].... I see no statutory basis or no basis of justification for the activity.' "[4]

FBI actions included: directing an agent to steal stationery from the Southern Christian Leadership Conference (SCLC), King's organization, in order to forge letters that would damage Andrew Young's campaign for Congress; actively discouraging financial donations to the SCLC by spreading false rumors that King had a Swiss bank account and that King had misused funds; scrutinizing King's tax returns; and rewriting agency reports which had determined that King was not a national security threat.[5]

One of the FBI actions with the most damaging effects was the "bugging" of King's hotel rooms, which yielded recordings of extramarital relationships.[6] Hoover took great delight in listening to these recordings and in giving them to President Johnson, Attorney General Robert Kennedy, congress members, and representatives of the press.[7] The Bureau sent a tape recording of these sexual affairs to King, along with an anonymous letter. The letter, King believed, was urging him to commit suicide.[8]

The FBI also focused on two of King's advisors who had had or might have had communist connections. Regarding the individual considered the "most dangerous," according to the report, "...when [an FBI] field office reported to FBI headquarters in 1964 that the Advisor was not then under the influence and control of the Communist Party, the FBI did not curtail either its investigations or discrediting program against Dr. King." The FBI continued the publicity campaign against King in regards to the advisor, falsely claiming the advisor was a communist agent. They passed this false information on to the president, congressional leaders, newspaper reporters, and others. After its hearings, the committee pointed out that "We have seen no evidence establishing that either of those Advisers attempted to exploit the civil rights movement to carry out the plans of the Communist Party."[9]

Perhaps the "evidence" segregationists cite most often as proof of King's association with communism is a 1957 photograph of him at the Highlander Folk School in Tennessee. Supporters of segregation started the false rumor that the school was a training school for the Communist Party, apparently because it had integrated facilities (in violation of a Tennessee law forbidding integrated schools) and supported civil rights and oppressed Appalachian workers. The FBI investigated and rejected the allegations, but people with racist views claimed that King and other movement leaders were trained by communists at Highlander.[10]

The Senate committee noted, "The FBI has stated that at no time did it have any evidence that Dr. King himself was a communist or connected with the Communist Party. Dr. King repeatedly criticized Marxist philosophies in his writing and speeches. The present Deputy Associate Director of the FBI's Domestic Intelligence Division, when asked by the Committee if the FBI ever concluded that Dr. King was a communist, testified, 'No sir, we did not.'"[11] Furthermore, FBI agent Sullivan wrote in his autobiography, *The Bureau: My Thirty Years in Hoover's FBI*, that King was definitely not a Communist.[12]

The FBI's overall campaign greatly inhibited the civil rights activities of Dr. King and the Southern Christian Leadership Conference. It also placed an enormous personal burden on the civil rights leader. As the Senate committee wrote in their final report, the FBI campaign comprised "a shameful chapter in the nation's history."[13]

APPENDIX 2

MARTIN LUTHER KING: THE IDEAL VS. THE REALITY

by Bill Drake

A version of this article appeared in the *Community Endeavor*, Nevada City, California. Permission to use the original article was granted by Su Lukasha.

Around 1990, it was reported that King had plagiarized some of his college papers, using quotes from other writers without giving them credit.[1] Much more serious were his extramarital affairs, which have been discussed in a number of books about King.

Understandably, his transgressions troubled him deeply. A month before his assassination, during a sermon at the Ebenezer Baptist Church, he told the congregation that, like all people, he had sinned but that he desired to be good.[2]

As David Garrow notes in *The FBI and Martin Luther King*, during his last months King became increasingly self-critical and felt undeserving of the public attention he was given.[3]

People who would condemn King for adultery would do well to remember the parable of Christ, in which he stops a mob from stoning to death a woman who had committed adultery. His message to the mob was, "Let you who are without sin cast the first stone." Even though we may not act on some of our impulses in the same way as Dr. King, we have to acknowledge whatever ways we are similar to him within our humanness.

When considering King's imperfections, it is important to remember the positive aspects of his character and his enormous accomplishments. As well as being a great philosopher and leader, he put his life on the line every day, exhibiting almost superhuman courage and conviction. He dedicated his life not only to civil rights but also to human rights.

Regarding his affairs, there is value in recognizing the enormous pressure King was under. This is not to justify them, but to understand how he might give in to this particular weakness.

Most importantly, it should be remembered that King was a human being. Like all of us, he had his share of insecurities and made his share of mistakes.

What makes his human shortcomings so hard for some people to accept is the fact that his humanness has generally been denied due to the tendency of our culture to deify him. Whenever we put someone on a pedestal, there is the potential for unfortunate results. He or she is not allowed human failings, while the rest of us who are looking up to the person tend to overlook our own potential for greatness. Then when the person's human frailties are revealed, the human tendency is to drop him or her beneath us in disgust, as if to say, "How could you be so human? We thought you were perfect!"

It is wonderful that we celebrate Martin Luther King Day, which gives us an opportunity to stop and honor not only the genuine greatness that King had but the entire civil rights movement, including its less famous leaders. But we must also do both King and ourselves a favor and acknowledge his complexity and human frailties.

APPENDIX 3
Most of this information can be found in Chapters 11 and 12.

A PHILOSOPHY OF SOCIAL ACTION

©2014 by Bill Drake, All Rights Reserved (Adapted from articles published by the Peace Center of Nevada County, CA), www.healracism.com

As a college student in the 1960s, I began my involvement in social action with the Vietnam War protests and the movement for students' rights on college campuses. In the decades that followed, I founded or co-founded and helped lead several organizations related to anti-nuclear efforts, environmental protection, and protection of Native American cultural resources. Like many others, I committed civil disobedience and went to jail for my beliefs. Since the beginnings of my activism, my view of social action has changed considerably.

"Us" vs "Them"
When I reflected on the 1960s protests during the mid-1970s, I was not only struck by how an "us" vs "them" approach, or polarization, was at the heart of the Vietnam War ("us"/good/U.S. vs. "them"/evil/Communists), but how it was also at the heart of our anti-war protests ("us"/good/protesters vs. "them"/evil/U.S. government), at least for some of us. To a degree, our polarizing approach to the U.S. Government reflected the same core problem that we were fighting against, and in that sense, we were modeling conflict even as we believed we were working for peace.

This is not to say that we were wrong to protest or oppose the war. In acting on one's beliefs or pursuing social justice, it is not always possible to avoid an "us" vs. "them" position, even if it is only in one's perception of others. What I would suggest is to try to be aware of this phenomenon if it is present and to take steps to lessen it if that is possible. It would be ideal to oppose other people's positions instead of the people themselves and avoid making personal attacks on others.

Knowing Oneself

Over the years since then, my involvement with social action taught me the importance of knowing oneself. On one hand, like other things, social change endeavors provide a valuable opportunity to learn about one's reactions and psychological motivations. On the other hand, the more one knows oneself, the more effective one can be at creating positive social change.

Self-Righteousness and Social Action

Looking back, I can see the degree of self-righteousness (related to unconscious anger) that pervaded my early social change efforts. When one strongly believes in a cause, there can be a human tendency to become self-righteous about it and to think that anyone who looks at the issue differently is wrong. After all, it makes so much sense (to me!), it is so "right" — shouldn't everyone else be able to see how "right" it is and change their thinking and behavior? Acting on what we believe without being self-righteous can be challenging, yet it is essential in order for us to respect others, to be heard by others, and — importantly — to listen to others. As I have grown older, and been influenced by meditation and other disciplines, I have learned to watch self-righteousness as it arises, which can allow a softening, even a humility, and increases the ability to communicate well.

Projections Onto Others

What we strongly react to in others can be "projections" of qualities within ourselves that are usually unconscious. (This does not mean that other people do not have the qualities. They may or may not.) To see that in the 1960s I manifested the same essential behavior that I was so angry at our country's leaders for manifesting made a big impact on me.

In the years since that insight, through self-observation and the influence of meditation, teachers like Byron Katie, etc., I have come to see how most, if not all, of the things I react to in the world can be found in my own mind or behavior, be it in the past or present. If I am concerned about racism, it is valuable for me to see my own prejudices and racism. (At least I can see that I am prejudiced against people who are prejudiced.) If I am angry about how a politician appears self-righteous, it is helpful to acknowledge that in that moment I am being self-righteous. I am energized about my being "right" and his or her being "wrong." If I am upset that there might be a class of people that is greedy and exploitative, it is valuable to acknowledge that I can be or have been greedy and exploitative at times. And within my own human nature, if I search deeply enough, are aspects of both the Dalai Lama and Hitler. As I recognize and accept this about me, I am better able to accept it about others and come less from a place of separateness.

We See the World as We Are, Not as It Is[1]

At the same time, I have come to see how subjective my individual world is. In a quote sometimes attributed to writer Anais Nin, it is suggested that we see the world as we are, not as it is. To recognize this is to realize how our reactions to those we oppose can say as much, or more, about us as about them. As we come to understand ourselves and our tendency to project onto others, we have more humility and less judgment of other people. This breaks down the concept of "enemy" and increases our abilities to communicate and be more effective. In working to change racism, for example, it can make a big difference if I have recognized my own prejudices and seeds of racism and am not just projecting them onto so-called "racists."

To some degree, because of our background experiences, etc., we already have certain opinions or inclinations, and we are likely to seek information that reinforces them. If we are of liberal persuasion, we seek out liberal media. If we are of conservative bent, we may listen to conservative radio talk shows. In either case, we tend to believe we have the only real truth, and people of the opposite view are idiots. Our view of those who believe differently from the way we do tends to reflect both our subjectivity and an "us vs them" approach.

In looking at things this way, I can see that in some ways, in my humanness, I am not really different from my perception of some of our politicians that I have been quick to judge. I can also see that my perception of them was never an accurate view of who they really were. While we often focus on differences, we are psychologically more like others than different from others. (This is not to say that we cannot oppose some of our politicians' decisions and policies.)

Most People Do the Best They Can

It is my belief that most people do the best they can in any situation. They do their best considering their beliefs, conditioning, experiences, insecurities, etc. This includes people doing destructive or hurtful things. If they could do better, they would, and maybe in the next moment they will. In hindsight, I can see how I did racist things when young because of ignorance and false information about others, family conditioning, my insecurities, and pain related to an abusive childhood. My behavior was unfortunate, but it was all I knew to do. In later years, I have also seen myself act in ways I did not like in spite of knowing better. For example, there have been times I have not been able to open my heart, even though I wanted to. Seeing this about ourselves as well as others — *while not condoning hurtful behavior* — shows us our "sameness" with others and softens the aspect of blame. It also suggests that the behavior of others can be more about them than about us, even when we seem to be a target for them. We do not need to take some things personally. When we take things personally, we can create a reaction in us that clouds perceptions and reduces effectiveness.

Some Ideals for Social Action I Have Adopted
Over the Years

(1) It is usually better to be *for* instead of *against* something or someone. Acting *for* something is more positive, less abrasive and polarizing, and more effective in the long run. (2) It is generally better to come from a place of "action" rather than "reaction," perhaps depending on the situation. Such a position is less tainted by judgments of others, self-righteousness, and one's own emotions, and can be less polarizing. (Emotions can provide energy for taking positive action, but be aware that they can also impede the clarity of one's actions and have a negative impact.) (3) Making lasting changes will most likely come through love — love for all concerned, for example, not just love for those who might be called "victims," but for so-called "perpetrators" as well. (4) There is value in putting one's heart behind an endeavor, while not being attached to the outcome, although one can have goals. In my experience, regardless of my efforts, the outcome is usually not in my hands, and attachment to an outcome is a good set-up for frustration. A better approach is to be open to whatever outcome occurs. (5) It is valuable to see our "sameness" *and* "differences" (with multi-cultural work, recognize and respect differences of culture and experiences of racism, for example) (6) Patience with ourselves and others, and with situations and "the world" is ideal. (7) Only when we accept ourselves as we are can we really accept others as they appear to be to us; otherwise, our self-rejection can be projected onto others as a rejection of who they are (as we perceive them). (8) It is imperative that we try to be OK with the fact that we will make mistakes and will even fall far short of our ideals at times. (9) It is important to hold ideals for which to strive while being aware of the "reality" of a situation *and* being able to handle the gap between the two. This was one of Martin Luther King's strengths. It is within this gap that learning, growth, and change tend to happen. (10) When we can, it is ideal to act in a way that diminishes barriers between people rather than increases them. This is not always possible.

Conclusions

We can only come to integrate such positive ideals into our daily lives when we learn to know ourselves. As long as we are unconsciously projecting onto others, have a need to be right, are self-righteousness and arrogant, have anger related to our childhood issues, have a tendency to overreact, etc., we will probably be less successful in the long run. In this light, the adage, "know thyself," is essential for effective social action. Self-knowledge makes it more likely we will come more from a place of love instead of fear, hate, or anger. It makes it possible for us to realize within ourselves the changes we want the world to have (paraphrasing words often attributed to Gandhi).

I have spent a lot of time looking at how we separate ourselves from each other. But what interests me more is how I separate myself from those whose actions or ideals I oppose. Within my human insecurities, what labels, stereotypes, or concepts do I use to feel better than them and judge them? Can I work for what I believe in, perhaps through social action, without losing my connection to them, without an "us vs them" approach — or can I *at least* hold that as an ideal? *And, most fundamentally, can I allow myself the great privilege of loving them?*

Two Exercises to break Through the Illusions of "Enemy," "Us vs Them," Separation from Others

"Just Like Me" Exercise

When around others, look directly at one person after another, and as you look at each one, say to yourself one or more phrases which refers to your common human experience. Pick a quality you imagine, or have recognized, about yourself and say, "Just like me, this person _____ " (fill in the blank: has jealousy at times, can be insecure, wants to be happy, has anger sometimes, has a good heart, etc.). You could do this while sitting on a park bench, shopping, walking down the street, seeing other drivers on your way to work, etc. Try to feel each statement rather than just doing it as a habit. If you do it often enough, gradually it can change your life. (A number of teachers teach this Buddhist practice. This variation is similar to one taught by Aura Glaser ["The Hidden Treasure of the Heart," Aura Glaser, *Shambhala Sun*, http://www.shambhalasun.com/index. php?option=com_content&task=view&id=3106&Itemid=247 {accessed August 6, 2013}])

"Without a Story" Exercise

Byron Katie, author of *Loving What Is*, teaches that our stressful stories about ourselves and others keep us from opening our hearts. When we let go of our stories, we have the possibility of accessing the love that is within us. Here is an adaptation of an exercise of hers that you can do in a quiet space. Pick someone you have issues with. (Do not start with someone with whom you have had a traumatic experience.) First see the person in your mind's eye while you remain aware of your story about him or her. Observe how you react as you do this. What do you feel? How does your body respond? Then take a moment to clear your head of your story, your feelings, and the person's image. Then imagine seeing the person again, but without any story about who he or she is. See how the person appears to you, how that feels, and what you observe in yourself.

Four Helpful Resources:

Difficult Conversations, How to Discuss What Matters Most, Douglas Stone, Bruce Patton, and Sheila Heen, c1999. (An excellent book on communicating.)

Radical Acceptance, Embracing Your Life With the Heart of a Buddha, Tara Brach, c2003. (Focuses on self-acceptance and acceptance of life experiences. This book by a psychotherapist comes from the Buddhist tradition but has universal applications.)

Radical Self-Acceptance, Tara Brach, 3-CD set. (This set comes from the Buddhist tradition but has universal applications.)

The Story Factor: Inspiration, Influence, and Persuasion Through the Art of Storytelling, Annette Simmons, 2nd edition, c2006. (Chapter 7 of this book discusses the importance of finding common ground [similar desires, ideals, etc.] with someone you want to influence. The chapter offers a number of valuable insights for social activists who want to create positive change by motivating or influencing others. Chapter 8 stresses the importance of listening to people we want to change.)

APPENDIX 4

The following are ideas I believe are important to share with young people when addressing the issues of prejudice, discrimination, and social justice. I often include these ideas when co-leading workshops in schools. (In my community, most of the students I work with happen to be white.) Most of this information can be found in Chapters 11 and 12.

SOME THOUGHTS FOR YOUNG PEOPLE ABOUT PURSUING SOCIAL JUSTICE AND OVERCOMING PREJUDICE[xxxviii]

©2014 by Bill Drake, All Rights Reserved,
www.healracism.com

Why Work to Overcome Prejudice and Create a Better World?

Some of us are naturally drawn to care about social justice, fairness, and creating a better world for all people. Some of us act out of having awakened to unconditional love, love not as an idea but as a reality that is lived, or perhaps, "lives you." When this love is present, and not distorted by our thoughts, beliefs, and other feelings, it naturally moves toward kindness and away from prejudice and doing harm. Martin Luther King spoke of this love. But even if we do not yet know this love, are not attracted to social justice, or do not think social justice matters, working to end prejudice in ourselves and our society personally benefits us. It helps us be more whole, make connections with others, and be more able to give and receive love. It adds meaning to our lives and makes them more rewarding in the long run. Most of us have many years left on the planet. As long as we are here, why not make our time more rewarding?

---

xxxviii "Prejudice" refers to judgments of, or biases against, others that are not based on facts.

Becoming Aware of White Privilege

As a white person, "white privilege" (i.e., having the advantages of being white) can be hard to see because it is so much a part of my life. Yet, if I look, it is everywhere: throughout my life, society, and the world I live in. I would never have gotten some of the jobs I have had were I not white. I would never have been able to rent some of the apartments I have lived in were I a person of color. In many stores, were I a person of color, I would have been looked at with suspicion instead of respect. Many of the advantages I have had in my life have been because of my whiteness, and my advantages existed because of others' disadvantages.

Not Letting Guilt and Shame Get in Our Way

We all feel guilt or regret at times. Two areas of guilt have come up for me as a white person: (1) guilt for racism or prejudice that arises within me in the present, or has arisen in the past, in thoughts, feelings, and/or actions for which I am responsible; (2) guilt for what I did not create, but have inherited as a white citizen (racist history/society, white privilege, etc.). Guilt can be useful if it is not excessive and if it encourages us to make amends and avoid repeating our mistakes. Negative prejudiced thoughts may arise — we are all human — but we can recognize and question them instead of acting on them. The healthiest response is to forgive ourselves when appropriate and put what we have learned to good use. (Shame — the belief that we are bad rather than that we have done something wrong — is never useful.)

Those of us who have unintentionally inherited, and benefit from, systems that have been oppressive or destructive in other ways can realize that these things are not our creation or our fault. As anti-racism activist Tim Wise has pointed out, we can look for ways to change them.

The feeling of shame can get in the way of seeing and functioning clearly and being a good ally to people of color. For example, it can cause us to hold back from doing something that could be helpful and positive. It can also cause us to interact with people of color in a way that is distorted or off balance because of our feeling uncomfortable. Shame can also eat away at us and have a negative effect on our well-being.

Endeavor to accept yourself as you are, including your prejudices and other parts you would feel shame about. Self-acceptance does not mean acting on undesirable impulses or condoning racism or prejudice, nor does it preclude working toward overcoming some of your limitations. When you deny or suppress aspects of yourself that you consider undesirable, they tend to become less conscious and can bear a greater influence on you. When you are aware of and accept them, they are more likely to be transformed, or at least to have a less destructive influence on you.

Focusing on What is Possible and Avoiding Becoming Overwhelmed

It is easy to look at the news, or what seems to be the troubling state of the world, and feel overwhelmed or hopeless. (For the moment, let's put aside the fact that news tends to focus on negative events and ignore positive ones and is not at all an objective picture.) It is a mistake to think our small positive efforts are inconsequential due to the "big picture" that seems so negative.

Each step we take toward creating a less prejudiced world — and, especially, each step we take toward overcoming our own prejudices, making connections with others, and being more open-hearted — has enormous consequences over time, if not in the short run. Fifty years ago I realized racism and prejudice were wrong. Because of shifts in my understanding and my taking steps to overcome some of my prejudices over the past decades,

I have directly and indirectly affected the lives of thousands of people. This is not to boast, but to give you a real life example. As I grew and changed, how I related to people changed, and I had a more positive effect on others. This involved connecting with many people through several media (writing, personal interactions, radio programs, etc.). Many of the people I affected positively then went on to affect many people in their lives more positively. Just as this has been the case in my life, it can be the case in your life as well. The little things in our daily lives can have enormous effects in the world, just as a small pebble thrown into a still pond sends out countless ripples. But it is important to see that fundamentally this change begins within each of us. As we change ourselves, we make contributions to others and to the world, in more ways than we can ever know. Instead of getting lost in what you think is the big picture, especially if it seems overwhelming or hopeless, focus more on what is in front of you, especially on the work you can do on yourself.

APPENDIX 5

QUESTIONS FOR CLASS DISCUSSIONS, BOOK CLUBS, OR INDIVIDUAL REFLECTION

Bill Drake, www.healracism.com

These questions are designed to help readers think, learn something about themselves, learn something about the experience of others, grow to be a more loving and balanced person, and/or feel inspired to work toward a more loving and just society. Questions can be addressed in a journal and/or a group discussion.

Chapter 1: The Roots of My Family's Racism

1. Do you know, or can you imagine, what prejudices your ancestors might have had? If so, what sorts of experiences or situations could have contributed to those prejudices?

2. Do you know, or can you imagine, if they were targets of prejudice? If so, what might they have experienced?

3. Are there things your ancestors did that you consider positive? Things you would consider negative? Explain.

4. Do you believe that your ancestors had certain qualities — either positive or negative — that were passed down to your own family? If so, what are they?

5. What beliefs, values, or prejudices that you possess might have been passed down from your ancestors?

6. How do you think the institution of slavery, and laws that supported it, have affected race relations today?

Chapter 2: My Family and Jim Crow

7. How might a hundred years of Black Codes and then Jim Crow laws have affected the views of blacks and whites about themselves and others today?

8. How might the system of segregation have contributed to perpetuating false myths about black people?

Chapter 3: My Mother's Legacy

9. Which of your mother's beliefs were also held by her parents?

10. Are you aware of any prejudices your mother had or has? If so, what are they? What are possible reasons for these prejudices?

11. In what ways has your mother influenced the way you are? In what ways are you like her? In what ways are you different from her?

12. Has your mother had any prejudices that you have also seen in yourself? If so, what are they?

Chapter 4: In My Father's Shadow

13. What beliefs that have been held by your father were also held by his parents?

14. Are you aware of any prejudices your father had or has? If so, what are they? What are possible reasons for these prejudices?

15. In what ways has your father influenced the way you are? In what ways are you like him? In what ways are you different from him?

16. Has your father had any prejudices that you have also seen in yourself? If so, what are they?

Chapter 5: My Brothers and Me

17. If you have siblings, how have they influenced you?

Chapter 6: A Life-Changing Friendship

18. Have you had a friend or mentor who has had a strong influence on your life? If so, what has been the effect on you?

Chapter 7: Waking Up to My Own Racism

19. What prejudices, past or present, have you noticed within yourself? Have you questioned them? If so, what experiences have influenced you to question them?

Chapter 8: Significant Experiences Along the Way

20. What experiences related to prejudice have affected or influenced you in a significant way?

Chapter 9: My Spiritual Journey into Greater Awareness

21. Have religious teachings influenced your thoughts or feelings about groups of people who are different from yourself? If so, how?

22. Have your religious or spiritual beliefs or practices changed during your life? If so, how? What influences or experiences caused them to change?

23. Have you had any spiritual experiences that have affected how you view or feel about others? If so, what were they? How did they affect you?

Chapter 10: Some Causes and Effects of Racism and Other Forms of Prejudice

24. Have you experienced prejudice from others? If so, how has that affected you?

25. What groups of people might you be prejudiced toward? If you can, explain why.

26. How does prejudice hurt the target of prejudice?

27. How does prejudice or racism hurt the person who is prejudiced or has racist beliefs?

28. How does the oppression of one race by another cause harm to both races?

1. Learning Prejudice

29. How have your observations of role models in your life influenced you with regard to prejudice?

30. Have you had prejudices that you were taught to have by others? If so, what are they? Do you still believe what you were taught? If not, what caused you to change your beliefs? Do you ever notice yourself acting as if you still believe them? If so, explain.

2. Generalizing from Negative Experiences

31. Have you had negative experiences of people different from you that have resulted in your holding negative beliefs or prejudices about whole groups of people? If so, explain.

3. Perceiving Others as "Different" Leading to Feelings of Fear and Separation

298 • *Almost Hereditary*

32. How might fear of someone we think is different from us contribute to prejudice? Give examples of this.

33. Are there times in your life that feeling separate from others made it easier for you to hurt them in some way? If so, give examples. Do you think that if you had made a positive personal connection with them, you would have behaved differently? If so, explain.

4. Low Self-Esteem in Both Victims and Perpetrators of Prejudice

34. Give examples you have seen (including examples related to political and business leaders, books, television programs, movies, advertisements, etc.) which might encourage the view that white people should have more value than people of other races. How might these affect nonwhites? Whites?

35. How might low self-esteem or insecurity contribute to prejudice? Are there times when you may have been critical of others to make yourself feel better in some way? If so, give examples.

5. Judging Faults We Perceive in Others That Are Unconscious Within Ourselves

36. Have you ever had anyone judge you for something that you believe is true about them? If so, give examples.

37. Are you aware of having judged someone for something that is true about you? If so, give examples.

6. Stereotyping

38. How is stereotyping harmful?

39. Have you experienced being stereotyped by others? If so, how did that affect you?

40. Have you ever had stereotypes about a racial, ethnic, or other group? If so, explain.

41. Did you ever treat members of a group differently because of a stereotype? If so, how might that have affected them?

42. Give examples of groups of people being stereotyped in your community or society, in the past or present.

43. What is the problem with using labels like "racist" or "redneck"? Have you ever done this? If so, explain.

44. List all the derogatory labels you can think of that stereotype people according to race, ethnicity, or any other group designation. Have you ever used any of them? If so, which ones? How do you feel about it now?

45. Give an actual or a hypothetical example of a self-fulfilling prophecy that relates to a stereotype.

7. Scapegoating

46. How is scapegoating harmful?

47. Have you experienced being scapegoated by others? If so, explain. How did that affect you?

48. Have you ever scapegoated a racial, ethnic, or other group by blaming them for a problem in society? For a problem you have had? If so, explain. Did you treat members of the group unfairly? If so, how might that have affected them?

49. Give examples of groups of people being scapegoated in your community or society, in the past or present.

8. Lack of Awareness of One's Racism That May Cause Unintentional Harm

50. Have you ever unintentionally hurt someone out of ignorance that what you said or did was harmful? If so, how did it affect the other person? How do you feel about it now?

Chapter 11: Healing Racism and Prejudice in Ourselves

51. If we want to heal racism and prejudice in our communities and society, why is it important to start with ourselves?

1. Broadening Our Understanding through Education and Life Experiences

52. Have you had experiences that have helped you overcome or diminish prejudices in yourself? If so, what were they and how did they affect you?

53. How can education help diminish prejudices? Are there ways educational experiences have lessened your own prejudices? Explain.

54. What books, courses, or workshops might help one to reduce prejudice? Which, if any, are you inclined to seek out for yourself?

2. Some Steps to Overcome Prejudice and Develop Compassion

55. What experiences or techniques might you try in order to help you overcome or lessen prejudices you might have? List steps you could take. If you are willing, follow through. How can you find support to help you with this?

3. Becoming Aware of and Examining Our Judgments and Stories About Others

56. What are some judgments you have about qualities, behaviors, and/or beliefs you see in other people who particularly bother you? Try to find several that are true about you in the present or have been true about you in the past.

57. Have you ever questioned one of your judgments and discovered that it was not valid or not completely valid? If so, give examples.

58. In what ways are criticisms you have, or have had, of your mother true about yourself? Of your father?

59. Describe a story you believed about someone that kept you from liking or loving them.

60. What does the statement, "We tend to see the world as we are rather than how it actually is," mean to you?[1]

4. Overcoming Self-Righteousness

61. How might feeling "right" or self-righteous block communication?

62. Have there been times you have been so stuck in being "right" that you have not been able to open up to or communicate well with someone else? Give examples.

63. If you experience being self-righteousness, what would help you overcome it in order to make a more positive connection to other people?

5. Developing Self-Awareness

64. Why is self-awareness important?

65. What might you do to increase your self-awareness?

6. Accepting Ourselves

66. In terms of seeing parts of yourself that you might not admire, such as prejudice, why is self-acceptance important?

67. What is the problem with denying or suppressing parts of yourself you might not admire?

68. Have you become more accepting of so-called negative qualities within yourself and, as a result, become more accepting of others who appear to have the same qualities? If so, give examples.

69. What is the difference between *having* negative thoughts and feelings and *acting* on them?

70. How might it be helpful to acknowledge and embrace emotional pain or a feeling such as anger (without acting it out)?

71. How might shame or excessive guilt lessen white people's abilities to be good allies for nonwhites who experience discrimination?

72. How might a moderate amount of guilt be to our benefit?

73. How might it be valuable for you to forgive yourself for having done something harmful to someone else?

74. What qualities that you admire in others can you see in yourself?

7. Overcoming Separateness by Seeing Our Sameness

75. Describe several ways all people are the same or similar.

76. Describe several ways human beings are interdependent.

77. If you are not a member of a group that has suffered oppression, when or how have you felt oppressed in your life? As a child around some adults? As a student around some teachers? As a young person being targeted for prejudice by other young people? As a woman treated unfairly by men? Give some examples. Do those experiences give you more empathy with oppressed people, even though your experiences may seem trivial compared to theirs?

8. Honoring Diversity

78. How might it be of value to experience and appreciate the lives and culture of people who are different from us, including those from different races and ethnic groups?

79. What could you do to learn more about people with cultures different from yours?

80. What might be the problem with being "colorblind" and seeing all people in the same way?

9. Understanding and Accepting Unintentional Racist Behavior

81. Have you ever said or done something that hurt another person without meaning to? If so, give examples.

82. Have you ever felt hurt by another person because you misunderstood something they said or did? If so, give examples.

83. Have you ever overreacted, or seen someone else overreact, to a situation due to a misunderstanding? If so, what happened.

10. Love

84. What does the statement, "When we start to love others, our experience of them improves," mean to you?[2] Have you experienced this? If so, give an example.

85. Have you ever experienced "agape," or unconditional love for all people? If so, what effect has the experience had on your relationship to others?

Chapter 12: Healing Racism and Prejudice in Our Communities and the World

1. Reducing Our Prejudices by Connecting with People Different from Ourselves

86. How might making a connection with and developing love for others against whom you are prejudiced help to heal that prejudice?

87. Have you ever had a prejudice change as a result of getting to know someone against whom you were prejudiced? If so, give an example.

88. How could you connect with people against whom you might feel prejudiced?

2. Becoming Aware of White Privilege

89. If you are white, list examples of situations in which your being white has given you an advantage over nonwhites.

90. Describe situations, if any, in which you have been disadvantaged due to your race, religion, beliefs, cultural identity, sexual identity, or your appearance to others.

91. How might society benefit if white privilege did not exist?

92. If you are white: If ending white privilege would mean that you would have fewer advantages or less power than you have had or now have, would you be willing to accept that? Elaborate.

3. Breaking Down Barriers Between Ourselves and Those Whose Beliefs and Actions We Oppose

93. What do you think Martin Luther King meant when he advocated focusing on opposing injustice, not a person or people perpetrating the injustice?[3]

94. Imagine someone growing up in a very different world from the one in which you grew up and how that person might be different from you because of it. How might the person's beliefs be different? His or her behavior?

95. How can two different people hold opposing views, yet each be just as convinced as the other that his or her view is right and the other person's view is wrong?

96. Do you tend to seek out things to read or listen to that support your point of view rather than challenge it? If so, what sources do you rely on that reinforce your point of view? What sources might you expose yourself to that would help you also understand the opposite view?

4. Acting Effectively Against Prejudice and Discrimination

97. Have you ever been around others who have used prejudicial or derogatory language (against blacks or gays, for example)? If so, how have you felt about it? Did you object? If so, how? What might you have done differently, if anything?

98. What steps could you take to take a stand against prejudice?

99. Why is how we communicate with those we oppose important?

5. Examining Our Motives

100. Why is it important to understand one's motives for doing social justice work and/or helping others to unlearn prejudice?

6. Addressing Prejudice in Educational Settings

101. Have you ever observed situations where bullying or prejudicial treatment was happening? How did you feel? Were you able to support the person or people being targeted? What might you have done differently?

102. Have you ever participated in bullying or prejudicial treatment? If so, how did that affect the targeted person or people? If so, why do you think you did that? How do you feel about it now?

103. If you are a student or an employee at a school, what might be done on your campus to lessen prejudice and foster appreciation of people of different races, backgrounds, etc.?

7. Not Overlooking the Trees for the Forest

104. In what ways can small steps to create social change have a big effect over time?

105. What small steps could you take toward healing prejudice in your life?

106. What small steps could you take toward healing prejudice in your community?

107. What small steps could you take toward healing prejudice in the world?

APPENDIX 6
FAMILY GENEALOGY

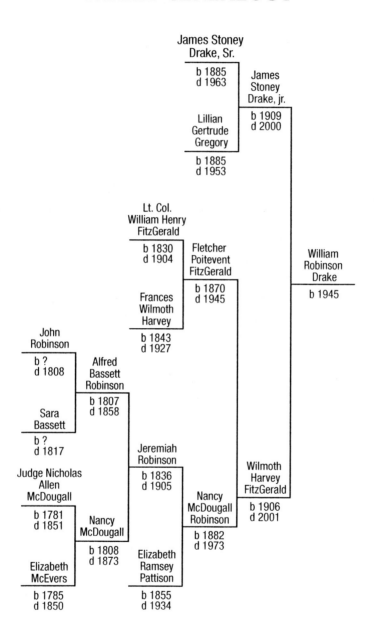

James Stoney
Drake, Sr.

b 1885
d 1963

James
Stoney
Drake, jr.

b 1909
d 2000

Lillian
Gertrude
Gregory

b 1885
d 1953

Lt. Col.
William Henry
FitzGerald

b 1830
d 1904

Fletcher
Poitevent
FitzGerald

b 1870
d 1945

William
Robinson
Drake

b 1945

Frances
Wilmoth
Harvey

b 1843
d 1927

John
Robinson

b ?
d 1808

Alfred
Bassett
Robinson

b 1807
d 1858

Sara
Bassett

b ?
d 1817

Jeremiah
Robinson

b 1836
d 1905

Wilmoth
Harvey
FitzGerald

b 1906
d 2001

Judge Nicholas
Allen
McDougall

b 1781
d 1851

Nancy
McDougall
Robinson

b 1882
d 1973

Nancy
McDougall

b 1808
d 1873

Elizabeth
Ramsey
Pattison

Elizabeth
McEvers

b 1785
d 1850

b 1855
d 1934

APPENDIX 7

SLAVE NAMES IN NANCY ROBINSON'S ACCOUNT BOOK

(Jan. 1, 1861-1865, including division of slaves in Alfred Robinson's estate)

I have included this appendix with the names of slaves owned by my maternal great-great-grandparents and their sons, Jeremiah and Douglas, as recorded by my great-great-grandmother, in order to acknowledge those individuals who suffered the pain of human bondage at the hands of my ancestors. Some slaves mentioned in Chapter 1 are not listed here.

Page numbers refer to page numbers in the account book.
? = name or initial can not be read with certainty

Adam (p.2, child) (p.4, Adam [?], Nancy's inheritance) (p.5, child, born April 1857)

Alfred (?) (p.4, Douglas' inheritance)

Alice (p.2, child) (p.5, child, born Nov. 20, 1862)

Alie (p.4, Douglas' inheritance)

Allen (p.4, Douglas' inheritance)

Alston (p.2) (p.3) (p.4, Alstin, Nancy's inheritance)

Amanda (?) J (?) (p.4, Jerry's inheritance)

Amelia (p.2) (p.3) (p.4, Nancy's inheritance)

Amelia (?) (p.4, Jerry's inheritance)

Amy (p.4, Jerry's inheritance)

Analine (?) (p.4, Jerry' inheritance)

Ann (p.2) (p.3) (p.4, Jerry's inheritance)

B George (p.4, Nancy's inheritance)

Becca, Rebecca (p.2) (p.3) (p.4, Becky, Nancy's inheritance)

Ben (p.2) (p.3) (p.4, Nancy's inheritance) (p.5, child, born Dec. 1852)

Bettie (p.4, Douglas' inheritance)

Bill (?) (p.4, Jerry's inheritance)

Claiborn (?) (p.4, Douglas' inheritance)

Caroline (p.4, Jerry's inheritance)

Caroline (p.4, Douglas' inheritance)

Cassy (?) (second name ?) (p.4, Jerry's inheritance)

Charlie (?) (p.4, Jerry's inheritance)

Clinton (p.4, Douglas' inheritance)

Dallis (Dullis?) (p.2) (p.3 Dallas?) (p.4, Dallis [?], Nancy's inheritance)

Daniel Whiteman (p.2, child) (p.4, Daniel, Douglas' inheritance) (p.5, Daniel Whitman, child, born May 17, 1862)

Dick (p.2) (p.3) (p.4, Nancy's inheritance)

Doctor Sykes (p.2, child) (p.3, Doctor S.) (p.4, Doctor, Nancy's inheritance) (p.5, child, born August 1859)

Eamona (?) (p.4, Douglas' inheritance)

Eli (p.4, Jerry's inheritance) (p.5, child, born Sept. 10, 1853)

Eliza (p.4, Douglas' inheritance)

Eliza Mc (p.2) (p.3 Liser Mc) (p.4, Nancy's inheritance)

Eliza R (p.2) (p.4, Nancy's inheritance)

Ella Mutitan (?) (Matilda ?) (p.2, child) (p.3, Ella) (p.5, Ella Matilda [?], child, born Nov. 1860)

Ellen (p.4, Douglas' inheritance)

Elva (p.2, child) (p.5, Elva Cornelia [?], child, born March 15, 1862)

Emma (p.4, Douglas' inheritance)

Esther (p.2) (p.3) (p.4, Ester [?], Nancy's inheritance)

Eugenia (second name?) (p.2, child) (p.5, Eugena [?], child, born June 1861 at Alban)

Fannie (p.4, Douglas' inheritance)

Filmore (p.2, child) (p.3) (p.5, child, born Dec. 1858)

Flora (p.2) (p.3) (p.4, Nancy's inheritance)

Forrest (p.2, child) (p.5, Gen. Forest, child, born Feb. 28, 1864)

Fredric (?) (p.3)

(Gen. [Nathan Bedford] Forest — see Forest [/Forrest])

(Gen. Robert Lee — see Lee)

(Gen. [William] Loring — see Loring)

(Gen. [Sterling] Price — see Price)

Genny (p.4, Douglas' inheritance)

(first initial ?) George (p.4, Douglas' inheritance)

George Carter (p.4, Jerry's inheritance)

George (p.2) (p.3) (p.4, George J [?], Jerry's inheritance)

George Jack (p.4, Jerry's inheritance [listed separately from "George J [?]")

Grace (p.4, Douglas' inheritance)

Grova (?) (p.4, Douglas' inheritance)

Guy (?) (p.4, Douglas' inheritance)

Hannah (p.4, Douglas' inheritance)

Harriet (p.4, Douglas' inheritance)

Harry (p.2, child) (p.3) (p.5, child, born May 1860)

Harry Wood (?) (p.2)

Haywood (p.3) (p.4, Nancy's inheritance)

Henrietta (?) (p.2, child) (p.3) (p.4, Nancy's inheritance) (p.5, child, born Sept. 27, 1853)

(initial ?) Henny (?) (p.2) (p.4, Henny [?],Nancy's inheritance)

Henry (p.2) (p.3) (p.4, Nancy's inheritance)

Henry B (p.4, Douglas' inheritance)

Howard (?) (p.2, child) (p.5, child, born July 15, 1862)

Howel (p.2) (p.3)

Howena (?) (p.4, Douglas' inheritance)

Inan (?) (p.2 [female])

Jack (p.2) (p.3) (p.4, Nancy's inheritance)

James (p.2) (p.3) (p.4, Nancy's inheritance)

Jaspen (p.4, Douglas' inheritance)

Jasper (?) (p.4, Douglas' inheritance)

Jim (p.4, Nancy's inheritance)

Joe Bell (p.2) (p.3) (p.4, Joe Ball [?], Nancy's inheritance)

Joe Gibson (p.2) (p.3?) (p.4, Joe Gib, Nancy's inheritance)

John (?) Gary (?) (p.4, Douglas' inheritance)

John Louie (p.2) (p.4, John L, Nancy's inheritance)

John Perry (p.2) (p.3, John Pery) (p.4, Nancy's inheritance)

John S. (p.3)

June (p.4, Douglas' inheritance)

Lanna (?) (Laura?) (p.4, Douglas' inheritance)

Leann (?) (p.4, Douglas' inheritance)

Lee (p.2, child) (p.5, Gen. Robert Lee, child, born Nov. 7, 1863)

Liser (?) R. (p.3)

Lizzie (p.2) (p.4, Douglas' inheritance)

Lizzie (p.4, Nancy's inheritance)

Loring (p.5, Gen. [William] Loring, child, born 1864 [?] [belonging to Douglas])

Louis J (?) (p.4, Douglas' inheritance)

Louis L (p.4, Douglas' inheritance)

Louis T (p.2) (p.3, Lewis [?] T) (p.4, Lewis Tul [?], Nancy's inheritance)

Lovey (p.4, Jerry's inheritance)

Lucinda (?) (p.2, child) (p.3) (p.4, Nancy's inheritance) (p.5, child, born July [5th?] 1851)

Lucy (p.4, Jerry's inheritance)

Manerva (p.2, child) (p.3, Minerva) (p.5, Manerva, child, born Sept. 1859)

Maria (?) (p.2 [female]) (p.4, Maria [?], Douglas' inheritance)

Maria (?) (p.4, Nancy's inheritance)

Mariah (p.3)

Margaret (p.2, child) (p.4, Jerry's inheritance) (p.5, child, born Sept. 1858)

Martha (p.2) (p.3, Marthey?) (p.4, L. [?] Martha [?], Nancy's inheritance)

Martha Jane (p.2, child) (p.3) (p.5, Martha [?] [second name ?], child, born April 8, 1863)

Mary B (?) (p.4, Jerry's inheritance)

Mary Jane (p.2) (p.4, Nancy's inheritance)

Mary (?) Johnson (p.4, Douglas' inheritance)

Mary Mc (?) (p.4, Douglas' inheritance)

Mary S (?) (p.4, Jerry's inheritance)

May (p.2, child) (p.4, May [?], Jerry's inheritance) (p.5, May Ronean [?], child, born April 30, 1863)

Mayset (?) (p.3)

Milly (p.2)

Molly (p.2, child) (p.3, Mollie) (p.4, Mollie, Nancy's inheritance) (p.5, child, born Sept. 1857)

Narcissa (p.2, child) (p.3) (p.5, child, born Sept. 1857 [1859?])

Nat (p.4, Jerry's inheritance)

Oliver (?) (p.4, Jerry's inheritance)

Paul (p.2) (p.4, Nancy's inheritance)

Peggy (p.2) (p.3) (p.4, Nancy's inheritance)

Peter (p.2) (p.3 Peter B.) (p.4, Nancy's inheritance)

Phillis (second name?) (p.2, child) (p.5, child, born August 1861 [at Alban?])

Preston (?) (p.4, Douglas' inheritance)

Price (p.2, child) (p.5, Gen. Price, child, born Nov. 28, 1863)

Pricilla (p.4, Douglas' inheritance)

Rebecca (p.2, child) (p.5, child, born Jan. 7, 1864)

Rhoda (p.3) (p.4, Nancy's inheritance)

Rosanna (Rosann?) (p.2, child)

Roxana (second name?) (p.2, child) (p.5, Roxana, child, born Aug. 1861 [at Alban?])

Ruthann (?) (p.2)

Sallie (p.2) (p.3) (p.4, Sally, Nancy's inheritance)

Sally (second name ?) (p.4, Nancy's inheritance)

Sarah (p.2) (p.3)

Sarah Lana (?) Ann (?) (p.2) (p.3 Sarah Law) (p.4, Sarah Landen [?], Nancy's inheritance)

Simon (p.4, "not remembered in division" of Alfred's estate)

Sisey (p.3)

Susan (p.4, Douglas' inheritance)

Sylvia (?) (p.4, Jerry's inheritance)

T. (?) Bete (p.3)

Thomas (?) (second name ?) (p.4, Nancy's inheritance)

Toby (p.4, Douglas' inheritance)

Tom (p.2) (p.3) (p.4, Nancy's inheritance)

Tom (?) G. (?) (p.4, Jerry's inheritance)

V. (?) Henry (p.3)

Victone (?) (p.4, Douglas' inheritance)

Wm (?) Taylor (?) (p.5, child, Louis and Leona [?], born Jan. [?] [2?] 1865)

Y (initial ?) Pete (p.2) (p.4, Nancy's inheritance)

Totally illegible:
p.2: 1 child name
p.3; 4 names
p.4 Jerry's inheritance: 16 names
p.4 Douglas's inheritance: 5 names
p.4 Nancy's inheritance: 5 names
p.5: 1 child born 1865

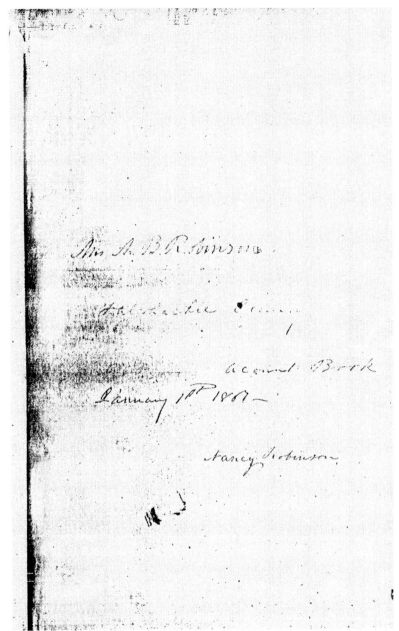

Title page (page 1) of Nancy Robinson account book: "Mrs. A. B. Robinson
/ Talahatchie County / Account Book / January 1ˢᵗ 1861 / Nancy Robinson"
(Tallahatchie is misspelled.) Copy of document courtesy of the Mississippi
Department of Archives and History.

Page 5 of account book: "Negro children (ages) belonging to Mrs. A. B. Robinson" Some of the children were named after friends or Confederate generals, including Dr. Sykes, Gen. Robert Lee (the commanding general of the Confederate forces by the end of the war), Gen. Price (Gen. Sterling Price), Gen. Forest (Gen. Nathan Bedford Forest), Gen. Loring (Gen. William Loring). Twenty-nine children are named with birth dates that range from 1851 to 1865. Copy of document courtesy of the Mississippi Department of Archives and History.

ACKNOWLEDGMENTS

Many people played a hand in the creation of this book. First and foremost is my wife, Joan Ramsey. I thank her for her loving support; her sharing of her professional expertise as a psychotherapist that added insights to my discussions of psychological phenomena; her collaboration on the discussion questions; and her extensive editing and proofreading.

Francisco Lovato appeared as my publishing coach at the right stage of the endeavor. His expert guidance was essential for turning the writing into an actual book that could get into other people's hands. He also did an outstanding job of scanning and photoshopping most photographs used in the book.

Joanna Robinson and poet Molly Fisk served as writing coaches for the initial draft in the early '90s, and Joanna proofread that version. Their important assistance gave *Almost Heredity* a good start, and it might not exist without their contributions.

I am also indebted to three people who encouraged me to revisit that draft I had put aside so long ago. Jeff Ackerman, publisher of *The Union* newspaper, and Jim Olsen, both of whom read the earlier version, saw it as a project of considerable value. Steve Sanfield who, after listening to mounds of verbiage related to my resistance to resuming work on my book, said — as any Haiku-writing Zen poet worth their salt might say — "Just do it!"

Jeff Toussaint, PhD, of Old Dominion University, was the first professor to adopt my book for a university class. He has been a strong advocate for the book, and he and the students of his class, "The Cultural Politics of Peace," provided me with invaluable advice regarding revisions that the original edition needed. I am very appreciative of Dr. Toussaint's considerable support and assistance.

A number of other people read drafts of this book and provided advice or editing assistance, including my brother James Stoney Drake, 3rd, Jeff Eppes, Amelia Nebenzahl, Lisa Randall, Colleen McKinnon, Jeannie Wood, Richard Tewes, Mary Enright, Norma Watkins, Jennifer Ritterhouse, Michael Jenaye, Pat Lane, Doris Schroeder-Smith, Erica Randall, Chris Bennett, Marina Bokelman, Barbara Brown, and Neil Chesney.

I am grateful for Byron Katie, whose teachings allowed me to approach my story with an entirely different perspective.

I am indebted to community radio station KVMR FM in Nevada City, California, for giving me the opportunity to broadcast numerous programs during their annual Martin Luther King Day celebrations. Program Director Steve Baker's support for the broadcasts is especially appreciated. These programs created a foundation for some of my writing. I am also grateful to Station Manager David Levin for granting Jamal Walker, Lew Powell, and me the rights to the recording of a 2012 Martin Luther King Day program we participated in. This recording can be accessed through my website: www.healracism.com.

Encouragement has been provided by my colleagues with whom I have helped high school students unlearn prejudice: Jamal Walker, Cindy Santa Cruz-Reed, and Rev. Lew Powell, as well as our consultant Isoke Femi. During the course of our work many students, faculty members, and administrators in Nevada County, California have, in their own way, provided inspiration for this book. Among them are former Nevada County Assistant Superintendent of Schools Stan Miller; principal Dan Frisella, librarian Jill Sonnenberg, and teacher Molly Starr at Nevada Union High School; and teachers Emily Zionts and Amelia Nebenzahl at John Woolman Semester School.

Katy Hight's formatting of the book was a valuable contribution.

In the beginning, Margot Silk Forrest provided me with some very useful feedback, and Joe McHugh was kind enough to encourage me to do "something" with my family history.

I am also grateful to Su Lukasha for permission to publish writing I did for the *Community Endeavor* newspaper, and my sister-in-law, Nancy Drake, for allowing me to use my brother Fletcher's photographs. I owe a major debt to Mick Hennen and his colleagues at the Mississippi Department of Archives and History (MDAH). The MDAH provided me with a number of important photographs and documents related to my ancestors and gave me permission to reproduce them along with Nancy Robinson's diaries (which are now in the public domain). Their generous assistance has been invaluable.

I am indebted to my fellow students in Molly Fisk's "Writing Your Life" class who shared their stories and listened to mine when this book was just being conceived.

Prayers and support from the Tibetan monks from Garden Shartse Monastery in India and African elder Malidoma Somé and his friends are deeply appreciated.

Harmeet Dhillon and Priya Brandes of the San Francisco law firm Dhillon and Smith did a considerable amount of research concerning the "fair use" of material from other writers whose works I have cited. I also received assistance from Michael Chesney, Hans Larsen, and intern Dan Bollinger of the Frantz Ward law firm in Cleveland.

Ivy Cone's generous assistance resulted in the You Tube video of a presentation I did on Martin Luther King Day, January 19, 2015. The video, educational in nature, conveys to the viewer an idea of what this book is about. Laurie Woodum and Lu Mellado played important roles in the creation of my book's website.

Thanks also go to Anita, an employee at the Tallahatchie County Courthouse in Charleston, Mississippi, who did me the favor of searching every floor of the courthouse to see if she could find a portrait of Lt. Col. William Henry FitzGerald, my great-grandfather.

Mike Rounds of Rounds, Miller, and Associates provided helpful advice on epublishing.

Ed Skopal, guest lecturer at Virginia Polytechnic Institute and State University, has graciously shared my book with professors at several universities. His support for *Almost Hereditary* is much appreciated. David McKay was kind enough to scan and photoshop several of the book's photographs. His ability to improve some of my old pictures was remarkable. Thanks to photographer Chris Harada, Chapter 14 has a good picture of Jamal Walker and me. Thanks to cousins Martha Mims Johnson and Elsie Maynard for photographs of Lt. Col. William Henry FitzGerald and Frances Wilmoth Harvey FitzGerald, and to cousin William Barksdale Maynard for the photograph of Lieutenant Colonel FitzGerald and some of his men. Jan Hillegas conducted research on my great-grandfather, Lt. Col. William Henry FitzGerald. My cousin Lucie Lee Lanoux, Reinette Senum, Gangaji, Maggie McKaig, Ann Todd Jealous, Norma Watkins, Lucinda Porter, Stephenie Clague, Michael Brackney (Brackney Indexing Service), and Marjorie Fox are among those who provided helpful support, assistance, or advice.

I acknowledge my brother Fletcher, who gave the right answer to my question about race, an answer that changed my life by beginning my own journey of unlearning prejudice. Had he lived, he would have been delighted to see this book. Finally, I offer appreciation for my great-great-grandmother Nancy McDougall Robinson and the written record of her life that fell into my hands in the early '70s but was left unread for twenty years. I am honored to be able to add her words to mine. Perhaps together we can heal the wounds of our family's past.

NOTES

Introduction

1. After my great-great-grandfather died in 1858 and his plantations and slaves were divided between his wife and two children, the family owned 136 according to my great-great-grandmother's account book. The account book, which was a record of the family's slaves, has entries from January 1861 to early 1865. It lists the slaves that she and her sons inherited from Alfred's estate as well as a number of slave children born after Alfred's death. A Mississippi relative of mine, who farms some of the old plantation land, believes that the family owned at least six or seven thousand acres in that state at one time. If he is correct, since most of this would have been in Alfred's estate, he might have had more than 136 slaves during some years. Slaves were bought at different times, but many died of illness, with about 40 dying in one year. My guess is that the family could have had as many as 200 slaves. Due to these considerations, I used the estimate of "136 to 200."

2. *Harold and Maude*, movie. Regarding: "it seems to be the nature of human beings to be inconsistent," which paraphrases a quote in the movie located 41:30-41:33 minutes into the DVD version.

3. Bonastia, *Southern Stalemate*, 104.

4. Regarding my great-great-grandmother's use of different names for the same plantation, Beulah Plantation is probably what is sometimes referred to by her as both "the river place" and "the Tallahatchie place." Albion Plantation (sometimes spelled "Alban," with both names misspellings of Albin) is probably the same as "the Cassidy place."

PART I: MY FAMILY HISTORY AND ROOTS OF MY RACISM

Chapter 1: The Roots of My Family's Racism

1. Davis, *Inhuman Bondage,* 184.

2. Ibid, 197; Milton R. Konvitz, *A Century of Civil Rights* (New York: Columbia University Press), 11; and Schneider and Schneider, *Slavery in America*, 53. As a source for his demographic information, Davis refers to: "Robert William Fogel, *Without Consent or Contract: The Rise and Fall of American Slavery* (New York, W. W. Norton & Co., 1989)." Konvitz cites

"Lloyd, *The Slavery Controversy, 1831-1860*, note 17 and 226-227, 229 and 243; and Phillips, *The Central Theme of Southern History*, 34 AM. HIST. REV. 31 (1928)." Davis indicates that three-quarters of Southerners were not involved in slavery, whereas Schneider and Schneider indicate two-thirds. Konvitz considers the belief in the inferiority of blacks to be the main theme of the history of the South.

3. Berlin, Favreau, and Miller, eds., *Remembering Slavery*, xxix.

4. *Unchained Memories*, DVDs.

5. Schneider and Schneider, *Slavery in America*, 88-89.

6. Ibid, 89.

7. Kolchin, *American Slavery*, 113.

8. Escott, *Slavery Remembered*, 38-39. Escott's assessment that, "the necessities of life, as most slaves described them, were simple but supplied in adequate quantity" is based on his detailed analysis of slave narratives. My own reading of hundreds of the narratives leads me to agree with him. Rawick, who, like Escott, is an authority on the slave narratives, seems to express a different opinion in that he says it was commonly the case that slaves "were poorly fed, clothed, and housed." (*From Sundown*, p.55). I have adopted Escott's view because it seems to be the most research-based but it is possible Rawick's view is more accurate.

9. Ibid. See the notation for the preceding endnote.

10. *Mississippi, Slave Narratives,* 115.

11. *Georgia,* Part 3, *Slave Narratives,* 5-6.

12. Ibid, 105.

13. Escott, *Slavery Remembered*, 38.

14. *North Carolina,* Part 1, *Slave Narratives,* 168-169.

15. Tadman, *Speculators and Slaves*, 126. Tadman gives a quote from the 1830s from Ethan Andrews and cites "Andrews, *Slavery and the Domestic Slave Trade*, 166."

16. *North Carolina*, Part 1, *Slave Narratives*, 68-69.

17. *Mississippi*, *Slave Narratives*, 119.

18. *Alabama*, *Slave Narratives*, 260.

19. Davis, *Who is Black?*, 38.

20. *Mississippi*, *Slave Narratives*, 157-158.

21. *North Carolina*, Part 1, *Slave Narratives*, 49.

22. Boyle, *The Desegregated Heart*, 69.

23. Kolchin, *American Slavery*, 118-119.

24. Even though slave owners usually named the slaves, according to *Remembering Slavery*, on some plantations slaves were successful in pressuring their owners to allow them to name their babies after one of the parents. The book, along with *Slavery Remembered*, also notes that, although slave owners only knew first names for slaves, a number of slaves had secret surnames that connected them to some degree of a heritage or lineage. (References: Berlin, Faureau, Miller, eds., *Remembering Slavery*, xl-xli; also Escott, *Slavery Remembered*, 50.) After being freed, a number of ex-slaves took the last name of their former master, while others intentionally took a different last name.

25. A few of Nancy's slaves did receive last names. Among these exceptions were four of Nancy's slaves born during the war, whom she named after Confederate generals. One was named after General Robert Lee, the general who, by the end of the war, was the commander of the Army of Northern Virginia and the commanding general of the Confederate army. Another was named General Forest, after Gen. Nathan Bedford Forest, whose soldiers murdered over three hundred black men, women, and children at Fort Pillow, Tennessee in 1864, after the fort surrendered. Most of the blacks murdered were Union troops.

26. Burns, *The Civil War*, episode 1, DVD; "The Origin and Nature of New World Slavery," The Gilder Lehrman Institute. The Gilder Lehrman Institute makes the point about malnutrition. The other points in my sentence can be found in both sources.

27. *Georgia*, Part 3, *Slave Narratives*, 88-89.

28. Ibid, 93.

29. *Missouri*, 90, 102-103.

30. Ibid, 102-103.

31. *Alabama, Slave Narratives,* 54.

32. Rawick, *From Sundown,* 55; Kolchin, *American Slavery,* 120-121.

33. Escott, *Slavery Remembered,* 42-43.

34. Rittenhouse, *Growing Up,* 32.

35. Douglas, *Life and Times,* 66.

36. Berlin, Favreau, and Miller, eds., *Remembering Slavery,* 280. This story was part of a radio documentary detailed in the book's appendix. The source for the story is not cited.

37. *Georgia,* Part 3, *Slave Narratives,* 80.

38. *North Carolina,* Part 1, *Slave Narratives,* 65.

39. *Alabama, Slave Narratives,* 333.

40. Berlin, Favreau, and Miller, eds., *Remembering Slavery,* xvi.

41. Berry, *The Hidden Wound,* 6-7.

42. Escott, *Slavery Remembered,* 25.

43. *North Carolina,* Part 1, *Slave Narratives,* 214.

44. Kolchin, *American Slavery,* 121 (regarding Southern literature encouraging the fair treatment of slaves). Kolchin has the following citation: "Charles C. Jones, *The Religious Instruction of the Negroes. In the United States* (New York, 1969; org. pub. 1842), 159, 165; 'Rules on the Rice Estate of P. C. Weston' (1856), in Ulrich B. Phillips, ed., *Plantation and Frontier,* Vol. 1 of John R. Commons et. al., eds., *A Documentary History of American Industrial Society* (Cleveland, 1910), 116."

45. *Texas,* Part 1, *Slave Narratives,* 186.

46. *Alabama, Slave Narratives,* 102.

47. Ward, with Burns, and Burns, *The Civil War,* 26-30.

48. Foner, *History of Reconstruction,* 7.

49. "An Index to *The Civil War,*" Burns, *The Civil War,* DVDs (booklet accompanying the PBS DVD series); Burns, *The Civil War,* episode 5, DVD (regarding the figure of 3½ million soldiers who fought in the war); Cohen, "Civil War Deadlier." Ken Burns and others use the commonly cited figure of 620,000 deaths during the war. Jeannie Cohen, however, explains that historian J. David Hacker refutes that figure. His research indicates that there were probably between 650,000 and 850,000 deaths. (Historians tend to think that about two-thirds of the war's fatalities related to illness.)

50. Kelly, "Battle of Gettysburg."

51. Thompson, "Battle of Cold Harbor."

52. Foote interview "Men At War," in *The Civil War,* Ward, 270.

53. Lord, "Mississippi," 31.

54. "Victory From Within," Andersonville National Historic Site.

55. Horton and Horton, *Slavery and the Making of America,* 205.

56. Lord, "Mississippi," 33

57. Ibid, 33-36, 39.

58. *North Carolina,* Part 1, *Slave Narratives,* 156.

59. *Missouri, Slave Narratives,* 117.

60. *North Carolina,* Part 1, *Slave Narratives,* 66.

61. Ibid, 168.

62. Lord, "Mississippi," 33-36, 39.

63. *Texas,* Part 1, *Slave Narratives,* 49-50 (Frank Bell).

64. *North Carolina,* Part 1, *Slave Narratives,* 120-121.

65. *Texas,* Part 1, *Slave Narratives,* 34.

66. *Missouri, Slave Narratives,* 54.

67. *North Carolina,* Part 1, *Slave Narratives,* 13.

68. Ibid.; *The American Heritage Dictionary,* s.v. "spiritualism."

Chapter 2: The Jim Crow Era and My Family

1. Konvitz, *Century of Civil Rights,* 12-13. He cites: "Miss. Black Code, Laws of Miss.,1865, at 82."

2. Ibid, 13-14.

3. Ibid.

4. *Texas,* Part 1, *Slave Narratives,* 123.

5. Rittenhouse, *Growing Up,* 3-6.

6. Chafe, Gavins, and Korstad, *Remembering Jim Crow,* xxiii, xxix, 1.

7. Litwack, *Trouble in Mind,* 19-20.

8. Ibid, 95, 98-99.

9. Osborne, *Miles to Go,* 29.

10. George, *Life Under Jim Crow,* 39.

11. Ibid, 37.

12. Packard, *American Nightmare,* 102-103.

13. George, *Life Under Jim Crow,* 73.

14. Osborne, *Miles to Go,* 20.

15. Woodward, *The Strange Career,* 98.

16. Lesher, *George Wallace*, 101-102. Lesher's footnote 38 cites "interview with (former governor) Jim Folsom, March 15, 1956."

17. *Missouri, Slave Narratives*, 81-82.

18. Equal Justice Initiative, "Lynching in America: Confronting the Legacy of Racial Terror."

19. Fears, "Atlanta, Ready to Revisit."

20. Davis, *Who is Black?*, 53.

21. Litwack, *Trouble in Mind*, 297, 285-286. Regarding the relationship of hatred of blacks to lynching, Litwack quotes Atlanta's Bishop Warren A. Candler who did a study of Southern lynchings. Litwack cites: "Clark, *Southern Country Editor*, 227; Ayers, *Vengeance and Justice*, 247; Wells, *Crusade for Justice*, 154-155."

22. *North Carolina*, Part 1, *Slave Narratives*, 172-173.

23. Davis, *Who is Black?*, 31, 56. Regarding acting black being equal to being black Davis cites "Joel Williamson, *New People: Miscegenation and Mulattoes in the United States*, New York: The Free Press 1980, 98-108."

24. "Separate but Equal," Separate but not Equal.

25. Rittenhouse, *Growing Up*, 14, 19, 73.

26. Ibid, 82-83, 85-90.

27. Lesher, *George Wallace*, 54.

28. Packard, *American Nightmare*, 64.

29. Bonastia, *Southern Stalemate*, 17, 86-88, 94. Bonastia cites "Benjamin Muse, *Virginia's Massive Resistance* (Gloucester, Mass.: Peter Smith, 1961), 75; 'The Voices for the Schools,' editorial, Norfolk *Virginian Pilot*, September 24, 1958, 4; Alexander S. Leidholdt, *Standing Before the Shouting Mob: Lenoir Chambers and Virginia's Massive Resistance to Public-School Integration* (Tuscaloosa: University of Alabama Press, 1997), 59; James W. Ely, Jr., *The Crisis of Conservative Virginia: The Byrd Organization and the Politics of Massive Resistance* (Knoxville: University of Tennessee Press, 1976); and James J. Hershman, Jr., 'Massive Resistance Meets Its Match:

The Emergence of a Pro-Public School Majority,' in Matthew D. Lassiter and Andrew B. Lewis, ed., *The Moderate's Dilemma: Massive Resistance to School Desegregation in Virginia* (Charlottesville: University Press of Virginia, 1998)."

30. Ibid, pp. 1, 106. Bonastia cites "Pearson quoted in Lucy Daniels, 'Blackout in Prince Edward County,' *Coronet*, August 1960, 110; Roy R. Pearson, *Setting Up Private Schools* (Farmville, VA: Prince Edward School Foundation, 1961), Special Collections, LU; 'Roy R. Pearson, 63, Retired Oil Executive, School Leader, Dies,' *Farmville Herald*, July 18, 1969, 1; R. C. Smith, *They Closed Their Schools: Prince Edward County, Virginia, 1951-1964* (Chapel Hill: University of North Carolina Press, 1965; repr. Farmville, VA: Martha E. Forrester Council of Women, 1996)."

31. Chafe, Gavins, and Korstad, *Remembering Jim Crow*, 323 (regarding today's racism having evolved out of Jim Crow).

Chapter 3: My Mother's Legacy

1. King, *Strength to Love*, 96-98. See my book's Appendix 1: Campaign to Discredit Martin Luther King.

2. "Martin Luther King, Jr. and Watts Rebellion."

Chapter 5: My Brothers and Me

1. Southern Christian Leadership Conference, *The Poor People's Campaign*. Each photographer who contributed to the book, including my brother Fletcher, retained the copyright for each of their photographs.

PART II: MY PERSONAL GROWTH AND JOURNEY OUT OF RACISM

Chapter 8: Significant Experiences Along the Way

1. Sullivan, *The Bureau*, 137-138.

2. Drake, "Message to the Black Community of Norfolk." This is a slightly edited version of my original letter.

3. Katie, "The School."

PART III: UNDERSTANDING AND HEALING PREJUDICE

Chapter 10: Some Observations on Racism
and Other Forms of Prejudice

1. *New Oxford Dictionary*, s.v. "prejudice."

2. *Webster's All-In-One*, s.v. "racism."

3. Adyashanti, meditation retreat; Isaacson, *Einstein*, 391. Adyashanti mentions specific factors that condition us whereas Einstein refers to the fact that we are very conditioned.

4. Drake, letter to the editor, January 20, 1997.

5. Vasquez and Femi, *No Boundaries*, "Handout 10: Racism is Harmful to White People." The first two points of my sentence ("…the person with racist beliefs lives with a view of the world that is distorted by false beliefs about his or her race and the race of others, is likely to have unreasonable fears of others solely due to their race. . .") were influenced by this reference.

6. See: King, *Stride*, 88; Kidwell, Noley, and Tinker, *Native American Theology*, 48-51; Lupton, *James Welch*, 23-24; *The Little Book of Bleeps*, 6, 78 (re: physicists Hagelin and Teller).

7. Berry, *The Hidden Wound*, 103.

8. Wise, *White Like Me*, 165-166.

9. Williams, *Eyes on the Prize*, 20-21.

10. Burns, speech at University of California at Davis.

11. "Why does the color 'flesh' not appear?"

12. "Do you still manufacture Indian red?"

13. Heimann, *Golden Age*.

14. 1960 Census.

15. Heinmann, *Golden Age*, 332-333.

16. Merton, "The Root of War is Fear," 276.

17. Taylor, "Education to Counter Oppression."

18. Ibid.

19. Ostrow, "Black and Asian Teens." The article referenced the Partnership at Drugfree.org for some of its information.

20. Szalavitz, "Study: Whites More Likely;" Ostrow, "Black and Asian Teens;" Price, "Study: White Kids." Szalavitz mentions the date the study was released. Price points out that participants in the study were from every state. The other details are in Ostrow's article.

21. Ostrow, "Black and Asian Teens."

22. Szalavitz, "Study: Whites More Likely."

23. Washington, "Arrest Puts Focus on Racial Profiling;" McGoey, "Shoplifter Profiling." McGoey's article is cited in regards to polls related to black men being racially profiled in stores and the fact that most shoplifters are white. The other content in my paragraph pertains to Washington's article.

24. *American Heritage Dictionary*, s.v. "self-fulfilling."

25. Mlodinow, *Subliminal*, 113.

26. Dweck, *Mindset*, 6-7, 75-76. Regarding pages 75-76 in her book, in her endnote 75 Dweck cites: "Claude M. Steele and Joshua Aronson, 'Stereotype Threat and the Intellectual Test Performance of African Americans,' *Journal of Personality and Social Psychology* 68 (1995), 797-811."

27. Ibid, 77.

28. Mlodinow, *Subliminal*, 50-51, 152-153, 156. On page 153, Mlodinow refers to research at the University of Washington which indicated that stereotyping usually occurs unconsciously. Mlodinow references this information with the following footnote: "Anthony G. Greenwald et al., 'Measuring Individual Differences in Implicit Cognition: The Implicit Association Test,' *Journal of Personality and Social Psychology* 74, no. 6 (1998): 1464-80; see also Brian A. Nosek et al., 'The Implicit Association Test at Age 7: A Methodological and Conceptual Review,' in *Automatic Processes in Social Thinking and Behavior*, ed. J. A. English (New York: Psychology Press, 2007), 265-92."

29. Rawls, *Indians of California*, 185, 201. Rawls cites: "Carl Meyer, *Bound for Sacramento: Travel Pictures of a Returned Wanderer*, Translated by Ruth Frey Axe, Introduction by Henry R. Wagner (Claremont, California: Sunders Studio Press, 1938) 279; *Marysville Express*, April 16, 1859; *Sacramento Union*, May 13, 1861; and *Marysville Appeal*, February 20, 1863."

30. Heizer, *The Destruction of California Indians*, 220-226. Heizer's text includes "An Act for the Government and Protection of Indians, April 22, 1850," and "Amendments in 1860 to the Act of April, 1850" (California Indian Indenture Act). He cites: "Chapter 133, Statutes of California, April 22, 1850; and Chapter 231, Statutes of California, April 8, 1860."

31. Murphy, "The Plight of the Native Americans," 33.

32. Heizer, *The Destruction of California Indians*, 219, 230. On page 230 Heizer quotes a Letter to Honorable Charles E. Mix, July 23, 1861, from George M. Hanson, Superintendent of Indian Affairs, Northern District, California. Heizer cites: "U. S. National Archives, Office of Indian Affairs, RG75, Letters received, California, 1861 (Document No. H275)."

33. Rawls, *Indians of California*, 176. Rawls cites: "Sherburne F. Cook, *The Conflict Between the California Indian and White Civilization: The American Invasion, 1848-1870*, Ibero-Americana, no. 23 (Berkeley: University of California Press, 1943), 111 and 115."

34. "Anti-Chinese Movement."

35. "The Apology Act, CA SB670;" Frame, "Mexican Repatriation." The second and third sentences of the paragraph relate to Frame's article. The remaining information came from the Senate bill.

36. Chadwick, and Varoqua, "New Jersey Muslims."

37. Robinson, "Aftermath of 9-11."

38. Mecoy, "Arab Americans Suffer."

39. Hassan, CAIR, November 5, 2001.

40. "Timeline," Carbone. The Sikh who was mistaken for an Arab and murdered on September 15, 2001 was Balbir Singh Sodhi.

Chapter 11: Healing Racism and Prejudice in Ourselves

1. Samuels, and Samuels, *Seeing With the Mind's Eye.*

2. Slazberg, *Loving Kindness*, cassettes.

3. Smith, "Loving-Kindness Meditation."

4. Bernhard, "Straw Into Gold."

5. "Gentleness," Open Dharma.

6. Slazberg, *Loving Kindness*, cassettes.

7. Dhammarakkhita, "Metta Bhavana."

8. Crouch, "Loving Kindness Meditation."

9. Salzberg, "Simple Yet Powerful."

10. Dhammarakkhita, "Metta Bhavana."

11. Carter, "Greater Happiness."

12 Bernhard, "Benevolence Toward Beings."

13. "Gentleness," Open Dharma.

14. Crouch, "Loving Kindness Meditation."

15. The process of generating and projecting light is similar to one described by Wallace in *The Four Immeasurables*, 135-139. As is the case with other teachers, Wallace encourages the practitioner to imagine the object of the meditation and generate a strong desire to relieve suffering.

16. Working with color and texture seems to be a traditional approach. Gyatso in *Eight Steps to Happiness*, 172-181, suggested inhaling black smoke and exhaling wisdom light. In *The Great Path of Awakening*, 15, Kongtrul worked with black tar and rays of moonlight.

17. Several teachers encourage being creative, for example, Wegela in *The Courage to be Present*, 82-85, and Chodron in *Start Where You Are*, 38-39.

18. In *Tonglen*, 39, Chodron encourages avoiding the story related to the suffering.

19. Buddhist scholar Berzin makes the point that doing the exercise will not cause you harm in "Tonglen- Giving and Taking."

20. In "Tonglen, Part 2 — Detailed Instructions," Traub writes about using tonglen as you go about your day.

21. Focusing on friends, a neutral person, then a difficult person seems to be a traditional approach. Wallace discusses it in *The Four Immeasurables*, 135-139.

22. On the *Tonglen Intensive* cassette program, Chodron discusses the need to gradually progress from easy situations to more difficult ones.

23. The general process of this alternative approach was influenced by teachings of both Chodron (*Tonglen Intensive* [cassettes], and *Tonglen*, 48-49) and Sogyal Rinpoche (*The Tibetan Book of the Dead*, 203-204). What I describe as an alternative approach, the first sentence in this paragraph, is drawn specifically from Sogyal Rinpoche's exercise in *The Tibetan Book of the Dead*, 203-204.

24. The general process of my meditation was influenced by teachings of both Chodron (*Tonglen Intensive* [cassettes], and *Tonglen* 48-49) and Sogyal Rinpoche (*The Tibetan Book of the Dead*, 203-204).

25. Jung, *Memories, Dreams and Reflections*, 247.

26. Rothberg, talk at Mountain Stream; Rothberg, e-mail messages to the author January 5, 2002 and January 17, 2002.

27. This example of mine is similar to one Rothberg used during his talk at Mountain Stream.

28. Rothberg, talk at Mountain Stream; Rothberg, e-mail messages to the author January 5, 2002 and January 17, 2002.

29. Katie, *I Need Your Love*, 22-25. The second chapter of her book gives instructions for using her inquiry process. Michael Katz, who assisted with the writing of *I Need Your Love*, found my use of the four questions to be acceptable (email from Michael Katz, August 9, 2013).

30. Regarding: "we tend to see the world as we are rather than how it actually is," this paraphrases the following statement on p.124 of Anais Nin's novel *Seduction of the Minotour*: "Lillian was reminded of the talmudic words: 'We do not see things as they are, we see them as we are.' "

31. Wallace, Buddhist retreat.

32. Progoff, *Journal Workshop*, 11.

33. Wallace interview.

34. Tarrant, *The Dark Within the Light*, 170.

35. Schneider and Schneider, *Slavery in America*, 3.

36. Ibid, 1, 4, 14.

37. Zeller, "The Politics of Apology."

38. Lovato, *Survivor*.

39. Hodge, *Handbook of American Indians*, 597-600.

40. Hanh, *Anger*, 32-34,164-166.

41. Information obtained from Don Williams, a chiropractor at the Vibrant Living Center in Grass Valley, CA. Williams studied under Dr. M. T. Morter and was authorized to practice and teach his method.

42. See: *The Little Book of Bleeps*, 6, 78 (re: physicists Hagelin and Teller); Kidwell, Noley, and Tinker, *Native American Theology*, 48-51; Lupton, *James Welch*, 23-24.

43. King, *Trumpet*, 71-72.

44. This view of mine is echoed by Reverend King in *Strength to Love*, 19.

45. King, *Where Do We Go*, 181.

46. King, *Stride Toward Freedom*, 88. While the words in my book to which this endnote refers echo King's views, I have held the same beliefs for many years, and they have been expressed by spiritual teachers from different

religious traditions. James Baldwin made the same observation in "In Search of a Majority," *Collected Essays*, 220-221.

47. Some meditation teachers, such as Chade-Meng Tan and Mirabai Bush call the practice "Just Like Me." Aura Glaser and others use the term "Equality Practice" which is probably a more traditional name.

48. A number of teachers teach this ancient practice. This variation is similar to ones taught by Glaser in "The Hidden Treasure," Wegela in *The Courage to be Present*, 100, and Chodron in *Tonglen*, 8.

49. Tan, "Cultivating Compassion;" Mirabai interview in Goldstein, "Mindfulness at Work." Acknowledging what is held in common is discussed by both writers. Mirabai mentions having statements read to participants. Adding positive wishes is referred to by Tan.

50. Goldstein, "Mindfulness at Work."

51. Hopkins, *Cultivating Compassion*, 33-37. His version offers a particular phrase to repeat that is fairly traditional. Hopkins' meditation is similar to a practice offered by Wallace in *The Four Immeasurables*, 135, 138.

52. Goldstein, "Mindfulness at Work."

53. Adapted from Byron Katie's teachings. Michael Katz, who assisted with the writing of *I Need Your Love*, considers my version of this exercise, with the citation used, to be acceptable (email from Michael Katz, August 9, 2013).

54. Wise, *Colorblind.*

55. Robertson, "A Battle Over Language."

56. Ibid.

57. Robertson, "Councilwoman Apologizes."

58. Drake, "Recalling the Dream."

59. Barks, *The Essential Rumi*, 36. This poem appears in many translations of Rumi. This is one such translation.

60. Regarding the statement "when we start to love others, our experience of them improves," a quote similar to this is sometimes attributed on the internet

to a "David Grayson." That is the name of a contemporary poet living in the San Francisco area. It is also a pseudonym for Ray Stannard Baker, an author who died in 1946. I have not been able to find an exact source for the quote. The contemporary poet informed me by email that the quote did not originate from him (email correspondence from David Grayson, April 5, 2012).

61. Matthew 12:31.

62. Ibid, 5:44.

63. King, *Trumpet*, 74.

64. King, *Stength*, 38.

65. Ibid, 34; *Where Do We Go*, 37. In *Strength* King mentions the importance of love in overcoming the world's problems. In *Where Do We Go* he notes that power used appropriately incorporates love as well as justice.

Chapter 12: Healing Racism and Prejudice
in Our Communities and the World

1. Creamer, "Personal Ties Pivotal."

2. Mlodinow, *Subliminal*, 158-160.

3. Ibid, 174-175.

4. Janius, "AP Poll: A Slight Majority of Americans." Re: "In an Associated Press poll conducted in late 2012 51 percent of Americans expressed anti-black sentiments. When statements that implied a negative view of blacks were taken into account, the number of Americans with anti-black sentiments increased to 56 percent. In a 2011 survey, almost identical percentages were noted in terms of non-Latino whites' views of Latinos." The 2012 assessment of Americans' views of blacks was slightly more negative than a 2008 study. In 2008, 48 percent were overtly negative. The figure increased to 49 percent when statements that implied a negative view were taken into account. Regarding views of Latinos by non-Latino whites, the 2011 survey determined that 52 percent expressed anti-Latino sentiments. When statements implying a bias were taken into account the figure increased to 57 percent.

5. Dalton, *Racial Healing*, 4-5.

6. Sawyer, host, *True Colors*, ABC Primetime.

7. Wise, *Affirmative Action*, 4.

8. Wise, "The Pathology of White Privilege."

9. Dalton, *Racial Healing*, 222-224. Dalton cites "Derrick Bell, 'Brown and the Interest-Convergence Dilemma,' in *Shades of Brown: New Perspectives on School Desegregation*, ed. Derrick Bell (New York: Basic Books, 1992)."

10. Haskell, and Jealous, *Combined Destinies*.

11. King, *Stride*, 84.

12. Hanh, *Peace Making*, CDs.

13. Carter, *Eye of the Hurricane*, 42-43.

14. Adyashanti, meditation retreat.

15. Isaacson, *Einstein*, 391.

16. Fisher, "Voters Seek Own Spin."

17. Regarding the statement "when we start to love others, our experience of them improves," a quote similar to this is sometimes attributed on the internet to a "David Grayson." That is the name of a contemporary poet living in the San Francisco area. It is also a pseudonym for Ray Stannard Baker, an author who died in 1946. I have not been able to find an exact source for the quote. The contemporary poet informed me by email that the quote did not originate from him (email correspondence from David Grayson, April 5, 2012).

18. Rosenberg, *Nonviolent Communication*, 6.

19. Ibid, 150-152.

20. Taylor, "Education to Counter Oppression."

21. King, "Letter from Birmingham City Jail," in *Testament of Hope*, 291. This essay of King's offers an example of his view that non-violent protest, rather than creating racial tension, brings it to the surface so it can be dealt with.

PART IV: THE JOURNEY CONTINUES

Chapter 13: The Journey Continues

1. Drake, "Recalling the Dream."

2. Arbuckle, "An Apology."

3. Although she has since died, at the time of this writing, Ricky Sherover-Marcuse's essays can still be found on the web at www.unlearningracism.org. (Accessed April 4, 2012)

4. Isoke Femi has been a consultant and professional trainer in the area of unlearning prejudice for over twenty-five years. She is the founder and co-director of the Todos Institute, and co-authored an intercultural alliance building manual, *No Boundaries*. She also developed Leading with Soul, a cultural leadership curriculum. (Source: http://www.aloveoflearning.org/about_us/people/staffandboardbios, accessed February 28, 2013.)

5. Drake, and Walker, "Unlearning Prejudice, An Expanded Proposal."

EPILOGUE

Mississippi Revisited

1. Carter, *An Hour Before Daylight*. Former President Carter's wonderful book makes it clear that his positive experiences of the poor blacks in his rural Georgia childhood environment helped him avoid developing racist views.

APPENDICES

Appendix 1: The Campaign to Discredit Martin Luther King

1. *The FBI, COINTELPRO*, Church Committee. Two newspaper articles that contain detailed information on the Senate hearings are: Horrock, "Senate Intelligence Panel," and Horrock, "FBI Aide." An excellent book on the FBI's overall role in trying to destroy King and the Civil Rights Movement is Garrow's *The FBI and Martin Luther King*. Six hundred pages from the FBI's files on Martin Luther King can be found in Friedly's and Gallen's *Martin Luther King, Jr.: The FBI File*. For a detailed assessment of the FBI's role in undermining King's last major campaign, see McKnight's *The Last Crusade*.

2. Ibid, 5-7.

3. Ibid, 20.

4. Ibid, 9.

5. Horrock, "Senate Intelligence Panel;" *The FBI, COINTELPRO*, Church Committee, 73, 143. Horrock discusses the stealing of stationary from the SCLC in order to forge letters damaging to Young and the rewriting of FBI reports. *The FBI COINTELPRO* pages cited discuss the other points in my paragraph.

6. *The FBI, COINTELPRO*, Church Committee, 105; Sullivan, *The Bureau*, 140-141. As well as in other sources, this subject is discussed in Garrow, *Bearing the Cross*, 372-375.

7. Garrow, *The FBI*, 165-166; Sullivan, *The Bureau*, 140-142. Garrow cites his endnote 38, 283 in regards to Hoover's fascination: "See Sanford Ungar, *FBI* (New York: Little, Brown, 1976), 269-70; Sullivan, *The Bureau*, 140-141; and Ovid Demaris, *The Director: An Oral Biography of J. Edgar Hoover* (New York: Harper & Row, 1975), 94." Garrow mentions Hoover's passing the recordings on to Johnson and Kennedy, and he cites endnote 43, 284 concerning Hoover's sharing the recordings: "Burke Marshall (Larry J. Hackman interview, 19-20 January 1970, Bedford, N.Y.), Kennedy Library, Boston 43." Sullivan discusses Hoover's sharing King recordings with the press, congress members, and President Johnson.

8. *The FBI, COINTELPRO*, Church Committee, 7.

9. Ibid, 11.

10. Garrow, *The FBI*, 24-25; Williams, *Eyes on the Prize*, 64-65; *The FBI, COINTELPRO*, Church Committee, 11. Garrow has the following citation: "10. The most complete account of the Labor Day (1957) incident is in Frank Adams, *Unearthing Seeds of Fire: The Idea of Highlander* (Winston-Salem: John F. Blair, 1975), pp. 122-27. These photographs [of King at a supposed Communist training at Highlander] later would adorn billboards across the South. Similar characterizations of King as the product of such a training school, which even the Bureau dismissed, are Alan Stang, 'The King and His Communists,' *American Opinion* 8 (October 1965): 1-14; James D. Bales, *The Martin Luther King Story* (Tulsa: Christian Crusade Publications, 1967); and Ralph de Toledano, *J. Edgar Hoover* (New Rochelle, N.Y.: Arlington House, 1973), p. 332." Garrow discusses the false rumor about Highlander. Williams mentions the Tennessee

law forbidding integrated schools. The Church Committee noted that the FBI rejected the allegations that Highlander was a Communist Party training school.

11. *The FBI, COINTELPRO*, Church Committee, 11.

12. Sullivan, *The Bureau*, 137-138.

13. *The FBI, COINTELPRO*, Church Committee, 13.

Appendix 2: Martin Luther King: The Ideal vs The Reality

1. "Boston U. Panel Finds Plagiarism," *New York Times*. This article cites an example of King's plagiarism.

2. Garrow, *The FBI*, 219, footnote 308. The footnote Garrow references pertains to King's speech "Unfulfilled Dreams," March 3, 1968, Ebenezer Baptist Church, Atlanta, 2-6.

3. Ibid, 216-219.

Appendix 3: A Philosophy of Social Action

1. Regarding: "we tend to see the world as we are rather than how it actually is," this paraphrases the following statement on p.124 of Anais Nin's novel *Seduction of the Minotour*: "Lillian was reminded of the talmudic words: 'We do not see things as they are, we see them as we are.'"

Appendix 5: Questions for Class Discussions, Book Clubs, or Individual Reflection

1. Regarding: "we tend to see the world as we are rather than how it actually is," this paraphrases the following statement on p.124 of Anais Nin's novel *Seduction of the Minotour*: "Lillian was reminded of the talmudic words: 'We do not see things as they are, we see them as we are.'"

2. Regarding the statement "when we start to love others, our experience of them improves," a quote similar to this is sometimes attributed on the internet to a "David Grayson." That is the name of a contemporary poet living in the San Francisco area. It is also a pseudonym for Ray Stannard Baker, an author who died in 1946. I have not been able to find an exact source for the quote. The contemporary poet informed me by email that the quote did not originate from him (email correspondence from David Grayson, April 5, 2012).

3. King, *Stride*, 84.

BIBLIOGRAPHY

NOTE: The following bibliography contains the main resources used for writing *Almost Hereditary*, not all the resources studied during the course of the writing. Almost all of the entries below were cited in the endnotes. See my website, www. healracism.com for some resource material, including three hundred excerpts from slave narratives, organized in categories. It also offers 165 excerpts from my great-great-grandmother's diaries. The majority of these diary excerpts were not used for this book. In addition my bibliography is presented in a much longer, annotated version on the website than it is here.

Categories used: * Black History, Black Writers; * Civil Rights; * Civil War; * Indians (Native Americans) * Jim Crow Era/After Civil War; * Jim Crow Photographs; * Martin Luther King, Jr., Southern Christian Leadership Conference; * Southern Christian Leadership Conference/Fletcher Drake Photographs; * Psychology, Personal Growth, Spirituality, Buddhism, Meditation, Mindfulness;* Racism, Healing Racism, Unlearning Prejudice; * Slavery; * Slave Narratives; * Photographs Related to Slavery; * White Privilege; * Miscellaneous Sources.

BLACK HISTORY, BLACK WRITERS

Gates, Henry Louis Jr. *Life Upon These Shores: Looking at African American History, 1513-2008*. New York: Knopf, 2011.

Gates, Henry Louis Jr., and Nellie Y. McKay, eds. *The Norton Anthology of African American Literature*. 2nd ed. New York: W. W. Norton and Company, 2003.

Green, Meg. *Henry Louis Gates, Jr.: A Biography*. Santa Barbara, CA: Greenwood, 2012.

Morrison, Toni, ed. *Baldwin, Collected Essays*. New York: Penguin Putnam, 1998.

CIVIL RIGHTS

Williams, Juan. *Eyes on the Prize: America's Civil Rights Years, 1954-1965*. New York: Viking Penguin, 1987.

CIVIL WAR

Burns, Ken. *The Civil War*. PBS, 1990, 6 DVDs.

Cohen, Jeannie. "Civil War Deadlier Than Previously Thought?" Article published June 6, 2011. http://www.history.com/news/civil-war-deadlier-than-previously-thought?cmpid=PaidMedia_Outbrain_HIS_HITH.

Foote, Shelby. "Men At War: An Interview with Shelby Foote." In *The Civil War, An Illustrated History,* Geoffrey C. Ward, with Ric Burns, and Ken Burns, 264-273. New York: Alfred A. Knopf, 1990.

"Fort Pillow Massacre." In *Encyclopaedia Britannica.* 2013. http://www. britannica.com/EBchecked/topic/214150/Fort-Pillow-Massacre. (Author not cited.)

Kelly, Martin. "Battle of Gettysburg." About.com American History, 2013. http://americanhistory.about.com/od/civilwarbattles/a/gettysburg_one.htm.

Thompson, Robert. "Battle of Cold Harbor: The Folly and Horror." Civil War Trust, 2013. http://www.civilwar.org/battlefields/coldharbor/cold-harbor-history-articles/. (From *Civil War Times Magazine*, http://www.historynet. com.)

"Victory From Within: Exploring the Stories of Prisoners of War." Andersonville National Historic Site, National Park Service. Accessed May 19, 2013. http://www.nps.gov/ande/index.htm. (Author not cited.)

Ward, Geoffrey C, with Ric Burns, and Ken Burns. *The Civil War, An Illustrated History.* New York: Alfred A. Knopf, 1990.

INDIANS (NATIVE AMERICANS)

Heizer, Robert, ed. *The Destruction of California Indians.* Lincoln: University of Nebraska Press, 1974. Introduction by Albert Hurtado was added in 1993.

Hodge, Fredrick W. *Handbook of American Indians North of Mexico.* Vol. 2. New York: Rowman and Littlefield, 1979. Originally published in 1907.

Kidwell, Clara Sue, Homer Noley, and George E. "Tink" Tinker. *A Native American Theology*. Maryknoll, NY: Orbis Books, 2001.

Lupton, Mary Jane. *James Welch: A Critical Companion.* Westport, CT: Greenwood Press, 2004.

Murphy, Rebecca. "The Plight of the Native Americans." *Sierra Heritage,* February 1998, 29-33.

Rawls, James. *Indians of California: The Changing Image.* Norman: University Of Oklahoma Press, 1984.

JIM CROW ERA/AFTER CIVIL WAR

"Act to Reorganize the Congressional Districts of the State," Mississippi Senate record, 1876, SB 166.

"An Act to Provide for Leasing Out the Penitentiary and Convict Labor of the State," Mississippi Senate record, April 7, 1876, SB 262.

Bonastia, Christopher. *Southern Stalemate, Five Years without Public Education in Prince Edward County, Virginia.* Chicago: The University of Chicago Press, 2012.

Boyle, Sarah Patton. *The Desegregated Heart: A Virginian's Stand in Time of Transition.* With a new introduction by Jennifer Ritterhouse and Boyle's letters added in 2001. Charlottesville: University of Virginia Press, 1962.

Chafe, William H., Raymond Gavins, and Robert Korstad, with Paul Ortiz, Robert Parrish, Jennifer Ritterhouse, Keisha Roberts, and Nicole Waligora-Davis. *Remembering Jim Crow: African Americans Tell About Life in the Segregated South.* New York: The New Press, 2001.

Davis, James F. *Who is Black?: One Nation's Definition.* University Park: Pennsylvania State University Press, 1991.

Equal Justice Initiative, "Lynching in America: Confronting the Legacy of Racial Terror," released February 10, 2015.

Fears, Daryl, "Atlanta, Ready to Revisit an American Evil," *The Washington Post,* January 28, 2002.

Foner, Eric. *A Short History of Reconstruction.* New York: Harper and Row 1990.

Fremon, David K. *The Jim Crow Laws and Racism in American History.* Berkeley Heights, N.J.: Enslow Publishers, 2000.

George, Charles. *Life Under the Jim Crow Laws.* San Diego, CA: Lucent Books, 2000.

Griffin, John Howard. *Black Like Me.* 3rd ed. New York: New American Library, 1977.

In the Land of Jim Crow: Growing Up Segregated. Phoenix Learning Group Home Edition, 2008, DVD.

Konvitz, Milton. *A Century of Civil Rights.* New York: Columbia University Press, 1961.

Lesher, Stephan. *George Wallace: An American Populist.* New York: Addison-Wesley, 1994.

Litwack, Leon F. *Trouble in Mind: Black Southerners in the Age of Jim Crow.* New York: Alfred A. Knopf, 1998.

Lord, Walter. "Mississippi: the Past that has not Died." American Heritage, 2011. http://www.americanheritage.com/content/mississippi-past-has-not-died. Originally published in *American Heritage*, June 1965, vol. 16, issue 4.

Osborne, Linda Barrett. *Miles to go for Freedom: Segregation and Civil Rights in the Jim Crow Years.* New York: Abrams, 2012.

Packard, Jerrold M. *American Nightmare: The History of Jim Crow.* New York: St. Martins Griffin, 2002.

"Resolutions," Mississippi Senate record, January 6, 1876.

Ritterhouse, Jennifer. *Growing Up Jim Crow: How Black and White Children Learned Race.* Chapel Hill: University of North Carolina Press, 2006.

"Separate but Equal: The Law of the Land." Separate but Not Equal: Brown vs Board of Education. Smithsonian National Museum of American History. Accessed May 20, 2013. http://americanhistory.si.edu/brown/history/1-segregated/detail/jim-crow-laws.html. (Author not cited.)

Slavery by Another Name. Directed by Sam Pollard. PBS, 2012, DVD.

Smith, Lillian. *Killers of the Dream*. Revised ed. New York: W. W. Norton, 1978. First published in 1949.

Tolnay, Stewart E., and E. M. Beck. *A Festival of Violence: An Analysis of Southern Lynchings, 1882-1930*. Chicago: University of Illinois Press, 1995.

Woodward, C. Vann. *The Strange Career of Jim Crow*. New York: Oxford University Press, 2002.

Wright, Richard. 1937. "The Ethics of Living Jim Crow: An Autobiographical Sketch." In *The Best American Essays of the Century*. Joyce Carol Oates, ed., 159-170. New York: Houghton Mifflin Company, 2000.

Wynes, Charles E. "The Evolution of Jim Crow Laws in Twentieth Century Virginia." Phylon (1960-2002), Vol. 28, No. 4 (4th Qtr., 1967), pp. 416-425. Accessed February 9, 2014. http://www.jstor.org/discover/10.2307/274293? uid=2129&uid=2134&uid=2478692297&uid=2&uid=70&uid=3&uid=2478 692287&uid=60&sid=21103414644807.

JIM CROW PHOTOGRAPHS
These photographs were accessed in 2013.

"A café near the tobacco market, Durham, North Carolina." Jack Delano, May 1940. Library of Congress, LC-USZ62-129840 (P&P). http://www.loc. gov/pictures/item/fsa1998006213/PP/.

"Christening of smallest Klansman, Wm.[?] Stanley, 8 weeks old." 1924. Library of Congress, LC-USZ62-23996 (P&P). http://www.loc.gov/pictures/ item/2012647921/.

"Detroit, Michigan. Riot at the Sojourner Truth homes, a new U.S. federal housing project, caused by white neighbors' attempt to prevent Negro tenants from moving in. Sign with American flag 'We want white tenants in our white community.'" Arthur S. Siegel, Feb. 1942. Library of Congress, LC-USW3-016549-C (P&P). http://www.loc.gov/pictures/item/owi2001018484/PP/.

"Drinking fountain on the county courthouse lawn, Halifax, N.C." John Vachon, April 1938. Library of Congress, LC-DIG-ppmsc-00216 (P&P). http://www.loc.gov/pictures/item/fsa1997003218/PP/.

"Lynching of MacManus." H. R. Farr, 1882. Library of Congress, LC-USZ62-2462 (P&P). http://www.loc.gov/pictures/item/2012646358/. Dates on and next to the photograph were removed with Photoshop.

"Negro going in colored entrance of movie house on Saturday afternoon, Belzoni, Mississippi Delta, Mississippi." Marion Post Wolcott, Oct.? 1939. Library of Congress, LC-USZ62-115416 (P&P). http://www.loc.gov/pictures/item/fsa1998013484/PP/.

MARTIN LUTHER KING, JR.,
SOUTHERN CHRISTIAN LEADERSHIP CONFERENCE

"Boston U. Panel Finds Plagiarism by Dr. King," *The New York Times Archives*, October 11, 1991. Accessed May 13, 2013. http://www.nytimes.com/1991/10/11/us/boston-u-panel-finds-plagiarism-by-dr-king.html. (Author not cited.)

The FBI, COINTELPRO, and Martin Luther King, Jr., U.S. Senate Select Committee to Study Governmental Operations with Respect to Intelligence Activities. S. Rep. (1976).

Garrow, David. *Bearing the Cross: Martin Luther King and the Southern Christian Leadership Conference.* New York: William Morrow, 2004.

Garrow, David. *The FBI and Martin Luther King.* New York: Penguin, 1995.

Horrock, Nicholas A. "Senate Intelligence Panel Told of FBI Attempt to Discredit Dr. King in 1964," *New York Times*, November 19, 1975, 16.

Horrock, Nicholas A. "FBI Aid Terms Effort to Vilify Dr. King Illegal," *New York Times*, November 20, 1975, 1, 30.

King, Martin Luther. "Letter from Birmingham Jail." In *A Testament of Hope: The Essential Writings and Speeches of Martin Luther King, Jr.*, edited by James M. Washington, 289-302. San Francisco: Harper, 1986.

King, Martin Luther. *The Strength to Love.* New York: Harper and Row, 1963.

King, Martin Luther. *Stride Toward Freedom: The Montgomery Story.* New York: Harper and Row, 1958.

King, Martin Luther. *The Trumpet of Conscience.* New York: Harper and Row, 1967.

King, Martin Luther. *Where Do We Go From Here: Chaos or Community?* New York: Harper and Row, 1967.

"Martin Luther King, Jr. and the Global Freedom Struggle: Watts Rebellion (Los Angeles, 1965)." Accessed March 12, 2013. http://mlk-kpp01.stanford.edu/index.php/encyclopedia/encyclopedia/enc_watts_rebellion_los_angeles_1965/ (Author not cited.).

McKnight, Gerald. *The Last Crusade: Martin Luther King, Jr., the FBI, and the Poor People's Campaign.* Boulder, CO: Westview Press, 1998.

Sullivan, William C. *The Bureau, My Thirty Years in Hoover's FBI.* New York: W. W. Norton, 1979.

Washington, James M. ed. *A Testament of Hope: The Essential Writings and Speeches of Martin Luther King, Jr..* San Francisco: HarperCollins, 1986.

SOUTHERN CHRISTIAN LEADERSHIP CONFERENCE
/FLETCHER DRAKE PHOTOGRAPHS

Southern Christian Leadership Conference. *The Poor People's Campaign, A Photographic Journal.* Atlanta: Southern Christian Leadership Conference, 1968. Contains photographs by my brother Fletcher Drake. Fletcher retained the copyrights to these pictures.

PSYCHOLOGY, PERSONAL GROWTH, SPIRITUALITY, BUDDHISM, MEDITATION, MINDFULNESS

Adyashanti. Meditation retreat, Mount Madonna, Watsonville, California, August 2007.

Bernhard, Toni. "Benevolence Toward all Beings: Lovingkindness as a Meditation Practice," The Elephant Journal. Article published March 20, 2012. http://www.elephantjournal.com/2012/03/benevolence-toward-all-beings-toni-bernhard/.

Bernhard, Toni. "Turning Straw Into Gold." Psychology Today. Accessed August 8, 2013. http://www.psychologytoday.com/blog/turning-straw-gold/201202/lovingkindness-practice.

Berzin, Alexander. "The Berzin Archives: Explanation of Eight-Verse Attitude-Training, Session Six: Tonglen — Giving and Taking; Verse Seven Continued and Verse Eight." Accessed August 6, 2013. http://www.berzinarchives.com/web/en/archives/sutra/level3_lojong_material/specific_

texts/eight_verse_attitude_training/explanation_eight_verse_attitude_tr/
transcript_6.html.

Brach, Tara. *Mindfulness Meditation: Nine Guided Practices to Awaken Presence and Open Your Heart.* Sounds True, 2012, 2 compact discs.

Brach, Tara. *Radical Acceptance: Embracing Your Life with the Heart of a Buddha.* New York: Bantam, 2003.

Brach, Tara. *Radical Acceptance: Guided Meditations.* Sounds True, 2007, 2 compact discs.

Brach, Tara. *Radical Self-Acceptance, a Buddhist Guide to Freeing Yourself from Shame.* Sounds True, 2000, 3 compact discs.

Brown, Brené. *I Thought It Was Just Me (But It Isn't): Making the Journey from "What Will People Think?" to "I Am Enough."* New York: Gotham Books, 2007.

Carter, Christine, "Greater Happiness in 5 Minutes a Day: How to Reach Kids; Loving-Kindness Meditation." The Main Dish. Article published September 10, 2012. http://www.greatergood.berkeley.edu/raising_happiness/post/better_than_sex_and_appropriate_for_kids.

(Center for Developing Healthy Minds, see http://www.investigatinghealthyminds.org/compassion.)

Chodron, Pema. *Start Where You Are.* Boston: Shambhala Publications, 1994.

Chodron, Pema. *Tonglen: The Path of Transformation.* Edited by Tingdzin Otro. Halifax, Canada: Vajradhatu Publications, 2001.

Chodron, Pema. *Tonglen Intensive.* Great Path Tapes, 1996, 4 cassette tapes.

Creamer, Anita. "Personal Ties Pivotal in Gay Marriage Views," *Sacramento Bee,* December 2, 2012.

Crouch, Ron. "Loving Kindness Meditation (Metta)." Aloha Dharma. Accessed August 9, 2013. http://www.alohadharma.wordpress.com/loving-kindness-meditation/.

Dhammarakkhita, Venerable. "Metta Bhavana: Loving-Kindness Meditation." Buddha Dharma Education Association. Article published August 2001. http://www.buddhanet.net/pdf_file/scrn_metta.pdf. (Author not cited.)

Dweck, Carol. *Mindset: How You Can Fulfill Your Potential*. London: Constable and Robinson, 2006.

Fisher, Marc. "Voters Seek Own Spin." *Washington Post*, printed in *Sacramento Bee*, January 21, 2012.

"Gentleness," Open Dharma. Accessed August 9, 2013. http://www. opendharma.org/static.php?left=blue&content=teachings/instructions/ heart_meditation/lovingkindnessmeditation&title=lovingpercent20kindness percent20meditation. (Author not cited.)

Glaser, Aura, *A Call to Compassion: Bringing Buddhist Practices of the Heart into the Soul of Psychotherapy*. Berwick, ME: Nicolas-Hays, 2005.

Glaser, Aura. "The Hidden Treasure of the Heart." Shambala Sun. Accessed August 9, 2013. http://www.shambhalasun.com/index.php?option=com_ content&task=view&id=3106&Itemid=247.

Goldstein, Elisha. "Mindfulness at Work: An Interview with Mirabai Bush." Mindful, November 26, 2012. http://www.mindful.org/mindful-voices/on-mental-health/mindfulness-at-work-an-interview-with-mirabai-bush.

Grayson, David. E-mail message to the author, April 5, 2012.

Gyatso, Geshe Kelsang. *Eight Steps to Happiness: The Buddhist Way of Loving Kindness*. 3rd ed. Glen Spey, NY: Tharpa Publications, 2012.

(Hanh, Thich Nhat, see Nhat Hanh, Thich.)

Harold and Maude. Directed by Hal Ashby. Paramount Pictures, 2000, motion picture on DVD.

Hopkins, Jeffrey, *Cultivating Compassion: A Buddhist Perspective*. New York: Broadway Books, 2001.

http://www.investigatinghealthyminds.org/compassion. Accessed August 30, 2014.

http://www.thework.com/index.php. Accessed June 23, 2013. Website for Byron Katie

Isaacson, Walter. *Einstein, His Life and Universe*. New York: Simon and Schuster, 2007.

Jung, Carl. *Memories, Dreams and Reflections*. New York: Random House, 1963.

Kabat-Zinn, Jon. *Guided Mindfulness Meditation, Series 1*. Sounds True, 2005. 2 compact discs.

Kabat-Zinn, Jon. *Mindfulness for Beginners*. Music Design, 2007. 2 compact discs.

Kabat-Zinn, Jon. *Mindfulness for Beginners: Reclaiming the Present Moment – and Your Life*. Boulder, CO: Sounds True, 2011.

(Katie, Byron, see: http://www.thework.com/index.php.)

Katie, Byron. *I Need Your Love — Is That True?: How to Stop Seeking Love, Approval, and Appreciation and Start Finding Them Instead*. With Michael Katz. New York: Harmony Books, 2005.

Katie, Byron. *Loving What Is: Four Questions That Can Change Your Life*. With Stephen Mitchell. New York: Harmony Books, 2002.

Katie, Byron. "The School." Joshua Tree, California, March 2003. "The School" is Byron Katie's nine-day training related to her teachings.

Kornfield, Jack. *Meditation for Beginners*. Sounds True, 2010. Compact disc.

Katz, Michael. E-mail messages to the author, August 9, 2013.

Kongtrul, Jamgon. *The Great Path of Awakening: The Classic Guide to Lojong, a Tibetan Buddhist Practice for Cultivating the Heart of Compassion*. Translated by Ken McLeod. Boston: Shambhala Publications, 2005.

The Little Book of Bleeps. Hillsboro, OR: Beyond Words Publishing, 2004.

Merton, Thomas. "The Root of War is Fear." In *A Thomas Merton Reader*, edited by T. McDonnell. New York: Doubleday, 1974.

Mlodinow, Leonard. *Subliminal: How Your Unconscious Mind Rules Your Behavior*. New York: Pantheon Books, 2012.

Nhat Hanh, Thich. *Anger*. New York: Riverhead Books, 2001.

Nhat Hanh, Thich. *Peace Making, How to Do It, How to Be It*. Sounds True, 2002. 2 compact discs.

Nin, Anais. *Seduction of the Minotour*. Chicago: Swallow Press, 1961

Progoff, Ira. *At A Journal Workshop*. New York: Dialogue House, 1975.

Rosenberg, Marshall. *Nonviolent Communication, A Language of Life*. 2nd ed. Encinitas, CA: PuddleDancer Press, 2003.

Rothberg, Donald. Speech given at Mountain Stream Meditation Center, Nevada City, CA, December 10, 2001.

Rothberg, Donald. E-mail messages to the author, January 5, 2002 and January 17, 2002.

Salzberg, Sharon. "A Simple Yet Powerful Way to Open the Heart and Connect with Others." Oprah.com. Accessed August 9, 2013. http://www.oprah.com/spirit/Opening-the-Heart-Through-Lovingkindness-Meditation/2.

Salzberg, Sharon. *Loving Kindness Meditation: Learning to Love Through Insight Meditation*. Sounds True, 1996. 2 compact discs.

Salzberg, Sharon. *Lovingkindness, The Revolutionary Art of Happiness*. Boston: Shambhala, 1995.

Salzberg, Sharon. *Real Happiness: The Power of Meditation, A 28-Day Program*. New York: Workman, 2011. Book and compact disc.

Samuels, Mike, and Nancy Samuels. *Seeing With the Mind's Eye: The History, Techniques and Uses of Visualization*. New York: Random House, 1975.

Simmons, Annette. *The Story Factor: Inspiration, Influence, and Persuasion Through the Art of Storytelling*. 2nd ed. New York: Basic Books, 2006.

Smith, Steven. "Loving-Kindness Meditation." The Center for Contemplative Mind in Society. Accessed August 13, 2013. http://www.contemplativemind.org/practices/tree/loving-kindness.

Sogyal Rinpoche. *The Tibetan Book of Living and Dying.* Edited by Patrick Gaffney, and Andrew Harvey. San Francisco: Harper, 1993.

Steele, Claude M. "Thin Ice: Stereotype Threat and Black College Students," *The Atlantic*, August 1999. http://www.theatlantic.com/magazine/archive/1999/08/thin-ice-stereotype-threat-and-black-college-students/304663/.

Stone, Douglas, Bruce Patton, and Sheila Heen. *Difficult Conversations, How to Discuss What Matters Most.* New York: Penguin, 1999.

Tan, Chade-Meng. "Cultivating Compassion: Meditation for Healthy Relationships." Huffington Post Healthy Living. Article published December 22, 2009. http://www.huffingtonpost.com/chademeng-tan/cultivating-compassion-me_b_401048.html.

Tarrant, John. *The Dark Within the Light.* New York: Harper, 1999.

Traub, Eric Lance. "Tonglen, Part 2: Detailed Instructions" Article published February 28, 2012. http://www.ericlancetraub.com/post/23771325158/tonglen-part-2-detailed-instructions.

Wegela, Karen Kissel, *The Courage to be Present: Buddhism, Psychotherapy, and the Awakening of Natural Wisdom.* Boston: Shambhala, 2010.

Wallace, Alan. Buddhist retreat, Lone Pine, California, July 2001.

Wallace, Alan, *The Four Immeasurables: Practices to Open the Heart.* 3rd ed. Edited by Zara Houshmand. Ithaca, NY: Snow Lion, 2010.

Wallace, Alan. Interview by Bill Drake, July 29, 2001. (Broadcast at a later date on KVMR FM, Nevada City, California).

RACISM, HEALING RACISM, UNLEARNING PREJUDICE

American Anthropological Association. "Statement on 'Race.' " May 17, 1998. http://www.aaanet.org/stmts/racepp.htm.

American Anthropological Association. "Statement on 'Race' and Intelligence." December 1994. http://www.aaanet.org/stmts/race.htm.

"Anti-Chinese Movement and Chinese Exclusion, The Chinese in California 1850-1925." Accessed November 16, 2013. http://www.memory.loc.gov/ammem/award99/cubhtml/theme9.html. (Author not cited.)

"The Apology Act for the 1930s Mexican Repatriation Program." California State Senate, SB 670. Introduced by Joseph Dunn (D-Garden Grove), February 22, 2005. http://www.leginfo.ca.gov/pub/05-06/bill/sen/sb_0651-0700/sb_670_bill_20051007_chaptered.html

Arbuckle, Janet. "An Apology to the Martin Family," *The Union* (Grass Valley, CA), July 2, 2011.

Berry, Wendell. *The Hidden Wound.* 2nd ed. Berkeley, CA: Counterpoint, 2010.

Burns, Ken. Speech given at University of California at Davis, January 11, 2002.

Carbone, Nick. "Timeline: A History of Violence against Sikhs in the Wake of 9/11." NewsFeed. Article written August 6, 2012. http://www.newsfeed.time.com/2012/08/06/timelline-a-history-of-violence-against....

Carter, Jimmy. *An Hour Before Daylight: Memoirs of a Rural Boyhood.* New York: Touchstone, 2001.

Carter, Rubin. Speech and Press Conference at University of California at Davis, January 30, 2002.

Carter, Rubin. *Eye of the Hurricane: My Path from Darkness to Freedom.* Chicago: Lawrence Hill Books, 2013.

Chadwick, John, and Eman Varoqua. "New Jersey Muslims Fear Backlash," North Jersey Media Group, September 12, 2001. http://www.bergen.com/news/muslimjc200109128.

Dalton, Harlon. *Racial Healing: Confronting the Fear Between Blacks & Whites.* New York: Doubleday, 1995.

"Do you still manufacture the Crayola Crayon color Indian red?" Accessed May 1, 2013. http://www.crayola.com/support/faq/another-topic/do-you-still-manufacture-the-crayola-crayon-color-indian-red/. (Author not cited.)

Drake, Bill. "A Message to the Black Community of Norfolk: I Apologize," *The Virginian Pilot* (Norfolk, VA); "You Can Change What You Think," *San Francisco Chronicle* (San Francisco, CA); guest editorial, *The Union* (Grass Valley, CA); January 19, 1998. (The same article was published in all three papers simultaneously on Martin Luther King Day 1998.)

Drake, Bill. Letter to the editor, *The Union* (Grass Valley, CA), January 20, 1997.

Drake, Bill. "Recalling the Dream, Grass Valley Man Reflects on Growing up in a Racist Family," *The Union* (Grass Valley, CA), January 17, 2011.

Drake, Bill, and Jamal Walker. "Unlearning Prejudice and Building Bridges: An Expanded Proposal," *The Union* (Grass Valley, CA), December 2, 2011.

(Facing History and Ourselves, see http://www.facinghistory.org.)

Frame, Craig S. "Mexican Repatriation A Generation Between Two Borders." 2009. http://www.public.csusm.edu/frame004/history.html.

Haskell, Caroline T., and Ann Todd Jealous, eds. *Combined Destinies: Whites Sharing Grief about Racism*. Sterling, VA: Potomac Books, 2013.

Hassan, Hodan. E-mail message to the author, November 5, 2001. Member of Council on American Islamic Relations (CAIR).

Heimann, Jim, ed. *The Golden Age of Advertising: the 60s*. Holn, Germany: Taschen GmbH, 2005.

http://www.facinghistory.org (Facing History and Ourselves). Accessed June 23, 2013.

http://www.pisab.org (The People's Institute for Survival and Beyond). Accessed July 3, 2014.

http://www.tolerance.org (Southern Poverty Law Center). Accessed June 23, 2013.

http://www.unlearningracism.org (Ricky Sherover-Marcuse). Accessed June 23, 2013.

http://www.untraining.org (The UNtraining, UNtraining White Liberal Racism). Accessed July 3, 2014.

"I, Too, Am B-CC," You Tube video, posted by students at Bethesda Chevy Chase High School, Bethesda, MD, January 17, 2015, http://www.youtube.com/watch?v=2KpKEFEpHms.

"I, Too, Am Harvard," campaign by students at Harvard University. Includes "I, Too, Am Harvard (Preview), March 3, 2014, https://www.youtube.com/watch?v=uAMTSPGZRil, and "Creating Space,", June 8, 2014, https://www.youtube.com/watch?annotation_id=annotation_4151841511&feature=iv&src_vid=uAMTSPGZRil&v=4JmQU_3v6gA.

Janius, Dennis, contributor. "AP Poll: A Slight Majority of Americans are now Expressing Negative View of Blacks," *The Washington Post*, Associated Press, October 27, 2012. http://www.washingtonpost.com/politics/ap-poll-majority-of-americans.

Kaolin. Talking *About Race: A Workbook About White People Fostering Racial Equality in Their Lives*. Roselle, NJ: Crandall, Dostie & Douglass Books, 2010.

Kivel, Paul. *Uprooting Racism: How White People can Work for Racial Justice*. 3rd ed. Gabriola Island, BC, Canada: New Society, 2011.

Lovato, Francisco. *Survivor: An American Soldier's Heartfelt Story of Intense Fighting, Surrender, and Survival from Bataan to Nagasaki*. Nevada City, CA: Del Oro Press, 2008.

McGoey, Chris E. "Shoplifting Profiling, A Retail Loss Prevention Tool." Accessed November 30, 2013. http://www.crimedoctor.com/shoplifter-profiling.htm.

Mecoy, Laura. "Arab Americans Suffer from Violent Backlash," *Sacramento Bee*, September 14, 2001.

Mecoy, Laura. "Hate Crimes Often Tough to Prosecute," *Sacramento Bee*, November 24, 2001.

Norris, Susan. E-mail message to the author, December 18, 2013. Permissions assistant, American Anthropological Association. She noted that I can use excerpts from the AAA's website statements related to race as long as correctly quoted and properly cited.

Ostrow, Nicole. "Black and Asian Teens Have Lowest Rates of Drug and Alcohol Use," *Businessweek*, November 9, 2011.

Price, Jay. "Study: White Kids More Likely to Abuse Drugs," *The Seattle Times*, November 12, 2011.

Robertson, Blair Anthony. "A Battle Over Language and Race Erupts at City Hall," *Sacramento Bee*, November 10, 2001.

Robertson, Blair Anthony. "Councilwoman Apologizes, But Qualifies That," *Sacramento Bee*, November 21, 2001.

Robinson, B. A. "Aftermath of the 9-11 Terrorist Attack, Attacks on Muslims." Ontario Consultants on Religious Tolerance. Accessed December 17, 2001. http://www.religioustolerance.org/reac_ter1.

Sawyer, Diane, host. *True Colors*. ABC Primetime, September 26, 1991. Part 1: http://www.youtube.com/watch?v=YyL5EcAwB9c; Part 2: http://www.youtube.com/watch?v=gOS3BBmUxvs. (Author not cited.)

(Sherover-Marcuse, Ricky, see: http://www.unlearningracism.org.)

(Southern Poverty Law Center, see: http://www.tolerance.org.)

Szalavitz, Maria. "Study: Whites More Likely to Abuse Drugs Than Blacks," *Time*, November 7, 2011.

Taylor, Jeremy. "Education to Counter Oppression at Starr King," 2004. Accessed February 2012. http://www.jeremytaylor.com/pages/socialjustice.html.

(The People's Institute for Survival and Beyond, see http://www.pisab.org.)

(The UNtraining, UNtraining White Liberal Racism, see http://www.untraining.org.)

Vasquez, Hugh, and Isoke Feme. *No Boundaries: A Manual for Unlearning Oppression and Building Multicultural Alliances*. Oakland, CA: TODOS: Sherover Simms Allinace Building Institute, 1993.

Washington, Jesse. "Arrest Puts Focus on Issue of Racial Profiling in Stores," Associated Press, *The Sacramento Bee*, November 30, 2013, B6.

"Why does the color 'flesh' not appear in the 1958 limited edition box of 64?" Accessed May 1, 2013. http://www.crayola.com/support/faq/another-topic/why-does-the-color-quotfleshquot-not-appear-in-the-1958-limited-edition-box-of-64/. (Author not cited.)

Wise, Tim. *Affirmative Action: Racial Preference in Black and White.* New York: Routledge, 2005.

Wise, Tim. *Colorblind, The Rise of Post-Racial Politics and the Retreat from Racial Equality.* San Francisco: City Lights Books, 2010.

Zeller, Jr., Tom. "The Politics of Apology for Japan's 'Comfort Women,'" *New York Times*, March 5, 2007. http://www.thelede.blogs.nytimes.com/2007/03/05/the-politics-of-apology-for-japans-comfort-women/?scp=2&sq=WWII+sex+slaves&st=nyt.

Zinn, Howard. *A People's History of the United States.* 5th ed. New York: HarperCollins, 2003.

SLAVERY

Davis, David Brion. *Inhuman Bondage: The Rise and Fall of Slavery in the New World.* New York: Oxford University Press, 2006.

Horton, James Oliver, and Lois E. Horton. *Slavery and the Making of America.* New York: Oxford University Press, 2005.

Kivisto, Peter. *Americans All: Race and Ethnic Relations in Historical, Structural, and Comparative Perspectives.* Belmont, CA: Wadsworth Publishing, 1995.

Kolchin, Peter. *American Slavery 1619-1877.* New York: Hill and Wang, 1993.

"Names of Slave Owners," Tallahatchie County, Mississippi, July 1860.

"The Origin and Nature of New World Slavery, Life Under Slavery Period: 1600-1860." The Gilder Lehrman Institute of American History, Gilder Lehrman History Online, 2001, http://www.gliah.uh.edu/database/article_display.cfm?HHID=74. (Author not cited.)

Schneider, Dorothy, and Carl J. Schneider. *Slavery in America.* 2nd ed. New York: Checkmark Books, 2007.

Tadman, Michael. *Speculators and Slaves: Masters, Traders, and Slaves in the Old South.* Madison: The University of Wisconsin Press, 1989.

SLAVE NARRATIVES

Over 575 testimonies by ex-slaves were studied for material to supplement this book's first chapter. "Born in Slavery: Slave Narratives from the Federal Writers' Project, 1936-1938," Library of Congress (http:// www.memory.loc.gov/ammem/snhtml/) offers access to over 2,300 slave narratives. Two hundred related photographs can also be accessed on the Library of Congress website (http://www.loc.gov/pictures/search/?q=federal percent20writers percent20project percent20slave percent20narrative) and downloaded for free. (LOC websites accessed June 2012.) The state name for each volume of the narratives reflects where the individuals were living when they were interviewed, not necessarily what state or states they lived in when they were slaves.

Alabama Narratives. Vol. I, *Slave Narratives: American Slave Interviews.* San Bernadino, CA: Mountain Waters Pty Ltd, 2012. Prepared by the Federal Writer's Project of the Public Works Administration for the State of Alabama. Washington 1941.

Berlin, Ira, Marc Favreau, and Steven F. Miller, eds. *Remembering Slavery: African Americans Talk About Their Personal Experiences of Slavery and Emancipation.* New York: The New Press, 1996.

Douglass, Frederick. *Life and Times of Frederick Douglass.* New York: Bonanza Books, 1962. Reprinted from the revised edition of 1892.

Escott, Paul D. *Slavery Remembered: A Record of Twentieth-Century Slave Narratives.* Chapel Hill: The University of North Carolina Press, 1979.

Georgia Narratives. Vol. IV, part 1, *Slave Narratives: A Folk History of Slavery in the United States From Interviews with Former Slaves.* Filiquarian Publishing/Qontro Classic Books. Prepared by the Federal Writers' Project of the Works Progress Administration for the State of Georgia. Washington 1941.

Georgia Narratives. Vol. IV, part 3, *Slave Narratives: A Folk History of Slavery in the United States.* Filiquarian Publishing/Qontro Classic Books. Prepared by the Federal Writers' Project of the Works Progress Administration for the State of Georgia. Washington 1941.

Glover, Jacqueline, and Thomas Lennon. *Unchained Memories*. HBO, 2003, DVD.

North Carolina Narratives. Vol. XI, part 1, *Slave Narratives: A Folk History of Slavery in the United States*. Filiquarian Publishing/Qontro Classic Books. Prepared by the Federal Writers' Project of the Works Progress Administration for the State of North Carolina. Work Projects Administration. Washington, 1941.

Rawick, George P. *From Sundown to Sunup: The Making of the Black Community*. Westport, CT: Greenwood Publishing Company, 1972.

Slave Narratives From the Federal Writers' Project, 1936-1938: Maryland. Bedford, MA: Applewood Books. In cooperation with the Library of Congress. Volume VIII in the Works Project Administration series.

Slave Narratives From the Federal Writers' Project, 1936-1938: Mississippi. Bedford, MA: Applewood Books. In cooperation with the Library of Congress. Volume IX in the Works Project Administration series.

Slave Narratives From the Federal Writers' Project, 1936-1938: Missouri. Bedford, MA: Applewood Books. In cooperation with the Library of Congress. Volume X in the Works Project Administration series.

South Carolina Narratives. Vol. XIV, part 1, *Slave Narratives: A Folk History of Slavery in the United States*. Filiquarian Publishing/Qontro Classic Books. Prepared by the Federal Writers' Project of the Works Progress Administration for the State of South Carolina. Work Projects Administration. Washington, 1941.

Texas Narratives. Vol. XVI, part 1, *Slave Narratives: A Folk History of Slavery in the United States*. Filiquarian Publishing/Qontro Classic Books. Prepared by the Federal Writers' Project of the Works Progress Administration for the State of Texas. Work Projects Administration. Washington, 1941.

Unchained Memories: Readings from the Slave Narratives. New York: Bulfinch Press, 2002.

Virginia. Vol. XVII, *Slave Narratives: A Folk History of Slavery in the United States*. Filiquarian Publishing/Qontro Classic Books. Prepared by the Federal Writers' Project of the Works Progress Administration for the State of Virginia. Work Projects Administration. Washington, 1941.

Washington, Booker T. *Up from Slavery.* New York: Dover, 1955. Washington's autobiography written in 1901.

Yetman, Norman R., ed. *When I Was a Slave.* New York: Dover, 2002.

PHOTOGRAPHS RELATED TO SLAVERY

PLANTATION HOUSES

"General view of plantation house — Melrose Plantation, State Highway 119, Melrose, Natchitoches Parish, LA." Frank, Hampson, 1980. Library of Congress, HABS LA,35-MELRO,1—4 (P&P). http://www.loc.gov/pictures/item/la0105/.

"Northwest front — Laurel Hill Plantation House, Rodney & Red Licks Roads, Rodney, Jefferson County, MS." Jack E. Boucher, 1972. Library of Congress, HABS MISS,32-ROD.V,1—1 (P&P). http://www.loc.gov/pictures/item/ms0191/.

SLAVE QUARTERS

"GENERAL VIEW AND WEST SIDE OF SLAVE QUARTERS, LOCATED SOUTHEAST OF POLK HOUSE HABS TENN, 31-BERSP, 2A-1 - Old Beersheba Inn, Polk House (Cottage), Armfield Avenue, Beersheba Springs, Grundy County, TN." Library of Congress, HABS TENN,31-BERSP,2—10 (P&P). http://www.loc.gov/pictures/item/tn0228.photos.153244p/.

"Historic American Buildings Survey James Butters, Photographer April 10, 1936 FRONT VIEW (WEST ELEVATION) — Concord Slave Quarters & Ruins, Natchez, Adams County, MS." Library of Congress, HABS MISS,1-NATCH.V,10—2 (P&P). http://www.loc.gov/pictures/item/ms0126.photos.092847p/.

"Historic American Buildings Survey John O. Brostrup, Photographer September 4, 1936 10:50 A. M. VIEW OF SLAVE QUARTERS FROM SOUTHWEST (front.) - Rock Hall & Slave Quarters, Dickerson, Montgomery County, MD." Library of Congress, HABS MD,11-____,4—6 (P&P). http://www.loc.gov/pictures/item/md0211.photos.081897p/.

"Historic American Buildings Survey W. N. Manning, Photography, June 13, 1933. LOG CABIN ON PLANTATION (FROM SNAPSHOT) — Womack-Crenshaw Plantation, County Road 54, Greenville, Butler County, AL." Dog trot house. Library of Congress, HABS ALA,7-____,4—17 (P&P). http:// www.loc.gov/pictures/item/al0042.photos.007744p/.

"Photograph of Slave Cabin and Occupants Near Eufala, Barbour County, Alabama." Between 1936 and 1938. Library of Congress. Digital ID: mesnp 010000 (P&P). http://www.memory.loc.gov/cgi-bin/query/D?mesnbib:1:./ temp/~ammem_WxnE:: http://memory.loc.gov/mss/mesn/mesnp/010/010000v.jpg.

SLAVES

"'Auction & Negro Sales,' Whitehall Street." George N. Barnard, 1864, Atlanta, GA, during Gen. Sherman's occupation of the city. Library of Congress, LC-DIG-cwpb-03351 (digital file from original neg. of left half) LC-DIG-cwpb-03350 (digital file from original neg. of right half) LC-B8171-3608 (b&w film copy neg.) (P&P). http://www.loc.gov/pictures/item/ cwp2003000884/PP/.

"Five generations on Smith's Plantation, Beaufort, South Carolina." Timothy H. O'Sullivan, 1862. Library of Congress, LC-B8171-152-A (P&P). http:// www.loc.gov/pictures/item/98504449/.

"Gordon as he entered our lines. Gordon under medical inspection. Gordon in his uniform as a U.S. soldier." Wood engraving from photograph by McPherson & Oliver, illustrated in Harper's Weekly, July 4, 1863. Library of Congress, LC-USZ62-98515 (P&P). http://www.loc.gov/pictures/ item/89716298/. Only the image of scars on his back was used for this book.

"A group of 'contrabands.'" Slaves taken from plantation owner by Union troops. Photographed at the Foller Plantation in Cumberland Landing, Pamunkey Run, Virginia by James F. Gibson, May 14, 1862. Library of Congress: LC-DIG-stereo-1s02760 (digital file from original stereograph, front) LC-DIG-stereo-2s02760 (digital file from original stereograph, back) LC-USZ62-57025 (b&w film copy neg. from dup. stereo) (P&P). http:// www.loc.gov/pictures/item/2011660086/. This double image picture was reproduced as a single photograph with Photoshop.

"Iron mask, collar, leg shackles and spurs used to restrict slaves." Created Samuel Wood, 1807. Library of Congress, LC-USZ62-31864 (P&P). http:// www.loc.gov/pictures/item/98504457/.

"Slave pen, Alexandria, Va." Interior view showing the doors of cells where the slaves were held before being sold. Photographed between 1861 and

1865. Library of Congress, LC-USZ62-46763 (P&P). http://www.loc.gov/pictures/item/98510275/.

"Wilson Chinn, a branded slave from Louisiana — Also exhibiting instruments of torture used to punish slaves." Photographed by Kimball, 1863. Library of Congress, LC-USZ62-90345 (P&P). http://www.loc.gov/pictures/item/96524703/.

WHITE PRIVILEGE

Kendall, Frances E. *Understanding White Privilege: Creating Pathways to Authentic Relationships Across Race*. New York: Routledge, Taylor and Francis Group, 2006.

McIntosh, Peggy. "White Privilege: Unpacking the Invisible Knapsack." Accessed May 2, 2013. http://www.amptoons.com/blog/files/mcintosh.html.

Rothenberg, Paula S. *White Privilege: Essential Readings on the Other Side of Racism*. 4th ed. New York: Worth Publishers, 2012.

http://www.timwise.org (Time Wise). Accessed June 23, 2013.

http://www.whiteprivilegeconference.org. Accessed August 13, 2014.

The White Privilege Conference, also WPC University, and Diversity University, see http://www.whiteprivilegeconference.org.

Wise, Tim. "The Pathology of White Privilege: Racism, White Denial, & The Costs of Inequality." Mt. Holyoke College, Massachusetts, October 2007. Videotape of speech. Accessed November 30, 2013. https://www.youtube.com/watch?v=8SIINVfqnxw.

Wise, Tim. *White Like Me, Reflections on Race from a Privileged Son*. 2nd ed. New York: Soft Skull Press, 2008.

MISCELLANEOUS SOURCES

1960 Census, Section 1: Population, table number 15, 26. Accessed on the internet May 1, 2013. *1961-02 Census report.pdf*.

The American Heritage Dictionary. 5th ed. New York: Houghton Mifflin Harcourt, 2012.

New Oxford American Dictionary. 3rd ed. New York: Oxford University Press, 2010.

Rumi. *The Essential Rumi*. Translated by Coleman Barks. Edison, NJ: Castle Books, 1997.

Webster's All-In-One Dictionary & Thesaurus. 2nd ed. Springfield, MA: Merriam-Webster, 2013.

Webster's American English Dictionary. Springfield, MA: Merriam-Webster, 2011.

Webster's New Universal Unabridged Dictionary. 2nd ed. New York: Simon and Schuster, 1983.

INDEX

Note:
Page numbers followed by "cap" indicate captions.
Page numbers followed by "def" indicate definitions.
Page numbers followed by "fig" indicate figures.
Page numbers followed by "map" indicate maps.
Page numbers followed by "n" indicate footnotes.
Page numbers followed by "n" or "nn" plus one or more numbers indicate numbered endnotes.
Page numbers followed by "ph" indicate photographs.
Page numbers followed by "q" indicate quotations.
Page numbers followed by "+fig," "+n," or "+ph," indicate discussions plus figures, footnotes, or photographs.

opening the heart, 210–211, 250
opposing injustice, 151, 247–248,
250, 255
See also working against
prejudice
opposing racial segregation and
discrimination, laws
against, 79
oppression, feeling of, 229–230
orphans, black: forced
apprenticeship, 73
Oteen, Sarah (former slave), 26q
others:
connecting with people who are
different, 240–241
loving others despite differences,
155, 235–237
understanding perpetrators' life
experiences, 247–250, 252
See also judgments of others;
projection (onto others);
separation/separateness
(from others)
overcoming fears, 206, 207, 224
overcoming hopelessness, 257–
259+n
overcoming racist conditioning,
203–214, 240, 263–266
affirmations, 207
Bill's difficulty in, 2, 147–148
Bill's work on, 1, 5, 145–150,
151–158, 203–204, 240,
242–243, 263–266
Drake family members' difficulty
in, 5
education and, 203–204
immersion approach, 206
through life experiences,
204–205
loving kindness meditation,
207–210, 228
personal benefits, 239
student exchange program, 205

visualization exercises, 207
workshops for, 206
See also working against
prejudice
overcoming self-righteousness,
220–223
overcoming separation/separateness,
224, 228–232
overprotectiveness of Bill's mother,
107, 155, 159
overseers (white), 26, 34, 41, 43
overwhelm, focusing on each step
vs., 257–259, 293–294

P
pain:
Bill's in confronting his family's
and his own racism, 4, 5,
71–72, 106, 266, 272–273
recognizing and embracing,
226–227
See also suffering
Parkes, Anna (former slave), 38q
Parks, Rosa, 133
Parkway internship (Bill), 145
Patillo, G. W. (former slave), 38q
patrollers:
black soldiers as, 58, 63
white patrollers, 42
peace/anti-nuclear group action
(Bill), 150–151
Pearl Harbor bombing, 195
People's Institute for Survival and
Beyond, 206
perception:
reflection as, 228
of self. *See* self-perception...
perception of difference: racism
from, 183, 223
perpetrators of injustice: breaking
down barriers between
ourselves and, 247–250,
252

personal benefits of working against
    prejudice, 239
petroglyph protection meeting, 190
"A Philosophy of Social Action"
    (Bill), 283–290
photography for SCLC, Fletcher's,
    118–119, 121–124ph
pilots story, 182
plantation houses, 21, 22ph
    Albin Plantation house (late
        1800s), 94ph
plantations, 15, 21
    the benevolent plantation myth,
        71–72, 89–90
    former slaves leaving/staying on,
        61–64
    relocation of slaves between, 37
    slave leaving permits, 42
    See also Robinson plantations
Plymouth (Bill), 110, 116
pneumonia among slaves, 30cap,
    35–36
poems by Bill:
    "A Handshake," 181, 263
    "Mama Don't Know," 198–199
    "Prayers of a Seeker," 168–169
    "The Purpose," 238
    "Through These Eyes," 267
poems by Nancy Robinson, 63, 64,
    71
police harassment of blacks, 75
political activity:
    Bill's, in/after college, 117,
        137–140, 141–142, 201;
        drug arrest and legal case
        re, 140–143
    Bill's peace/anti-nuclear group
        action, 150–151
    nonviolent protests, 151, 255
    See also social action
Poor People's Campaign
    photographs, Fletcher's,
        119, 123ph, 124ph

possessions: Bill's mother's pride
    in, 95–96
Powell, Colin, 187–188, 199+n
Powell, Reverend Lew, 264–265
"Prayers of a Seeker" (Bill),
    168–169
prejudice (social prejudices),
    177def, 215
    against homosexuals, 204
    Bill's experience of, 138–139,
        139–140, 190
    of Bill's father, 106, 180–181
    of Bill's mother, 92–93, 180–181
    experience of, 229–230; Bill's,
        138–139, 139–140, 190
    through insecurity, 179
    against interracial marriage, 106
    prevalence, 1, 9, 172, 223
    and separation, 217–218
    of white Southerners against
        Northerners, 53, 54, 56–57,
        72, 92, 155, 182–183
    working against. *See* working
        against prejudice
    See also judgments...; racist
        beliefs; racist conditioning
Presley, Elvis: "Love Me Tender,"
    105
price of slaves, 28
pride in one's heritage, 233
    Bill's mother's in her Southern
        heritage, 93–94, 198;
        slaveholding, 29, 89–90
Prince Edward County schools
    closure, 87
prisoners of war: Japanese
    enslavement of, 222
Progoff, Ira, 220
projection (onto others), 186–187,
    284–285
    racism from, 186–187, 253, 254
    self-awareness and, 224, 253, 254
prostitution by slaves, forced, 26

Santa Cruz-Reed, Cindy, 265–266
Sara Posey (S. M. Baldwin?), 70
Sawyer, Diane, 245
scapegoating, 194–196
  of blacks by white Southerners,
    58
scars from whipping of slaves, 40fig
schools:
  closure in Virginia, 87
  working against prejudice in,
    254–257
  See also education; Fishburne
    Military School; Virginia
    Tech
SCLC. *See* Southern Christian
    Leadership Conference
Scott, Janie (former slave), 28q
seat-kicking incident, 133–134, 153,
    219, 224
Seeing with the Mind's Eye
    (Samuels), 207
segregated café and movie theater,
    76ph, 77ph
segregation. *See* racial segregation
self-acceptance, 225–228, 293
self-awareness (knowing oneself),
    216
  developing, 223–224
  and projection, 224, 253, 254
  and social action, 284
  See also awareness
self-centeredness, 161–162
self-deception: racism and, 253
self-fulfilling racism. *See*
    internalized racism
self-hatred, 187
self-perception of blacks as inferior
    to whites, 186, 191–193,
    203, 244
  See also black inferiority
self-perception of whites as superior
    to blacks, 60–61, 111, 186,
    203, 244

See also white supremacy
self-righteousness:
  Bill's, 218, 220, 253, 284
  overcoming, 220–223
  and social action, 284
selfless service (Tibetan Buddhist
    teaching), 171
selling of slaves. *See* buying and
    selling of slaves
Senate committee on intelligence.
    See Church Committee
sensitivity of Nancy Robinson, 14,
    41, 69
separation/separateness (from
    others), 228–229
  overcoming, 224, 228–232
  prejudice and, 217–218
  racism from, 183, 223
  self-awareness and, 224
  stereotyping and, 191
September 11 attacks, 195–196
servants (black people), 81/85,
    90+ph, 91, 100
  The Help book discussion, 265
  mammies, 85–86+ph
sexist stereotyping, 190–191
sexual enslavement of women
    prisoners of war by
    Japanese troops, 222
sexual exploitation of slave/former
    slave women:
  in postbellum Klan attacks, 66
  slave owner rape/forced
    prostitution, 26, 34
shame, 225–226, 292–293
  breathing in and out, 213–214
share-cropping enslavement of
    former slaves, 58–60
Shea, Father Tom, 146
Sherover-Marcuse, Ricky, 264,
    340n3
shoplifting by racial groups, 189
sickness and dying of slaves, 35–36

Visit Bill Drake's website

www.healracism.com

- Links to:
    - You Tube videos of talks by Bill Drake
    - Audio recordings of radio programs with Bill Drake and others
    - Facebook page
    - Blog
- Additional excerpts from the interviews of former slaves and Bill's great-great-grandmother's diaries
- Annotated bibliography
- New information and links as the journey continues